$2.95

		DATE DUE	

THE STRUGGLE FOR PEACE

THE RT. HON. NEVILLE CHAMBERLAIN, P.C., M.P.

THE STRUGGLE
FOR PEACE

by

THE RIGHT HONOURABLE
NEVILLE CHAMBERLAIN, M.P.

TORONTO
THOMAS ALLEN
1939

Made and Printed in Great Britain at
The Mayflower Press, Plymouth. William Brendon & Son, Ltd.

CONTENTS

3

FOREWORD

THE countless letters I have received from men and women all over the world during the last six months have impressed deeply upon my mind the intense desire for the preservation of peace that exists among the peoples of every country.

Since that day at the end of May 1937 when I was first summoned to be Prime Minister I have striven with all my power to dispel the nightmare of war which has so long hung over Europe. My efforts have been mocked at by some and denounced by others, but I believe that by the majority they have been approved, and if peace has not yet been securely established, we have at any rate so far escaped the calamity of war.

It is in the hope of making clear the aim and purpose I have had in mind that I have consented to the publication in a collected form of the speeches I have made on this subject since I have held my present office.

In order to remind readers of the exact circumstances under which each speech was made, it has been found essential to add connecting links with explanatory notes; and for these I am indebted to Mr. Arthur Bryant who has kindly undertaken the task for me.

I have described myself as a man of peace to the depths of my soul. As such, with ideals which must always be tempered by the realities of life, I have sought after an international harmony in which nations may live together, each developing its national aims and characteristics without fear of threats or violence from its neighbours. On such a basis alone can confidence be established, and without confidence there can be no betterment of the lot of the peoples and no development of the spiritual side of our civilisation.

To me war is not only the cruellest but the most senseless method of settling international disputes. But man of peace as I am, there is one claim which, if it were made, must, as it seems to me, be resisted even, if necessary, by force. That would be a claim by any one State to dominate others by force, since if such a claim were admitted, I see no possibility of peace of mind or body for anyone.

Let no one suppose that resistance to such a claim would involve the denial of the right of any nation to put forward its grievances, its difficulties or its desires, and to have them examined by others in a spirit of understanding and goodwill. I admit frankly that during the past twenty years there have been faults and failures in this direction, and that some at least of our present troubles might have been avoided if greater wisdom had been shown at an earlier stage.

But I believe that the lessons to be learned from these failures have not been unnoticed and that the world, weary of perpetual excursions and alarums, would to-day gladly join in a new effort to rule itself more wisely if it were given the chance.

Therefore I shall not abandon my efforts for this much longed for Peace and I trust that my readers, whoever and wherever they may be, if they share my ideal, will give me their good wishes and, so far as they can, their help, in the cause to which I am devoting myself.

Neville Chamberlain.

ON ACCEPTING A TRUST

On 31st May, 1937, three days after he became Prime Minister, Mr. Chamberlain was elected Leader of the Conservative Party at a meeting at the Caxton Hall, Westminster. Lord Derby moved a resolution, seconded by Mr. Winston Churchill, assuring him of the loyal and whole-hearted support of the Party in the task that lay before him.

"I SUPPOSE I need hardly say to you that the resolution which has just been read to me is very gratifying to me at this moment when I have just assumed the duties and responsibilities that attach to the office of Prime Minister. I am entering on them at an age when most people are thinking of retiring from active work, but I have hitherto led a sober and a temperate life. I am informed that I am sound in wind and limb, and I am not afraid of the physical labours which may be entailed upon me. Indeed, I do not think it is the long hours or the hard work that form the most alarming aspect of the duties of a Prime Minister. It is rather, as it seems to me, the knowledge that in all the perplexities and the problems which rise up day after day in front of any Government in these troublous times, the ultimate responsibility of the final decision must rest upon the shoulders of the Prime Minister. No major point of policy can be decided, no real fateful step can be taken without the assent, either active or passive, of the Prime Minister, and if things go wrong he can never escape the reflection 'I might have prevented this if I had thought or acted differently.'

"I believe it is that ultimate and inescapable responsibility which is the real root of the anxieties which have worn down the energies of our recent Prime Ministers, and it is that responsibility which now lies in front of me. And so, while I have been waiting in that little room to know what is to become of me, I have not been so much racked by anxieties as to the result of your deliberations, but I have rather been thinking how much easier my sleep would be to-night if your choice had fallen upon somebody else. But, though I have never sought this or any other office, I have never thought it right to shirk any duties which other people thought me capable of performing. I shall have the good fortune to be able to count upon the assistance of a lady whose affection and understanding have for many years made all my troubles seem light.

" There is only one thing which is essential if the Government of which I am now the head is to be an effective force for the things which you and I want to see done, and that is that you and I should work together in mutual confidence and trust. And it is because this resolution has not only declared your choice of me as your leader but has also promised me your whole-hearted support that I shall gladly and definitely accept the charge, and on my side I promise you to devote myself with all my strength to an endeavour to prove worthy of your trust. The pleasure that you have given me by passing this resolution has been very much increased by the knowledge that it was proposed and seconded by Lord Derby and Mr. Churchill. I would like to thank them very warmly for consenting to do so, and for their words, which, although I was not here to listen to them, I know them well enough to be able to guess were both gracious and generous.

"I know you will forgive a personal note if I say that ever since Friday last my thoughts have reverted continually to my father and to my brother. Both of them had qualifications far greater than I for the highest Ministerial office. Both of them might have attained it if it had not been that, by the chances of political fortune, they had to choose between their natural ambition and national interests which seemed to them to be paramount. I look upon my position to-day as the continuation—perhaps I may say the consummation—of their life work, and it has therefore been a matter of the keenest satisfaction to me that my election should have been proposed by two men for both of whom I have long entertained the highest respect and admiration, and of whom I would like particularly to remember to-day that each of them began his political career with the strong interest and approval of my father, and each of them subsequently became the personal friends of my brother until the date of his death.

" I am very conscious of the difficulty of succeeding one who led our party for so many years, and who had succeeded in obtaining from them such an unusual amount of respect and affection. I know well that I do not possess some of those qualities which have specially distinguished Mr. Baldwin and have given him his great place. My only consolation is that I do not know anyone else who does possess them. He and I have known each other now for 14 years, during which I have been his close personal friend, and, in spite of differences of temperament which are almost as obvious as our differences in personal appearance, our outlook on politics and on people has been very much the same. Although every man must have his own method of work, the main principles which guided him are the ones which I shall endeavour to follow. Like him, I regard it as of the first importance to preserve the unity of the Conservative Party, to-day the most powerful political instrument in the country.[1]

" I recall that I myself was not born a little Conservative. I was brought up as a Liberal, and afterwards as a Liberal Unionist. The fact that I am here, accepted by you Conservatives as your Leader, is to my mind a demonstration of the catholicity of the Conservative Party, of that readiness to cover the widest possible field which has made it this great force in the country and has justified the saying of Disraeli that the Conservative Party was nothing if it was not a National Party. But to-day the Conservative Party is only an element, although it is the largest and strongest element in a National Government, and like Mr. Baldwin I am convinced that the best interests of the country will be served by the continuance of the national character of that Government. These next two years may well be critical in the history of Europe, and, whether they end in chaos or in a gradual appeasement of old enmities, and the restoration of confidence and stability, will depend very likely upon the part played by this country, which is bound to be important, and may well be decisive.

" If we are to exert our full influence in the right direction, we shall require something more than the devotion and the

---

[1] It was the unity behind the Prime Minister of a democratic national government, containing representatives of the Conservative, Liberal and National Labour Parties, which fifteen months later was to enable Mr. Chamberlain to go to Berchtesgaden, to Bad Godesberg and to Munich with an authority no less than that of the dictators and to avert a war which up to the very last hour had seemed inevitable to the whole world.

loyalty of purely party followers, valuable and even indispensable as that is. If we are to produce the deepest impression, we must be able to mobilise the widest possible public opinion here and throughout the Empire. To attain that result, I feel satisfied that our best course is to continue the combination of the three parties which has so successfully commanded the adhesion of the country during the last 5 years.

"The new Government, then, remains National, like the one which it has succeeded. It will continue our programme, now well under way, of the re-establishment of our defensive forces. It will combine with that a sustained effort to remove the causes which are still delaying the return of confidence in Europe. It will not cease to promote the development of industry and the improvement of agriculture. And, finally, it will seek to raise still further the standards of our people whenever and wherever that can be done consistently with the maintenance of the credit of the nation, and with due regard to the burden of the taxpayer.

"I thank you once again for your confidence and for the encouragement that you have given me this morning. The National Government has built up a great record of achievement, but there remains still before us a vast field from which energy, wisdom and statesmanship can extract incalculable benefits for the people of this country. Let us, then, join together in our determination to make the most of our opportunities and to ensure that the record of the remaining years of this Parliament shall not be less fruitful than that which has gone before."

" A RESPECTABLE TRADESMAN "

On the 28th June, Mr. Chamberlain received the honorary freedom and livery of the Cordwainers' Company. Members of his family have belonged to the Guild for some 200 years, and his brother, Sir Austen Chamberlain, was Master of the Guild at the time of his death.

"... LORD BALDWIN has mentioned that I am Prime Minister. I do not think it is so often present in my mind as perhaps it used to be in his. But I do like to think that this invitation from the Court was not given to me because I was Prime Minister. It was extended months before that event took place, and when you could not possibly know that it ever would take place. It was not even given to me because I was Chancellor of the Exchequer, though I know that this is something for which everybody has frequently expressed their thankfulness.

"The invitation was given to me on account of my long family connection with the Company. We go back for 200 years, when William Chamberlain was admitted to the Company in 1739. For those 200 years there never has been a time when some members of my family have not been on the Court of the Company.

"Although I cannot boast of the blueness of the blood in my veins or of the fame of my forebears, I am yet prouder of being descended from those respectable tradesmen, as they were called, than if my ancestors had worn shining armour and carried great swords.[1]

"It is many years since we had a business connection with cordwaining. I do not think that even in those palmy days its profits were such as to have qualified my ancestors for liability to N.D.C., if N.D.C. had then been in existence. We found other means of keeping body and soul together, but we have not yet forgotten our old connection.

"Now I am the latest recruit to your ranks, and I do most deeply appreciate your feeling that you would like to keep up this long connection between my family and your Company, and I am glad to think that after I am gone, it may be continued by my brother's descendants."

[1] It was with an umbrella, it will be recalled, that Mr. Chamberlain flew across Europe on his mission of peace. The reference, in the light of later events, seems to make the speech too significant to omit.

THE CHANCE WHEN IT COMES

On 3rd July, Mr. Chamberlain spoke in his native city of Birmingham at a Banquet given at the Council House.

"AS I have been listening, my Lord Mayor, to your kind and friendly words and looking round this familiar room, my thoughts have gone back to another occasion thirty-one years ago when another member of my family was similarly honoured. I can well remember my father's emotion on that occasion. Indeed, I never saw him nearer to a breakdown than he was in making that speech, when he strove to express his sense of the obligations that had been so constantly showered upon him by the city of his adoption; and now it is my turn to try to find words to say how deeply I appreciate all the kindnesses that have been shown me by my fellow-citizens throughout my life, and particularly to thank you for the signal honour you have bestowed upon me by asking me to be your guest to-night as the first son of Birmingham to become Prime Minister of the United Kingdom.

" I should like to add that the value of the compliment you have paid me is more than doubled by the gracious tribute you have been kind enough to pay to my wife—a lady on whom I think some thoughtful good fairy bestowed at her birth just those very qualities that are so desirable and which are not always found in the wife and helpmeet of a statesman.

" Well, my Lord Mayor, I suppose that in time I shall get used to being addressed as Prime Minister, but at present I feel rather like one of those centenarians who are interviewed by enterprising representatives of the Press and are summoned to account for the good fortune that they do not appear obviously to have deserved. I have been running over in my mind various answers which these venerable gentlemen give on these occasions, but I am afraid they do not seem exactly to suit my case. I cannot pretend I have been a lifelong abstainer from alcohol, or from tobacco, or that I am in the habit of spending a few minutes in simple exercises every morning before breakfast. If I told you that I have never told a lie, I suppose probably you would not believe me. Any suggestion that the moment I stepped out of my cradle I formed the ambition to become Prime Minister before I died I am afraid has not the slightest foundation in truth. And so, I suppose, the only explanation I can give is that I was born and bred in Birmingham. And when I have said that, what other explanation is necessary?

" After all, there can be only a few Prime Ministers in a generation, and there must always enter an element of chance into the question as to whether the office falls to one or another of those who are capable of filling it. In my case, unlike my father and my brother, the die has been cast in my favour; but I should not be my father's son if I did not recognise that what matters is not the luck that assigns the office, but what is made of it when it comes.

" I regard my present position not as a prize, but as an opportunity for service, and any satisfaction I may derive from it will not be permanent unless I can feel when I lay it down that I have used my opportunity wisely and in the interests of the country as a whole.

" We are living in a time of transition, a time when conditions are changing almost from day to day, and no one can say how they will ultimately settle down. When we look abroad we see new systems of government being tried, and although they differ fundamentally from one another, they are alike in this : that in every case their enthusiastic adherents claim they have found the only practical method of dealing with modern conditions. We see every nation vehemently asserting its desire for peace, and every one of them arming as feverishly as if they meant to go to war ; and, similarly, every nation declares that it wishes to see freer trade, and yet the barriers that hinder trade seem as firmly fixed as ever.

" Well, perhaps these inconsistencies and incongruities are not really as inexplicable as they may appear at first sight. There is a wide difference between what a nation desires and what it feels it can venture to do in order to attain those desires.

" It seems to me that in these days the task of statesmanship is to find ways and means of inducing Governments to put aside their mutual fears and suspicions and to give rein to the longing which, I believe, is at the heart of every one of them—namely, to live at peace with its neighbours, and to devote its energies and resources to the advancement of the happiness and prosperity of its people.

"Well now, my Lord Mayor, in that task I am convinced that His Majesty's subjects, through their respective Governments, may play an important part. The members of the British Commonwealth of Nations have already set a striking example to the rest of the world in the establishment among themselves of relations of mutual trust and confidence and in the complete abandonment of any idea that the use of force is a possible remedy for their differences, if ever they should have any.

"It was my privilege to preside over the later meetings of the Imperial Conference which was concluded a few weeks ago.[1] Around our Board there were sitting representatives of countries divided from one another by vast distances, inhabited by peoples speaking different languages, and living very different lives. With some of them we ourselves had actually been at war within living memory, and yet there was not one of them sitting round that Board who did not feel a sense of kinship with the others. There was not one of them who was not convinced that in any great and serious crisis all of us would be actuated by the same motives of sincerity, honesty and humanity.

[1] The Imperial Conference met in May 1937, immediately after the Coronation, under the chairmanship of Mr. Chamberlain. It declared, *inter alia:* "That for each member of the Commonwealth the first objective is the preservation of peace," and that the members of the Conference, though "themselves firmly attached to the principles of democracy and to Parliamentary forms of government," held "that difference of political creed should be no obstacle to friendly relations between Governments and countries, and that nothing would be more damaging to the hopes of international appeasement than the division, real or apparent, of the world into opposing groups." At the close of the Conference, Mr. Chamberlain used these words:

"On all the big issues on which the welfare of mankind ultimately depends, we think alike; and when you consider the nature of the countries whose representatives are gathered round this table, how they are inhabited by many different races, speaking many different languages, with different climates, religions, conditions of neighbourhood, and separated by vast distances of sea and land, surely this solidarity of opinion is profoundly impressive, and cannot fail to exercise its influence far beyond the boundaries even of the British Empire."

" I hope the citizens of the United States will not think me presumptuous if I say that we have the same confidence in their outlook upon these great questions which affect the lives of men and women as we have in that of the British Empire.

" If these several nations, in spite of all their differences, can feel this trust in one another, surely it is not fantastic to imagine that some day all the States which subscribe to the Covenant of the League of Nations may consent to drop their recriminations and to settle down in peace to see how they can make life more worth living for the peoples that inhabit them.

" When I served as a member of the Birmingham City Council, I learned one lesson which I have never forgotten, and that is that in this imperfect world a man cannot have everything his own way, and that those who get things done are those who are ready to work with and for others, and who are prepared to give up something themselves in order that they may receive something in return. There is always some common measure of agreement if only we will look for it, and there is but little satisfaction in standing out for the last item of a programme on which we have set our hearts if, by so doing, we are going to miss the opportunity of obtaining anything at all.

" Those maxims that apply to individuals apply to nations too. We in the British Empire have gone far to solve our problems by mutual accommodation ; and if, by our example, by exercising that great and powerful influence which we have in the world, we can induce others to follow the same prescription, why then we shall have justified our faith in ourselves and our mission among the nations of the earth."

THE FALL OF THE AVALANCHES

On 25th June, a few days before Mr. Chamberlain spoke at Birmingham he had made his first speech as Prime Minister in the House of Commons on Foreign Affairs. The subject was the Spanish Civil War which had broken out a year earlier, when the Army and the Catholic North had risen in arms against a Popular Front Government on the grounds that it had deliberately failed to preserve the elements of order and to secure the rights of worship. This bitter internecine conflict had been complicated by the intervention of large numbers of volunteers from almost every country in the world, including the four great Continental Powers, Soviet Russia, Italy, France and Germany. A cockpit was thus provided for a miniature world war between what seemed to some the champions of Fascism and Democracy and to others of Fascism and Communism. From the start it was plain that the situation might well precipitate a world war—a disaster which the British Government consistently endeavoured to avert by the expedient, admittedly imperfect, of the London Non-Intervention Committee, on which representatives of the Powers concerned were officially joined together to discuss ways of evacuating those foreign combatants who were already in Spain and of preventing the arrival of new ones. In June, 1937, a serious crisis had arisen as a result of an attack made by Spanish Republican aircraft on the German battleship Deutschland *while on Non-Intervention patrol duty in the Mediterranean—an attack which had been avenged by a bombardment by German warships of the town of Almeria. As a result of a further though unsuccessful attack alleged to have been made on the German cruiser* Leipzig *by a Spanish Republican submarine, the Germans had withdrawn their ships from the Non-Intervention Patrol and the Italians had followed suit. Though this withdrawal actually operated to the advantage of the Republicans, it was made the occasion of a full-dress attack on the principle of Non-Intervention by the British Parliamentary Opposition, whose partiality for the Republican cause in Spain caused them to wish to raise the official ban on the import of arms to those with whom they sympathised, while retaining it only against the Spanish Nationalists, whom they alleged, on inadequate and highly partial evidence, to be receiving far more help from Italy and Germany than the Republicans were from Russia and other countries sympathetic to their cause. After Sir Archibald Sinclair, leader of the Liberal Opposition, had spoken condemning the Government's policy of Non-Intervention, the Prime Minister rose.*

" THE right hon. Baronet has given us a comprehensive thoughtful survey of the whole field of foreign affairs, and I have listened to him with all the more pleasure because here and there I heard a phrase with which I was not in disagreement. I do not rise at this moment for the purpose of replying to him, or indeed of developing most of the subjects on which he touched. My right hon. Friend the Secretary of State for Foreign Affairs (Mr. Eden) will have an opportunity of speaking later and I have no doubt he will be able to make reply to the points that have been raised. I rise only in order to say a few words about one aspect of foreign policy, and it is one which at present is uppermost in all minds in Europe, the situation arising out of the civil war in Spain. I do not think it ought to be necessary for me to state what is the policy of His Majesty's Government in regard to that situation, because it has already been so frequently repeated, but, all the same, I will state it again, because it seems to me that every now and then there is a tendency, amid the strong feelings that are aroused in this connection, to forget what it is that the Government really are aiming at.

" In this Spanish situation there is one peculiar feature which gives it a specially dangerous aspect. That is that to many people looking on from outside, it presents itself as a struggle between two rival systems each of which commands an enthusiastic, even a passionate body of support among its adherents in their respective countries, with the result that supporters of these two rival systems cannot help regarding the issue of the struggle in Spain as a defeat or a victory, as the case may be, for the side to which they are attached. I am not expressing an opinion as to whether that view of the struggle is correct or not, but I say that the fact that it is held constitutes a perpetual danger to the peace of Europe, because, if some country or Government representing one of these two ideas attempts to intervene beyond a certain point, then some other country taking the opposite view may find it difficult, if not impossible, to refrain from joining in, and a conflict may be started of which no man can see the end.

"In these circumstances, the policy of His Majesty's Government has been consistently directed to one end, and one end only, namely, to maintain the peace of Europe by confining the war to Spain. It is for that purpose that, in conjunction with France, we have worked to set up and, since then, to maintain the Non-intervention Agreement. No body could have had a harder task than the Committee, and we in this country have suffered the usual fate of those who have tried to be impartial. We have been deliberately accused by both sides of partiality towards the other. But although we have had to express as a Government our dissatisfaction with the failure of the scheme of non-intervention, we maintain, though it is true that intervention has gone on, and is going on in spite of the Non-intervention Agreement, that it is also true that up to the present we have succeeded in achieving the object which has been at the back of our policy the whole time. We shall continue to pursue that object and that policy as long as we feel that there is a reasonable hope of avoiding a spread of the conflict. I do not take the view myself that it is fantastic to continue this policy successfully even to the end.

"The situation is serious, but it is not hopeless, and, in particular, although it may be true that various countries or various governments desire to see one side or the other side successful, there is not a country or a government that wants to see a European war. Since that is so, let us to try to keep cool heads and neither say nor do anything to precipitate a disaster which everybody really wishes to avoid. I think we are bound to recognise that as long as this civil war is going on in Spain——"

MR. GALLACHER : " Invasion."

THE PRIME MINISTER : " Incidents are bound to occur which involve foreign Powers. The very duties which foreign Powers have imposed upon themselves in trying to stop the importation of weapons and ammunition into Spain—[an HON. MEMBER: " What foreign Powers ? "]—

means that there must be an interference with the course of hostilities. Each side is being deprived of supplies of material of which it feels itself in urgent need."

MR. S. O. DAVIES : " Rubbish, absolute rubbish."

THE CHAIRMAN : " Order."

MR. DAVIES : " There is a limit."

MR. MORGAN JONES : " May I ask you, Sir Dennis, on a point of Order, whether Members of this House are to be precluded from expressing their disagreement with the speakers in the ordinary way ? "

THE CHAIRMAN : " In a case of this kind, where the Prime Minister is making a very important speech, I think that it is the general will of the House that, at any rate until he has concluded his speech, there should be no interruptions that would be likely to make it more difficult for the Committee to follow his statement."

MR. ATTLEE : " I quite agree that everybody should be given a free hearing in this House, and a fair hearing, but I cannot agree with you, Sir Dennis, with all respect, that we should make distinctions between one person and another. [HON. MEMBERS : " Oh."] Yes, I suggest that we are all on an equal footing in this House as Members, we all have the right of free speech, and we all have occasionally to submit to interjections, but I submit with great respect to you, that, while, when an important speech is being made we should all exercise the greatest restraint, this House should draw no distinctions between its Members."

THE PRIME MINISTER : " May I say that I am not making any complaint ? It is not a personal matter. It is a very grave subject, and I recognise that people hold very strong views on this subject, and may find it very difficult to restrain expression of those views. I am trying not to put the thing in a provocative way. As far as I am personally concerned, I am not making any sort of complaint. I was trying to put the case to the Committee that the very fact that we are trying to maintain a policy of non-intervention, which is exercised through a patrol by ships belonging to various Powers stopping ships taking arms and ammunition into Spain, involves an interference with the hostilities and, therefore, is bound to create strong feelings of resentment among those in Spain who feel that they are thus being handicapped. That leads to accusations of want of impartiality and counter-accusations, and then to such deplorable incidents as the bombing of the *Deutschland* and destruction by bombing. [An HON MEMBER : " And the bombing of Almeria."] And the bombing of Almeria. Once this chain begins, it goes on, first on one side and then on the other.

" I am not going to discuss the incidents in which the cruiser *Leipzig* was involved. The German officers on that ship were convinced, on what they thought was indisputable evidence, that they had been the subject of attack by torpedoes. I do not exclude the possibility of a mistake. I know that in the course of the Great War many British naval officers thought that they saw torpedo tracks when afterwards it was proved that there could have been no torpedo, and we did not think any the worse of them on that account. They were perfectly genuine in what they said and thought at the time. But whether the German officers are right or wrong, that is what they believe, and in those circumstances it seems to me that their claim, that they could not allow their ships to be exposed any longer to the risk of such incidents as that, was a reasonable claim, and ought not to be the subject of hostile criticism.

" In fact, I go a little further than that. When I think of what the experiences of the German Navy have been, the loss of life and mutilation of men on the *Deutschland* and the natural feelings of indignation and resentment which must be aroused by such an incident, with all that, I must say that I think the German Government in merely withdrawing their ships and then stating that this question is closed have shown a degree of restraint which we all ought to recognise. At any rate, the result of this disappearance of German and Italian ships from the patrol means that there should not be any longer any danger of further incidents of this kind and, in my view, the best thing we can do now is to turn our minds back again to the two practical steps which have to be taken, the first one being to fill the gap in the patrol which has now been left open and the other to re-start our endeavours to obtain the withdrawal of foreign volunteers in Spain.

" That is all I have to say at present, and I want to conclude

with a very earnest appeal to those who hold responsible
positions both in this country and abroad—and I am including
the Press and the Members of this House—to weigh their
words very carefully before they utter them on this matter,
bearing in mind the consequences that might flow from some
rash or thoughtless phrase. I have read that in the high
mountains there are sometimes conditions to be found when
an incautious move or even a sudden loud exclamation may
start an avalanche. That is just the condition in which we
are finding ourselves to-day. I believe, although the snow
may be perilously poised, it has not yet begun to move, and
if we can all exercise caution, patience and self-restraint, we
may yet be able to save the peace of Europe."

that admission and he says, ' There are 40,000 of my troops there,
and there are Generals and Field-Marshals whom I have con-
gratulated on their victories in Spain,' is it not the business of the
Non-Intervention Committee to tell him that those troops have
no right to be in Spain and that he must bring them away at once ?
If the number is only 40,000, then the less tax it will be on his
transport. He should be told that we shall not be satisfied in
this country unless those troops are taken away to Italy within
fourteen days."

*To this warlike suggestion the Prime Minister replied in
the closing speech of the Debate :*

"THE House always listens with pleasure to a speech from the hon. Member who has just addressed us, because he is always good tempered and always convinces us that he is speaking with complete sincerity. But good temper and sincerity are not sufficient to make an accurate analysis of the complicated foreign situation or to formulate a policy. If the hon. Member will forgive me, I should like to say that he is in the position in which the Leader of the Opposition accused the Government of being, namely, that he seems to me to be completely divorced from reality. He is a victim of phrases and words. He uses words over and over again without, it seems to me, making clear what he means by those words. He says that the Government have no policy, that he can never understand their foreign policy. What does the hon. Member mean by foreign policy? You can lay down sound and general propositions. You can say that your foreign policy is to maintain peace; you can say that it is to protect British interests, you can say that it is to use your influence, such as it is, on behalf of the right against the wrong, as far as you can tell the right from the wrong. You can lay down all these as general principles, but that is not a policy. Surely, if you are to have a policy you must take the particular situations and consider what action or inaction is suitable for those particular situations. That is what I myself mean by policy, and it is quite clear that as the situations and conditions in foreign affairs continually change from day to day, your policy cannot be stated once and for all if it is to be applicable to every situation that arises.

"Perhaps the hon. Member when he accused the Government of having no foreign policy was really thinking simply of the League of Nations, which was in fact the illustration he gave us when he went on to specify more particularly of what he complained. He complained that my right hon. Friend (Mr. Eden) did not once in the course of his speech state the

33

detestation of the Government for war and did not once mention the name of the League. Would it really have illuminated matters very much if my right hon. Friend had repeated what has been said hundreds of times—that this Government does detest war, and that we have done and are doing everything we can to maintain peace throughout the world? Would that have illuminated matters at all? Is not the real, practical question what action can we take in existing circumstances to carry that principle into effect? When the hon. Member says that my right hon. Friend did not mention the League, what is the use of saying for the thousandth time that we believe in the principles for which the League was founded and that our policy is directed to make those principles effective? That is not carrying us any further, and I cannot help thinking that the hon. Member forgets that the League is not an end in itself, it is a means towards an end, and if the League is temporarily unable to fulfil its function to achieve that end, what is the use of repeating parrot-like that we believe in the League?

"We believe in the principles for which the League was founded. We do believe that if it could be as it was, or as it was expected to be, a League of all the powerful nations in the world, it would be an effective instrument for carrying out the principles in which the hon. Member and the Government believe. The hon. Member says that the League is a guarantee against aggression. Unfortunately, experience has shown this to be absolutely untrue. The League as it is at present is not a guarantee against aggression, and pending a regeneration of the League or its development into an effective instrument, it is no use going on repeating 'the League.' We have to find practical means of restoring peace to the world.

"My right hon. Friend, in making the first speech in the Debate, confined himself to two subjects, and for the most part I think the Debate has followed his example. That seems to me to be right. I do not imagine that when the right hon. Gentleman the Leader of the Opposition (Mr. Attlee) expressed a desire for a Debate upon foreign affairs to-day, his purpose was merely to debate in an academic manner general questions of policy. I conceive that his purpose was to ascertain from

the Government what was their view as to the proper action
to be taken to deal with these two sources of difficulty and
anxiety with which we are faced to-day, and I propose myself
to devote a few of my remarks to the situation in Spain and
to the questions which have been raised in the course of the
Debate upon that subject, and also to say something about
the situation in the Far East.

" My right hon. Friend was imprudent enough to express
some satisfaction that the party opposite had come to the
conclusion that, in the present state of the world, they could
not refuse their support for the rearmament of this country.
I think he said he hoped that might lead to further agreement
between us. That, of course, was rash on the part of my
right hon. Friend, and it at once provoked a terrified effort
on the part of the right hon. Gentleman opposite to show
his friends behind him that there really was no truth in that
scandalous statement. We know that the right hon. Gentleman has his troubles. One of the greatest of his troubles,
who is not now sitting near him but—in another capacity—
may not be very far off, must have given him some anxiety
about the future. Therefore, I am not surprised that he
endeavours to dwell on that subject on which he hopes that
unity may still remain in his party, namely, criticism of the
Government's policy. But really, when in order to bring
that out he travesties the policy of His Majesty's Government
in the way he did in his speech, I think he should remember
that misrepresentations of that kind are apt to have their
repercussions. He suggested that for the Government there
was no question of right or wrong in the world save where
the material interests of the British Empire were concerned.
Let him take care that he does not find people taking for
granted that where British material interests are concerned,
the Labour Party has no interest itself in the matter, and
that the only objects for which they would be prepared to
use British armaments, British soldiers, sailors and airmen,
would be those in which there is no material British interest
involved. Let him beware of this, that when he is ridiculing
the policy of His Majesty's Government, he does not give
rise to misrepresentations of that kind.

" Let me come to the particular question of the Spanish

situation. Let us consider for a moment what our object should be with regard to the Spanish situation. Supposing that there had been going on in Spain to-day a civil war without any intervention of any foreign troops whatsoever, would the party opposite then have been urging us to intervene on one side or the other? [HON. MEMBERS: 'No!'] The right hon. Gentleman says 'No.' [An HON. MEMBER: ' There would be no war !'] The right hon. Gentleman has just admitted that in that case there would have been no desire and no suggestion that it was the duty of the Government of this country to intervene on one side or the other. He has, in fact, admitted that the problem in Spain is the intervention of foreign troops, of foreign soldiers fighting either on one side or the other. [HON. MEMBERS: 'No!'] That being so, it is clear that the best thing we can do is to try to get these foreign troops out of the country, and, seeing that the attitude of other countries towards the civil war in Spain is so largely dominated by their own ideas of what is suitable for their own countries, it is clear that if the policy of non-intervention had not been pursued, originally at the instance of the French Government but all through with the hearty and full co-operation of the British Government— if that policy had not been pursued, there was every prospect that the civil war in Spain might presently become a European war of unknown magnitude.

" The events of yesterday have, of course, very largely knocked the bottom out of this Debate. [HON. MEMBERS: ' Oh !'] I am only quoting what has been said by one hon. Member after another in the course of this afternoon. Hon. Members opposite cannot have listened to their own colleagues. A good many speeches which, no doubt, had been prepared on another assumption, have had to be torn up, and the right hon. Gentleman this afternoon was compelled to make a rapid shift of ground. So, instead of taunting us with truckling to dictators and with weakness in not breaking off negotiations if the Italian Government could not see their way to accept the invitation to the Three-Power conversations—instead of denouncing us for consenting to discuss this matter once again in the Non-Intervention Committee, he has had to take up different ground altogether and to throw doubts upon the good faith of the Italian Government. The right hon. Gentleman is quite entitled to have his suspicions. All I would say is that if in foreign affairs you are always going to begin with the assumption that the other party is not going to hold to anything that he promises, you will not make much progress. In the present case it appears to me that what happened yesterday is a full justification of the patience and persistence which my right hon. Friend has shown during these long drawn-out negotiations.

" The right hon. Gentleman asked one or two questions. One of them was, in what proportion were these withdrawals to take place, and he went on to say that if the proportions were to be as man for man on both sides, that would be grossly unfair to one side, and he specified which side. He said it would be grossly unfair to the Spanish Government. That, of course, is based on the assumption that there are far more volunteers on the side of General Franco than on the other side. What I would say, however, is that nobody knows how many volunteers there are on either side."

MR. DALTON : " The secret service ought to know."

THE PRIME MINISTER : " I repeat that nobody knows how many there are on either side. The first thing to do is to ascertain the numbers, and if they can be ascertained by an international Commission, as is proposed, then the proposal is that the withdrawals shall be in the proportion of those numbers as found on the two sides."

MR. ATTLEE : " That was not stated in the Italian Note. Is the Commission to go on and make arrangements for a total withdrawal ? The Italian suggestion was that first there should be a withdrawal of man for man on each side, and what I was asking was what would be the amount, because if I am correct, or if the general reports are correct, there are four or five times as many on the rebel side as on the Government side."

THE PRIME MINISTER : " That is the point that I was coming to. Let us be quite clear. The ultimate proposal is that all the volunteers should be withdrawn, and if that is so, obviously there must be more on one side withdrawn than on the other, if the numbers are greater on one side than on the other. The only question, therefore, is what is to happen in the meantime. It may take some time, and surely we are not going to wait and have no withdrawals at all until these figures are accurately ascertained. Therefore, the proposal is that what is called a token withdrawal should take place, of a comparatively small number, and that that number should be equal on the two sides."

MR. ATTLEE : " That is exactly what my point was—what kind of amount is meant by a token withdrawal."

THE PRIME MINISTER : " I said a comparatively trifling or small amount, but the number has not actually been fixed. Supposing it was 5,000. I do not say it is, for a moment—it may not be as many as that—but supposing it was 5,000 from either side, I do not think there is anything unfair in that. The surplus of volunteers on one side would remain exactly the same as before the withdrawals. The next question of the right hon. Gentleman was whether, while this withdrawal was taking place, it would be open to other Powers to go on pouring arms and munitions or weapons into Spain. Of course, anything of the kind would stultify the whole procedure, and the proposal is this, to see that there shall be no further intervention while withdrawals are taking place. Anyhow, the Government would not consider an arrangement at all satisfactory or acceptable which allowed further volunteers to be poured in while nominally we were withdrawing troops already there.

" Several questions were asked by the right hon. Member for Caithness (Sir. A. Sinclair). I am not going to answer all his questions, because I put it to him, What is the use of digging now into the past and giving figures of Italian troops alleged to have been landed here or landed there? But, as a matter of fact, as far as I can make out, there is no official confirmation of the landings of those troops which are alleged to have landed in Spain. But, whether it was the fact or not, if we are now going to get on with the business, there is no useful purpose to be served by digging into the past. We want to deal with the present and future rather than with the past.

" There is one point on which I do not want to forget to say something, and that is in reply to various questions that have been put to me, notably in the opening words of the hon. Member who spoke last, who made an appeal on behalf of the people of Gijon, a place which, according to the latest information, has now fallen. It is late in the day, but we have instructed our Ambassador to support with all the influence that he can bring to bear an appeal which has been made to General Franco by the French Government to use those who have been taken prisoner with all the humanity possible. While I am speaking of this place, I do rather resent the suggestions that were made by the Leader of the Opposition and by some others that the British Government in their humanitarian efforts have favoured one side. It was suggested that we had been very ready to help refugees from Franco's side but that there has not been equal willingness to assist those on the other side. There is no foundation for that."

MR. ATTLEE: "I suggested there were certain technicalities with regard to territorial waters that had not been objected to when it was a question of rescuing Franco, but which were said to be standing in the way of rescuing the supporters of the Government."

THE PRIME MINISTER: "I do not want to go into that, but the right hon. Gentleman will be surprised to hear that from this town of Gijon alone we have removed no fewer than 30,000 refugees in British ships under the protection of the British flag.

"I want to say a word about the Balearic Islands. It has been suggested that even if all goes well with the withdrawal of volunteers, nevertheless when the war is over we may find Italians still in Spain, still in possession of some of the Balearic Islands and possibly in possession of other parts which might be used for military purposes. These are very serious suggestions and I do not underrate them for a moment. I know that the idea that the Italian Government have some such notions in their minds is very widely held, not only in this country. But I believe that idea to be unfounded. We have had repeated and most categorical assurances from the Italian Government. Last September we received an assurance from that Government that they did not contemplate any deal with the Spanish insurgents for the cession of Ceuta, Spanish Morocco, or the Balearic Islands. This assurance was recalled in the exchange of notes of 31st December which was published as a White Paper. On that occasion the Italian Minister for Foreign Affairs wrote that:

B *

" ' So far as Italy is concerned the integrity of the present territories of Spain shall in all circumstances remain intact and unmodified.'

" Since then we have several times had reaffirmation of those assurances, and as lately as the 15th of this month our Ambassador, Lord Perth, was assured by the Italian Foreign Minister that Italy had no territorial, strategic or even economic designs on Spain. Moreover, the Italian delegate at Geneva declared to the French Foreign Secretary last month that Italy had no intention of making the smallest change in the territorial status of Spain and had no designs on the Balearic Islands, and that the integrity of the continental and insular territory of Spain would be respected.

" I accept those assurances as being given in good faith. I am very glad that they have been given. They relieve us of the necessity even of considering a situation which, if it had made any material change in the military conditions in the Western Mediterranean, would have been a matter of serious concern to His Majesty's Government. Happily that is not the case, and I hope very much that the change which took place yesterday in the Non-Intervention Committee may be taken as the commencement of a process which will presently remove the danger which has been so present to our minds all through, lest this conflict in Spain should spread outside the borders of that country, and that once the question of Spain is out of the way, we may get down to the deeper and more serious causes of European unrest and anxiety. I would like to say a word or two about the Far East."

SIR A. SINCLAIR : " What about the movement of troops into Libya ? "

MR. CHAMBERLAIN : " I thought the right hon. Gentleman must be aware that the movement of troops to Libya is carrying out a process the beginning of which was announced as long ago as April last, and we have no reason to suppose that it has any connection with current events."

MR. GALLACHER : " Nothing means anything."

MR. CHAMBERLAIN : " The Leader of the Opposition and also the right hon. Member for Caithness both expressed regret and surprise that my right hon. Friend (Mr. Eden) had not spoken again of the speech which was delivered by President

Roosevelt, although he and I took the first opportunity after that speech was made public of expressing our satisfaction at what President Roosevelt had said and our intention to co-operate with him as far as that might be possible. If I may quote the words I myself used, the right hon. Gentleman will see that he had no grounds for suggesting that we, in contradistinction to President Roosevelt, have no ideas and no policy and no word of welcome for the gesture made by the President from across the Atlantic. I said:

" ' In his declaration of the necessity for a return to a belief in the pledged word and the sanctity of treaties he has voiced the convictions of this country as well as of his own, and in his call for a concerted effort in the cause of peace he will have this Government whole-heartedly with him.'

I do not know what more I could have said. Since then there have been some developments. We now have arrangements made for the meeting of the Conference of the Powers which signed the Nine-Power Treaty and probably some other countries as well. That will be the occasion for the concerted effort of which the President spoke, and I would like to say this, that when the right hon. Gentleman demands that we should say here and now not only how we are going to begin that Conference but what will be our action if all sorts of hypo-thetical circumstances arise in the course of the Conference, I suggest that he is not there offering the words of wisdom which I should expect from his experience. To say before-hand, before consultation with any of those who are going to take part in the Conference, what you will do is the very worst way of getting that concerted effort which is what the President has asked for and which, I understand, the right hon. Gentle-man himself would like to see. No, Sir, we know perfectly well what the Conference is for. The Conference is to try to restore peace in the Far East[1]—and that is sufficient to go on

---

[1] Japan had invaded China in July 1937 on the pretext of preserving Japanese interests from anarchy. Many in this country held that since the League of Nations was not prepared to do so, Britain should intervene on behalf of China—an intervention which would not only jeopardise the peace of the rest of the world, but which, if undertaken with adequate force, would place us at the mercy of our European neighbours while our fleet was engaged in operations at the other end of the world.

with. Do not let us, then, adopt the suggestion of the Leader
of the Opposition and begin to say what we are going to do
if we find it impossible to make peace by peaceful methods.

"When the right hon. Gentleman suggests that he would
like to see us put an embargo upon Japan, by which I understand him to mean a financial and economic boycott of Japan,
let him consider carefully the analysis of the situation which
was made by the right hon. Member for Caithness. The right
hon. Gentleman said, ' It may be that if you can get certain
countries to join with you in this process of economic boycott,
you can put such pressure upon Japan that in time '—I do
not know how long, but in time—' she may be forced to
desist from further military operations in China, but you must
bear in mind that if you are going to do that, there may be
some counter action by Japan, and that if you are to meet that,
you must be assured beforehand of sufficient force to enable
you to overwhelm it.' He added, too, that we could not be
the country to lead in the application of that force and suggested that the lead, if it came from anybody, would have to
come from the United States. I commend that analysis to
the consideration of the House in general and the right hon.
Gentleman in particular. They may be able to measure in
their own minds what are the prospects of a successful application of economic pressure when one of the conditions behind
it is of that formidable nature.

"I suggest that it is altogether a mistake to go into this
Conference talking about economic sanctions, economic
pressure and force. We are here to make peace, not here to
extend the conflict. The first thing we have to do is to see
what means, by concerted effort, can be brought to bear in
order to bring about the peaceful solution of the problem.
Do not let us allow our minds to be distracted by hypothetical
considerations which have not yet arisen, but let us put our
whole force and our whole energy, with all the co-operation
we can get from others, into the task of saving those lives
which are daily being sacrificed in this terrible warfare which
is going on to-day."

AT THE LORD MAYOR'S BANQUET

On 9th November, 1937, Mr. Chamberlain, in accordance with historic custom, attended the Lord Mayor's Banquet at the Guildhall and responded to the toast of " His Majesty's Ministers."

"AS you have observed, this is the first time that I have attended this banquet as Prime Minister, and a new Prime Minister would, I know, always receive at your hands such a kindly and generous welcome as you have extended to me. But I am no stranger to the City, which has already had a long and varied experience of my activities in another capacity, and moreover I have my sponsors to-day in the shades of my ancestors, to whom you have so gracefully alluded, and who lived their lives and carried on their trades for a hundred years within a stone's throw of this ancient building. I thank you, then, both for myself and for my colleagues for what you have said about us, and I assure you that we value very highly your support and appreciation.

" It is customary at this dinner for the Prime Minister to give a general review of the situation abroad. But I make no apology for referring to the one great event of the year at home before I turn to consider affairs oversea. The memory of the Coronation, at which our young King and Queen dedicated their lives to the service of their many peoples, is fresh in our thoughts, and I am sure that you will wish to join me in expressing to Their Majesties the loyalty and good wishes which are felt by all their subjects.

" The Coronation Ceremony also marked the new stage which has been reached in the constitutional development of the British Empire. The participation of Dominion Prime Ministers and other representatives from oversea—and indeed the very form of the Coronation Service—showed that the King was being crowned as King not of this country alone, but of all the peoples and nations within the British Commonwealth. We were glad to welcome to this country all who in their public or private capacity came to attend this great and historic occasion, and I should like to take this opportunity to thank those—among whom the Corporation of the City of London took, as always, a leading part—who did their best to make our visitors' stay in this country pleasant and memorable.

" Immediately after the Coronation a meeting of the Imperial Conference was held in London for the discussion of matters of common concern to the members of the British Commonwealth of Nations. The Conference was not arranged for the purpose of solving any particular problems, but, as in previous cases, its object was to enable the representatives of the several parts of the British Commonwealth to exchange information, to examine the events of the past and the prospects of the future, and, by attaining a clear understanding of their respective interests and responsibilities, to establish a general harmony of aims and objects between His Majesty's several Governments. This object was fully attained. I have every reason to know that the Dominion Prime Ministers and the other members of the Oversea Governments whom we were delighted to welcome here felt at the conclusion of their labours that our full and frank discussions had brought about a clear perception of the issues involved, and that on all fundamental principles there was little or no difference between us. To use the words of the Prime Minister of Canada, the Conference showed once again how peoples pursuing common ideals, but preserving the full measure of their independence, can find means of working together for the common good.

" Since the outbreak of hostilities in China it has been the aim of His Majesty's Government to bring about a truce by frequent representations to both sides, at the same time keeping constantly in touch with the Governments of other countries concerned, especially with that of the United States. Unfortunately, these efforts have so far proved unsuccessful.

" When the League of Nations, on being appealed to by the Chinese Government, referred the question to the League Far Eastern Advisory Committee, His Majesty's Government heartily welcomed the recommendation of that Committee that the parties to the Nine-Power Treaty should consult among themselves in accordance with Article VII of that treaty. The most urgent necessity is that fighting should cease in order to allow of a settlement between the two parties on a proper basis, and we believe that the most hopeful means of achieving this purpose is through the Conference now being held at Brussels, whose mandate is to ' seek a method of putting an end to the conflict by agreement.'

" In our view an essential factor for success in any endeavour to bring about a settlement is the co-operation of the United States, whose influence and interests in the Far East are so considerable. We rejoice, therefore, that in the admirable exposition of the objects of the Conference which he gave in his opening speech Mr. Norman Davis made it clear that all the participating Governments are assured of the constructive co-operation of the United States Government. His Majesty's Government in the United Kingdom, for their part, are prepared, as the Foreign Secretary declared on the same occasion, to offer the very fullest collaboration to promote the success of the Conference. The prolongation of this unhappy conflict, with all the misery and suffering which it involves, can only result in increasing damage to each of the two great nations concerned, and we, who have a long tradition of friendly relations with both of them, will anxiously await the day when their differences shall be composed and they can once again turn their attention to the development of their resources and the welfare of their respective peoples.

" I have spoken of the pleasure with which His Majesty's Government received the news of the readiness of the Government of the United States of America to co-operate in the Brussels Conference. We regard that action as a first and most valuable step towards the fulfilment of the desire expressed by President Roosevelt at Chicago for a concerted effort by peace-loving nations for the sanctity of treaties and the settlement of differences by peaceful means. We are convinced that a closer understanding and a more complete community of purpose between our two nations may do much to assist the cause for which the President has pleaded, and which is also nearest to our hearts. We are now engaged in informal discussions with a view to the eventual conclusion of an Anglo-American trade agreement, and I earnestly hope that, in spite of all the difficulties to be surmounted, we may succeed in arriving at an accord which might well bring benefits to the world far transcending the immediate advantages to the trade of our respective countries.

". . . I wish it were possible for me to tell you that the general European situation presented no features of difficulty or anxiety. Few of us could have foreseen, when hostilities first broke out in Spain, that they would involve so many troublesome and complicated problems for others, and perhaps the only satisfactory aspect of the history of this affair from our point of view has been the close collaboration with the French Government which we have enjoyed throughout. In company with them we have continued our efforts to make the policy of non-intervention more effective. We have taken a prominent part in all endeavours to lessen the sufferings of the Spanish civilian population, and we have done, and will do, all in our power to prevent the conflict from spreading beyond the borders of Spain.

" For France the year has not been an easy one, for her people have been faced with serious financial and economic difficulties, which, however, are being met with courage and determination. I would like to take this opportunity of paying my tribute to the remarkable success achieved by the Paris Exhibition, in spite of the difficulties which attended its early stages.

" As regards our relations with the two great Powers which are now so closely associated in what is known as the Rome-Berlin axis, I will only say this. It is the sincere desire of His Majesty's Government to see those relations established upon a basis of mutual friendship and understanding, but as we believe that that understanding, which might well have far-reaching effects in restoring confidence and security to Europe, will be more hopefully pursued by informal discussion than by public declamation, I propose to abstain from further words upon the subject this evening.

" Before I conclude my review of foreign affairs I would say a word or two about the League of Nations. There are apparently some people whose faith in the League is so shallow that unless they keep repeating its name aloud at frequent intervals they feel themselves liable to forget all about it. The faith of His Majesty's Government goes deeper than that. To us the League is not a fetish but an instrument, the value of which is in direct proportion to its effectiveness. At the present time its effectiveness is seriously impaired because some of the most powerful nations in the world are not members or are not in full sympathy with it, but our aim must be to strengthen its authority and thus so to increase its moral and material force as to enable it to carry out fearlessly and successfully the purposes for which it was originally founded.

" And that leads me to make one further observation before I leave this subject. It appears to be the fashion in some quarters to decry any allusion to material interests, as if they were sordid considerations unworthy of a really high-minded people. I should be the last to suggest that we should exclude from our minds all thoughts of moral and spiritual aims, or that we should occupy ourselves solely with selfish endeavours to improve our material prosperity at the expense of other people's. But is there not a danger of running to the opposite extreme ? After all, the political, financial, and economic stability of this country and of the associated peoples of the British Commonwealth is one of the most important factors in the general well-being of the world. And in endeavouring to preserve that stability we are doing no injury to others, but on the contrary we are making a contribution, the value of which can hardly be over-estimated, to the preservation of the confidence and security of all.

" And now, having concluded my survey, in which I have found many grounds for a cheerful outlook interspersed with some sources of perturbation too real to be ignored, I want to direct your minds for a few minutes more to the consideration of a subject of serious import to us all—and not us only in this hall, but in the country and, indeed, throughout the world.

" Perhaps I may put my subject in the form of a question. What sort of future are we trying to create for ourselves and for our children ? Is it to be better or worse than that which we have inherited ? Are we trying to make a world in which the peoples that inhabit it shall be able to live out their lives in peace of mind and in the enjoyment of a constantly rising standard of all that makes life worth living, of health and comfort, of recreation, and of culture ? Or are we preparing for ourselves a future which is to be one perpetual nightmare,

filled with the constant dread of the horrors of war, forced
to bury ourselves below ground and to spend all our substance
upon the weapons of destruction?

"One has only to state these two alternatives to be sure
that human nature, which is the same all the world over,
must reject the nightmare with all its might and cling to the
only prospect which can give happiness. And for any Government
deliberately to deny to their people what must be their
plainest and simplest right would be to betray their trust
and to call down upon their heads the condemnation of all
mankind.

"I do not believe that such a Government anywhere
exists among civilized peoples. I am convinced that the aim
of every statesman worthy the name, to whatever country
he belongs, must be the happiness of the people for whom
and to whom he is responsible, and in that faith I am sure
that a way can, and will be found to free the world from
the curse of armaments and the fears that give rise to them
and to open up a happier and a wiser future for mankind."

FENCING IN A CHINA SHOP

Before the Houses rose for the Christmas vacation, the Opposition demanded another Debate on the international situation. It took place on 21st December. The Prime Minister rose, after Mr. Attlee, at half-past four on that winter afternoon.

" THIS Debate on foreign affairs is taking place at
the urgent request of the Opposition. We have
not thought it right to refuse to accede to that request,
but I must express my own personal regret that it has been
thought necessary to have another public discussion on
foreign affairs. It is so difficult to say anything that can do
good, and so easy to say much that might do harm. A china
shop is not the best or the safest place for a fencing match, and
if, in my reply to the right hon. Gentleman (Mr. Attlee), I am
not altogether as informative as he would like me to be, it
must be remembered that, even if the Opposition do not
feel any responsibility for the safety of the crockery, certainly
His Majesty's Government do. It is our responsibility.

" The right hon. Gentleman stated at the beginning of
his speech that there was a profound difference of view
between the Opposition and the supporters of the Government on foreign affairs, but I think that in listening to his
speech the House must have been surprised, after that
exordium, to find how much he had to say with which the
House itself was in general agreement. In particular, if I
may say so, His Majesty's Government fully realise what the
right hon. Gentleman said about the new methods of propaganda which have sprung up in recent years. They fully
realise that the old stand-upon-your-dignity methods are no
longer applicable to modern conditions, and that, in the
rough-and-tumble of international relations which we see
to-day, it is absolutely necessary that we should take measures
to protect ourselves from constant misrepresentation. The
objectives which the right hon. Gentleman put before us are,
I think, broadly speaking, common to us all. It is only
when one comes to the methods of achieving those objectives
that I am bound to say I found the right hon. Gentleman's
speech singularly lacking in constructive ideas. Nor could I
perceive what was the particular course which the right
hon. Gentleman would have had us take in the past,

53

unless it was to go to war with any Power with whom we disagreed. . . .

"The right hon. Gentleman has made some allusions to the various international conversations which have recently taken place, and I would like to touch upon those, and to begin with the visit of the Lord President of the Council to Germany. I have already told the House that the conversations which took place between the Lord President (Lord Halifax) and the German Chancellor and various prominent Germans were of a confidential character, and I am sure that hon. Members would not wish me to say anything which might be considered as a breach of the understanding upon which those conversations took place, but I may perhaps make one or two general observations which would supplement what has already been said upon this subject. It was never the expectation or the intention of His Majesty's Government that those conversations should produce immediate results. They were conversations, and not negotiations, and, therefore, in the course of them no proposals were made, no pledges were given, no bargains were struck. What we had in mind as our object, and what we achieved, was to establish a personal contact between a member of His Majesty's Government and the German Chancellor, and to arrive, if possible, at a clearer understanding on both sides of the policy and outlook of the two Governments.

"I think I may say that we now have a fairly definite idea of the problems which, in the view of the German Government, have to be solved if we are to arrive at that condition of European affairs which we all desire, and in which nations might look upon one another with a desire to co-operate instead of regarding each other with suspicion and resentment. If we are to arrive at any such condition as that, obviously it cannot be achieved by a bargain between two particular countries. This is rather to be considered, as we did consider it, as a first step towards a general effort to arrive at what has sometimes been called a general settlement, to arrive at a position, in fact, when reasonable grievances may be removed, when suspicions may be laid aside, and when confidence may again be restored. That obviously postulates that all those who take part in such an effort must make their contribution towards the common end, but, on the other hand, I think it must be clear that conclusions cannot be hurried or forced, that there must lie before us a certain period of time during which further study and exploration of these problems must take place, and that what has happened so far is only the preliminary to a more extended but, I hope, a more fruitful future.

"I do not think any greater service could be rendered to the cause of peace than by the exercise of restraint and toleration by the Press of both countries, whether they are presenting their account of current events or whether they are commenting upon policies and upon personalities. The power of the Press for good or for evil in international relations is very great, and a judicious use of that power, accompanied by a full sense of responsibility, may have far-reaching effects in creating an atmosphere favourable for the purposes at which we are aiming.

"Perhaps in this connection I might say one word about the mission which last March was entrusted to M. Van Zeeland by the French and British Governments. As the House is aware, M. Van Zeeland has made inquiries in a number of different countries as to the possibility of measures which might improve the general international economic situation and which might, by reducing barriers, once more stimulate the flow of international trade. I have some reason to suppose that his report is now nearly ready for presentation to the two Governments, and I should like to express my gratitude and appreciation of the public spirit shown by M. Van Zeeland in undertaking this work in the midst of all his other preoccupations and in personally giving his attention and his great ability to this important subject. But I would just like to add this observation, that, of course, all that M. Van Zeeland can do is to give us the benefit of any suggestions which he may make as the result of his investigations, but that the final decision as to whether or not those suggestions can be adopted must rest with the Governments concerned. Moreover, I do not think it is possible entirely to separate economic from political conditions. You may have a solution which is perfect from the economic point of view, but it may be of little avail if there is no disposition to examine it favourably and to try and adopt it. Therefore, while undoubtedly the economic problem must always be an important factor in any endeavour to bring about a better state of things in Europe, it is much more likely to receive favourable consideration if it has been preceded by some easing of political tension beforehand.

" Hon. Members will recall that soon after the visit of the Lord President to Germany, we had the pleasure of receiving a visit here from the French Prime Minister and Foreign Minister. I gave the House at the time a very full account of the conversations and of the happy result of that conference, and, therefore, I need not recapitulate it, but I may say again that the harmony which was proved to exist between the two Governments upon all the important issues which we discussed was, and is, a source of deep satisfaction to His Majesty's Government. Subsequently, M. Delbos, owing to the courteous initiative of the German Foreign Minister, had an opportunity of a brief but useful exchange of views with Baron Von Neurath in Berlin on his way out to visit a number of European capitals.

" There is just one other point that I would like to make before I leave the question of these conversations, although perhaps it is really unnecessary. I should like to say that in these conversations there has been no attempt, either on the one hand to break up or to weaken friendships and understandings already arrived at, or on the other hand to set up *blocs* and groups of Powers in opposition to one another. We believe that, although different countries have different methods of managing their own affairs, there is something which is common to them all, and that is the natural desire to improve their own condition ; and since we believe that the fulfilment of that desire can only be achieved by the help of others and by a real understanding and effort to meet others' needs, we conceive that any effort that we can make to promote harmony and to remove legitimate causes of grievances among the nations may well bring its own reward hereafter, if it should prove to have been a contribution to the general welfare of the world."

MR. A. V. ALEXANDER : " Before the Prime Minister leaves this point, with the statement issued after the French visit, is he going to say anything else about the very summarised details then given to the House, and may we take it that if we put questions later to-night to the Foreign Secretary, we may get far more information than we have had so far?"

THE PRIME MINISTER: "I do not think I can promise that the right hon. Gentleman will get far more information than what I consider is the rather full information already given, but perhaps he will put his questions, and then my right hon. Friend will see how far it is possible to meet him.

"Now I will pass to the question of Spain, on which the right hon. Gentleman the Leader of the Opposition was very critical of the actions of the Government. The record of the Opposition in the matter of Spain has not been altogether a happy one. The House will recollect that in July last, when the policy of non-intervention was in some considerable jeopardy, owing to the failure on the part of the nations concerned to agree upon the crucial points of belligerent rights and the withdrawal of volunteers, His Majesty's Government were invited by the other Powers to try and put an end to the deadlock by preparing some kind of compromise plan, but as soon as we had produced that plan, before even the Governments which had asked us to prepare it had had any opportunity of saying what they thought about it, the Opposition demanded the Adjournment of the House in order that they might condemn it and demand its withdrawal. The House did not agree with the Opposition on that occasion. What has happened since? The right hon. Gentleman described the policy of non-intervention as one dictated by expediency, and he said that the expediency had failed. He does not seem to have followed the actual circumstances of the case. What does he mean by expediency? If he means that the policy of non-intervention was designed to prevent the conflict spreading beyond the borders of Spain—and I agree that that was the object of the policy—then, so far from failing, it has been a complete success."

MR. DAVID GRENFELL: "The right hon. Gentleman is making a charge against a party. Was not the object of non-intervention to stop intervention?"

THE PRIME MINISTER: "The policy was designed with the object of confining the conflict to Spain. Although our plan, as we expected, had a mixed reception at first, and although a number of nations made reservations and others said that they did not like it at all, yet by degrees, one by one, the reservations have been withdrawn, until to-day the plan put forward by the British Government has been accepted by every other Government, from Italy on the one side right away to Soviet Russia on the other. That has been the basis of our appeal to the two parties in Spain, and if, as we hope, it will prove to be possible very soon now to send out the Mission to Spain, that Mission will go out on the basis of the British Government's plan.

"The right hon. Gentleman said that all that his party demanded was justice for the Government of Spain. Is it not perfectly clear to the House that his interpretation of justice for the Government of Spain means intervention on one side? That is the difference between the policy of the Government and the policy of the Opposition, that under cover of international law the Opposition desire to intervene on one side, whereas His Majesty's Government have tried to keep the balance even between both sides, and to back neither. I think we may fairly claim that during the past six months there has been a perceptible lessening of the tension in Europe. I put that down largely to the fact that the Spanish situation has become less acute. We may also claim that the policy of His Majesty's Government has played a most important part in averting a possible conflict outside Spain.

"One reason, no doubt, why we have been hearing less about Spain is that it has been eclipsed in our attention by the distressing events in the Far East. I am not proposing now to enter upon any discussion of the origin of what has now become a major war in everything but name. Whatever may be the true history of the matter, whether the Japanese have forced a war upon China or whether, as Japanese apologists seem to indicate, Japan was forced to defend herself against aggression by China, whatever may be the truth, it certainly is a fact that no attempt has ever been made by Japan to seek a settlement by peaceful means. The Brussels

Conference was called of the Powers which had signed the Nine-Power Treaty, together with certain other Powers which had important interests in the Far East, but Japan refused to attend. She refused even to enter into informal discussions outside the Conference. The result of that was that the Conference failed to achieve the purpose for which it had been convened, namely, to find some method of ending the war by peaceful means. That result was unfortunate, but it was not disgraceful to the Conference.

" There was only one way in which the conflict could have been brought to an end, as it proved, and that was not by peace, but by force. There was no mention of force in the Nine-Power Treaty, which provided the machinery, not taken advantage of by Japan, for consultation if a situation should arise which threatened peace. Coercion would not have obtained the support of any member of the Brussels Conference. Although the outcome of the Conference was so disappointing to the friends of peace, there was one feature of it, at any rate, from which we may draw some satisfaction, and that was that throughout we found ourselves in complete and harmonious agreement with the delegation of the United States of America on all the matters we discussed.

" Hon. Members are familiar with the latest developments in China, including the attack upon British ships in the Yangtse. They are aware of the repeated representations which we have made to the Japanese Government and the text of the Note we sent to them after the last incident had happened. What we are now doing is to await proof of the determination and the ability of the Japanese Government to prevent a recurrence of these incidents. From the beginning we have constantly offered our services with a view to trying to find some means of bringing this conflict to an end. We are still anxious to serve the cause of peace by any honourable means that are open to us, but it must not be thought that our desire for peace and our patience under repeated provocation mean that we are either indifferent to our international obligations, or that we are forgetful of our duty to protect British interests. It is now for the Japanese Government to show that they, in their turn, are not unmindful of the rights and interests of foreigners, and that their assurances and apologies mean something more than words.

" The right hon. Gentleman has alluded to the League of Nations and to the effect upon the League of the notice that has been given by Italy to terminate her membership. This notice, which cannot, of course, become operative for two years, does not make any real difference in the situation. There has been no Italian delegation to the League since May, 1936, and for more than a year no Italian has taken part in any committee or other organ of the League. Therefore, this public announcement makes no change in the facts of the situation ; it merely emphasises this point, that in its present condition the League is unable to discharge some of the functions with which it was invested when it was first created. Such a situation must necessarily cause great concern to all those who, like His Majesty's Government, still believe in those ideals of international co-operation which were present to the minds of the founders of the League. In spite of any anxiety which we may have, the League can still play a part in world affairs, and it will do so all the more effectively the more willing it is frankly to face the realities of the situation. We have in the League an organization that has proved itself in many ways, and that can continue its beneficent work in many other spheres. It can be of service to those who, like ourselves, wish to avail themselves of its services, and it will offer its services in no spirit of partisanship. We shall continue to give it our warmest support, believing that it can still afford the nucleus for the better and more comprehensive organisation which we believe is necessary for the maintenance of peace.

" The right hon. Gentleman said that he trusted I could give the House a message of hope. He did not paint a very optimistic picture of the situation of the world. He pointed out that there were present to-day in the situation all the elements which might conduce to another war. If we are to take his view that British commercial interests can only be protected by us if we protect all the interests of the world, and if we are to constitute ourselves in that way the policeman of the world—[Interruption]—how are we to protect the interests of the world if we are not the policeman of the world ? "

MR. ATTLEE : " It was precisely the object of the establishment of the League that the preservation of peace was a common interest of the world, and my point is that the right hon. Gentleman's Government has departed from that because it has always considered only the narrow Imperialist interest and not the world interest. He would be in a far better position to-day if it had realised that long ago."

THE PRIME MINISTER : " That seems to me to be only a repetition of the view that it is the duty of this country to protect interests all over the world, quite apart——"

AN HON. MEMBER : " What about others ? "

THE PRIME MINISTER : " Yes, in company with others. [HON. MEMBERS : ' Hear, hear ! '] Will the hon. Members who say ' Hear, hear,' tell us how we are to get others alongside us ? Are they completely blind and deaf to what has taken place ? Have they forgotten the efforts we have made to get other countries alongside us ? This seems to me to show once again that the Opposition are living in an unreal world. They are trying to put upon a mutilated League duties which it is not able to perform as it is constituted at present, and they are trying to throw upon this Government the onus of what is not the fault of this Government, but is the inevitable accompaniment of the present constitution of the League. We are not unmindful—we never have been in this country— of the abstract principles of justice, liberty and freedom, for which we stand in this country and the British Empire. But, although hon. Gentlemen opposite talk about our acting in concert with others, it takes two, at least, to bring about a concert, and we cannot act alone and stand up for these principles in all parts of the world. The right hon. Gentleman does, in fact, ask us to do that, because if the League fails hon. and right hon. Gentlemen opposite always say, ' It is entirely the fault of His Majesty's Government.' I should give the House no hope if I thought that that was all we had to depend on. When the right hon. Gentleman wants to know whether we are drifting or steering towards a port, I say, ' We are not drifting ; we have a definite objective in front of us.' That objective is a general settlement of the grievances of the world without war. We believe that the right way to go about that is not to issue threats, but to try to establish those personal contacts to which I have already alluded, and that only by friendly, frank discussion between the nations can we hope to arrive at a situation when once more we shall be able to remove anxiety from our minds."

TO MAKE FRIENDS OF FOES

The Prime Minister began the political new year with a speech to the Midland Union of Conservative and Unionist Associations, with which he had long been associated, at a luncheon in Birmingham on 4th February. In it he referred to the necessity for extensive and costly rearmament in the existing state of the world and to the folly of mankind that made such expenditure necessary.

" IN one of his famous essays Bacon says of men in great places that they have no freedom either in their presence or, he says, in their actions, or in their times, and I am reminded of a story which, I think, was related, or possibly invented, by the late Lord Grey of Fallodon about a Chinaman who, by living in the country and saying very little, achieved a reputation for immense wisdom. So great did his reputation grow that in due course a deputation of his fellow-countrymen waited upon him to ask him to accept the throne, and in reply, the story went, the Chinaman said nothing, but he went out quickly and washed his ears.

" I do not want you to take that story too seriously, or to think that I am anxious to be relieved of my office : I only tell it to imply that these burdens and responsibilities are considerable and that what are sometimes called the sweets of office lie not in the satisfaction of personal ambitions but in the opportunities that are afforded to make some contribution to the happiness and security of the British peoples, and perhaps sometimes to other peoples who are not fortunate enough to be included in the British Empire. I have no doubt that in the case of British Prime Ministers these opportunities are exceptionally wide. Nothing, I think, has impressed me more during the last eight months, in which I have had opportunities of conversation with many visitors from the smaller countries of Europe and elsewhere, than the unanimity with which they have expressed their confidence in the single-mindedness and the wisdom of Great Britain, and their desire to follow her lead.

" I can give you an instance of how this moral influence of our country does afford an opportunity of service to mankind by mentioning an incident which was made public only this week. You all know with what bitterness and barbarity this civil conflict in Spain is being carried on. Many prisoners have been taken on both sides, and in many instances these prisoners have been shot or have been maltreated, and the other day both sides in this conflict informed the British Government that they would be willing to entertain an exchange of prisoners—not only of non-combatants but actually of military and political prisoners, refugees and others, one condition being that we were to appoint a British arbitrator to prepare and carry out the arrangements. Is that not a wonderful instance of the confidence that is felt in British impartiality? It may mean some little expense, but we have expressed our readiness to undertake the responsibility, and if we can successfully carry through such an exchange as that, everybody will rejoice to think of the relief which will be afforded to hundreds of families who must to-day be suffering acute anxiety about the fate of their relatives.

" I should not like to leave you to suppose that in this striking instance the influence of the British people in world affairs is merely sentimental or depends upon the reliance upon our good intentions. The value of good intentions depends a great deal upon ability to carry them out, and I must record my conviction that the lessened tension, the increased feeling of security, which undoubtedly exists in Europe to-day, is largely founded upon the fact of British rearmament.

" I am glad to say that the task which the Government have undertaken of rebuilding our armed forces is one which has met with general approval throughout the country, and, indeed, I think the only anxiety which is felt about it is whether it is going fast enough and far enough. I don't think that there is any cause for serious anxiety upon that score. It is not to be expected that this vast programme of rearmament, by far the largest that this country has ever undertaken in time of peace, can be carried through without some delays and disappointments. We had let things go so far that extensive preparation was necessary before we could even begin production upon the scale which we were contemplating, but the initial difficulties have now been overcome. Our three Service Ministers and their staffs are untiring in their efforts, and the services of the Minister for the Co-ordination of Defence in watching over the whole programme, in preventing overlapping and seeing that every need is examined and met in proper priority, have been simply invaluable.

" It is only right that I should pay a tribute, too, to the services of the industries concerned who are co-operating with us in the fulfilment of our task. Both employers and workers are setting about their business with a full appreciation of the fact that what they are doing is vital in the national interest, and every month that passes bears fresh witness to their efficiency and their zeal. Here in the Midlands we can see on every side evidence of those activities in rearmament which for a long time will continue to keep our factories full and to find employment for the skill of our workpeople.

" That is something which may give us cause for satisfaction, but at the same time I must confess that the spectacle of this vast expenditure upon means of destruction instead of construction has inspired me with a feeling of revolt against the folly of mankind. The cost is stupendous, and the thought of the sacrifice that it must entail upon us, and upon those who come after us, drives the Government always to search for a way out, to seek to find some means of breaking through this senseless competition in rearmament which continually cancels out the efforts that each nation makes to secure an advantage over the others. We cannot hope by ourselves to discover a means of escape. It can only be done by frank and full discussion with others who share our desire, and by showing our readiness to make our contribution to the common cause of peace if others will do the same. This is not the time or the place to disclose what may be the prospects of fruitful discussions upon this subject, which is of such vital interest to great sections of humanity. All I would say is that the Government has given, and is giving, anxious thought to this question, and that in so far as good will and an earnest desire to succeed can contribute towards success, those qualities will not be lacking upon our part.

" It is a relief to turn from the troubled vision of international affairs to the calmer atmosphere that we find in our own country. I wonder sometimes if, in all our domestic history since the industrial revolution, you could point to any period in which such an upward trend of trade and commerce as we have witnessed during the last few years has been unaccompanied by any major industrial dispute. Surely that is a very remarkable tribute to the good sense of our employers and workers, and I hope I am not too optimistic in believing that this freedom from industrial warfare is no accident. It arises, as it seems to me, from something in the nature of a permanent change in the methods of arriving at a fairer distribution of the profits of trade and industry. That, in turn, has sprung from a more complete and a more scientific organisation of trade unions on the one side and of employers' associations on the other, with the effect that we have largely cut out the old personal antagonisms, and that in these days we can approach negotiations between employers and employed on a broader and a more objective basis.

" Whatever may be the cause of it, undoubtedly the result has been eminently satisfactory. During these last few years the profits of trade—and, may I, as an ex-Chancellor, add, the contribution which those profits make to the national revenue—have been very handsomely expanded, and the figures recently quoted by the Minister of Labour in the House of Commons, when he stated that last year the weekly wage rates of over 5,000,000 people had been increased by no less than £780,000, demonstrate most convincingly what benefits have accrued to the working people.

" If I were to try to put in a single word the greatest boon that any Government can bestow upon the country, I would say that it is in the establishment and maintenance of confidence. It is confidence that stimulates enterprise, and confidence that gives peace of mind to the people. I would say that in this country especially the establishment of confidence breeds a like result elsewhere. Only a little while ago there seemed to be some check to our confidence. I never believed that there was any foundation for such a check, and I think it has already passed off as far as we are concerned.

" Only in the last few days we have given proof of our confidence in our future, and in the future of our potential customers, by making certain relaxations in the regulations that govern the lending of money to foreign borrowers. I believe that that change will tend to stimulate international trade, and, after all, it is to international trade that we must chiefly look to take the place of our rearmament programme when it begins to approach its completion. If by joint effort we can succeed in securing some measure of political appeasement, that would bring in its train such a fresh accession of confidence as would give a new stimulus to industry and would bring new hope to the depressed areas of the world. To make this year of 1938 a starting-point of renewed confidence and security—that is the aim of His Majesty's Government. For that aim we ask your good wishes, and in the words of our West Midland poet :

> ' God's benison go with you, and with those
> Who would make good of bad, and friends of foes.' "

CONVERSATIONS WITH ITALY

Mr. Chamberlain made his first step towards international appeasement by responding to an approach from Italy, whose traditional friendship with this country had been broken by the Abyssinian War and further aggravated by the difference of outlook on the Spanish Civil War. A friendly gesture had been made by Signor Mussolini in July, 1937, in a message to the Prime Minister, to which the latter had cordially replied in a personal letter. But tension in the Mediterranean over the Spanish blockade and the decision of Italy to leave the League of Nations prevented further negotiations for a time. Early in February, 1938 however, came a chance of improving a worsening situation with an intimation of the Italian Ambassador's, following some friendly conversations between him and Mr. Anthony Eden, the British Foreign Secretary, that the Italian Government was ready at any time to open conversations with the British Government covering every question of dispute between the two countries, including the broadcast propaganda in the Middle East, the foreign volunteers in Spain and the formal recognition of the Abyssinian conquest. Mr. Eden had replied that, though Great Britain was bound to act as a loyal member of the League of Nations, a settlement between the two countries as a contribution to general appeasement would no doubt influence the League's attitude towards Italy. A week later Mr. Eden resigned on the grounds that the time for negotiations had not yet arrived, and that Italy must first agree on certain conditions precedent before discussions could commence. Mr. Chamberlain, supported by the rest of the Cabinet, held that this was not a practicable method of negotiation. On the afternoon of 21st February, after the House had listened to the statements of the Foreign Secretary and Under Secretary, Lord Cranborne, on their resignations, the Prime Minister rose to explain the Government's policy.

"THE House has followed with the keenest attention and with deep personal sympathy the statement of my right hon. Friend the late Foreign Secretary upon the reasons which have led him to the grave decision to resign his office. He has been followed by my Noble Friend the Member for South Dorset (Viscount Cranborne) in a statement of the reasons which have caused him to follow the example of my right hon. Friend. To the great majority of hon. Members this decision must have come with a shock of surprise, and I cannot wonder that they have been surprised, because, until only a few days ago, none of his colleagues had anticipated that there was any danger of an event which has been extremely painful to us all. If I may say so, it has been especially painful to myself, because my relations with my right hon. Friend have been those of a friend, as well as of a colleague, and if there have been, from time to time, differences of opinion between us, as there must be between the best of colleagues, they have never been exacerbated by hard words, but have always been discussed between us in the friendliest and most amicable manner.

"When, only a little over a week ago, some organs of the Press were declaring that there were serious differences of opinion between my right hon. Friend and myself, I was under the impression that we were in complete agreement, and I must add that, to the rest of the Government, including myself, it did not seem that such differences of opinion as have arisen upon the immediate question at issue were of sufficient importance to make it necessary for my right hon. Friend to leave us. My right hon. Friend took a different view. He has said, and said truly, that each man must be the keeper of his own conscience. I do not for one moment doubt or question the sincerity of his conviction, that the course which he has felt it necessary to take is the one which would best serve the interests of the country.

"In order that the House may have before it as complete a

73

picture as possible of the events which have led up to the present situation, I must ask for their indulgence while I endeavour to state once again my own views upon certain aspects of foreign policy—views which have never altered, and which have been shared by all my colleagues. On a former occasion I described that policy as being based upon three principles—first, on the protection of British interests and the lives of British nationals; secondly, on the maintenance of peace, and, as far as we can influence it, the settlement of differences by peaceful means and not by force; and, thirdly, the promotion of friendly relations with other nations who are willing to reciprocate our friendly feelings and who will keep those rules of international conduct without which there can be neither security nor stability.

" It is not enough to lay down general principles. If we truly desire peace, it is, in my opinion, necessary to make a sustained effort to ascertain, and if possible remove, the causes which threaten peace and which now, for many months, have kept Europe in a state of tension and anxiety. There is another fact which points in the same direction. We are in this country now engaged upon a gigantic scheme of rearmament which most of us believe to be essential to the maintenance of peace. Other countries are doing the same. Indeed, we were the last of the nations to rearm, but this process of general rearmament has been forced upon us all, because every country is afraid to disarm lest it should fall a victim to some armed neighbour. I recognise the force of that hard fact, but I have never ceased publicly to deplore what seems to me a senseless waste of money, for which everyone will have to pay dearly, if they are not paying for it already. I cannot believe that, with a little good will and determination, it is not possible to remove genuine grievances and to clear away suspicions which may be entirely unfounded.

" For these reasons, then, my colleagues and I have been anxious to find some opportunity of entering upon conversations with the two European countries with which we have been at variance, namely, Germany and Italy, in order that we might find out whether there was any common ground on which we might build up a general scheme of appeasement in Europe. It is not necessary now to enter upon a discussion upon our relations with Germany, because it is not over those that this difference has arisen. I would only observe that the visit of the Lord President of the Council to Germany marked the first attempt to explore the ground, and that we hope, in the light of the information which we then obtained, to pursue that matter further at a convenient opportunity. In the case of Italy there has been what my right hon. Friend has alluded to as the gentlemen's agreement of January, 1937, an agreement which it was hoped was going to be the first step in the clearing up of the situation between ourselves and the Italian Government. Speaking of this agreement in the House of Commons on 19th January, 1937, my right hon. Friend said :

" ' A series of statements were made in both countries, one by the Prime Minister '

that was Lord Baldwin—

' which indicated a desire to improve relations. To do this it was decided to attempt to seek agreement upon a joint declaration. This declaration is neither a treaty nor a pact, but it marks, we hope and believe, the end of a chapter of strained relations.'

My right hon. Friend went on to tell the House how well this declaration had been received by other countries, who regarded it as likely to be of service towards an appeasement in the Mediterranean. Unfortunately, there intervened in Spain the events to which my right hon. Friend has alluded. Nevertheless, there remained good reason for continuing to watch to see whether a suitable opportunity might arise in order to improve relations. Towards the end of July, after a speech which was made by the Foreign Secretary in the House of Commons on the 19th of that month, the Italian Ambassador, Count Grandi, informed my right hon. Friend that that speech had made an excellent impression in Italy and that the situation seemed to be so much easier that he was encouraged to deliver to me, as Prime Minister, a message which Signor Mussolini had authorised him to make use of when he thought that the moment was propitious.

" Accordingly, I arranged for Count Grandi to come to see me on 27th July. The message which he brought me from Signor Mussolini was of a friendly character. I felt that we were presented with an opportunity for improving our relations which ought not to be missed. I decided to take what I considered then, and what I consider now, to be the course which was best calculated to serve the purpose, namely, to put aside ordinary diplomatic formalities and send a personal reply in cordial terms by way of response. Perhaps I may remind the House of the words which I used on this subject in reply to the hon. Baronet the Member for South-West Bethnal Green (Sir P. Harris), who asked whether I could publish in a White Paper the correspondence between Signor Mussolini and myself. My reply was as follows:

" ' No, Sir. That correspondence was personal, but I have no objection to telling the House the purport of it. At the end of July last the Italian Ambassador brought me a message from Signor Mussolini of a friendly character. I took advantage of the opportunity to send Signor Mussolini a personal letter expressing my regret that relations between Great Britain and Italy were still far from that old feeling of mutual confidence and affection which lasted for so many years. I went on to state my belief that those old feelings could be restored if we could clear away certain misunderstandings and unfounded suspicions, and I declared the readiness of His Majesty's Government at any time to enter into conversations with that object. I was glad to receive from Signor Mussolini, immediately, a reply in which he expressed his own sincere wish to restore good relations between our two countries and his agreement with the suggestion that conversations should be entered upon in order to ensure the desired understanding between the two countries.'

" This letter was followed up by instructions to our Ambassador in Rome to inform the Italian Government that it was hoped that conversations might begin in September. Unfortunately, certain incidents took place in the Mediterranean which, in our opinion, rendered it impossible that conversations at that time could have any chance of success. Nevertheless, it is well to remember something which my right hon. Friend omitted to mention in his account of past history, namely, that he was successful at Nyon in arriving at an agreement with the Italian Government about the patrolling of the Mediterranean."

Hon. Members : " They were not there."

Mr. Arthur Henderson : " Is it not a fact that at the conference at Nyon the Italian Government were not represented ? "

The Prime Minister : " That is only a minor correction. The hon. Member knows perfectly well that the original agreement which was made between ourselves and the French was joined in by the Italians—with my right hon. Friend's help—who agreed to take their share in the patrolling of the Mediterranean by French, Italian, and British warships, and once more I hoped that this agreement might be followed by further discussions upon the Spanish situation, which in turn would open up the way for those conversations which had been the subject of the correspondence between Signor Mussolini and myself. There once again I was disappointed, and the situation became clouded by the difficulties experienced in the Non-Intervention Committee over the withdrawal of volunteers, difficulties which did not arise in one quarter only, and when later Italy gave notice of her intention to leave the League it was difficult to see how the conversations could proceed.

" I think it is well to consider how these successive obstacles to conversations affected the situation as between Italy and ourselves. It cannot be denied that during all those months which had lapsed since the original interchange of letters between Signor Mussolini and myself the state of Anglo-Italian relations had seriously and steadily deteriorated. It has always seemed to me that in dealing with foreign countries we do not give ourselves a chance of success unless we try to understand their mentality, which is not always the same as our own, and it really is astonishing to contemplate how the identically same facts are regarded from two different angles. I am informed from many sources that all this time when to us it appeared that the obstacles to conversations had arisen entirely by Italian action, exactly the opposite view was being held in Rome. (Laughter.) Hon. Members may laugh at that, and it is very funny, but if we are to make progress in the task of improving our relations with other countries, we must at least understand what their point of view is.

" All this time the suspicion was growing in Rome that we did not want conversations at all and that we were engaged in a Machiavellian design to lull the Italians into inactivity while we completed our rearmament, with the intention presently of taking our revenge for the Italian conquest of Abyssinia. I should not be at all surprised if hon. Members opposite had laughed at my description of this suspicion. Not only to hon. Members opposite, but to all of us the idea seems fantastic. It is one which never entered our heads, but when there is an atmosphere of ill will, suspicion breeds suspicion. The result of this suspicion was a series of activities on the Italian side, the movement of troops, the stirring-up of propaganda, and other matters to which my right hon. Friend alluded, but which I need not repeat, because everybody is aware of them. But it is in these circumstances, in a steadily worsening atmosphere over-hanging our relations with Italy, that a fresh opportunity arose to break out of this vicious circle. It arose on the 10th of this month.

" Following on some amiable conversations between the Italian Ambassador and my right hon. Friend, the Ambassador called at the Foreign Office and stated that these conversations had been sincerely welcomed in Rome and that he had been instructed to report that the Italian Government were ready at any time to open conversations with us. He added that he desired the conversations to be as wide as possible, embracing, of course, the question of the formal recognition of the Abyssinian conquest, but also not excluding Spain. In reply, the Foreign Secretary pointed out that we in this country were bound to act as loyal members of the League, but he added that it seemed to him that the attitude of the League and especially that of the Mediterranean Powers would no doubt be considerably influenced by the fact, if fact it came to be, that we and the Italian Government had come to an agreement which was a real contribution to a general appease-ment. My right hon. Friend emphasised that this was a factor which would have great weight with public opinion, not only in this country, but also in France and in the other Mediterranean States and, which is important, in the United States of America also.

" In all this my right hon. Friend was not merely expressing his own personal opinion, he was speaking for the Government as a whole, and those views which he expressed to the Italian Ambassador were particularly coincident with the views that I hold myself. I have always taken the view, for instance, that the question of the formal recognition of the Italian position in Abyssinia was one that could only be morally justified if it was found to be a factor, and an essential factor, in a general appeasement. That was the view of all of us, including my right hon. Friend, and it will be seen that the trend of these conversations which I have just reported was definitely favourable to a further discussion, which would include all outstanding questions, including the question of Abyssinia. All outstanding questions, it is important to recognise, did include the question of Abyssinia, and I emphasise this because of the point of view that has been expressed by my Noble Friend (Lord Cranborne).

" I am sure the House will not have failed to notice that in his view the issue is one quite different from that which was put forward by my right hon. Friend. [HON. MEMBERS : ' No.'] Let me remind the House that my right hon. Friend said quite clearly—I took his words down at the time—that the issue is : Should conversations be opened in Rome now ? That is not the point of view of my Noble Friend. He says that this is not a question of detail ; this is a question of fundamental principle. He went on to say that that fundamental principle was the principle of international good faith."

MR. EDEN : " Hear, hear."

THE PRIME MINISTER : " If that is the principle upon which my Noble Friend found it necessary to separate himself from us now, what has happened to alter the position since those conversations which I have described to the House ? There was no reason why we should not proceed in due course to discuss with Italy all outstanding questions. A week later our Ambassador in Rome reported a conversation with the Italian Foreign Minister at which the latter had told him he had instructed Count Grandi to urge earnestly that an early start should be made with the conversations. On the same day I suggested to my right hon. Friend that it would be useful if he and I had a talk with Count Grandi. My right hon. Friend in his statement was anxious to put the situation as objectively as he possibly could, but I must ask him to forgive me if I say that at one point he was not quite fair. He represented to the House that the Italian Government had called upon us to enter upon conversations now or never, and that we were being asked to submit to a threat. There is nothing in any of the communications which passed between us and the Italian Government which, in my judgment, would justify that description."

MR. ATTLEE: "As the Prime Minister is alluding to a number of communications and conversations, I take it that we shall have a White Paper to enable us to judge for ourselves?"

THE PRIME MINISTER: "I do not think there is anything in what I have alluded to which I should be in the least afraid to publish so that judgment might be exercised upon it. I repeat that in my judgment, and, I am sure I can say, in the judgment of my colleagues, with the exception of my right hon. Friend (Mr. Eden), nothing that has been said on behalf of the Italian Government would justify anybody in saying that they have used threats. It is, therefore, not fair to the House to suggest that they are being asked to submit to demands from another Government to which it would be derogatory to our dignity to submit. I have stated that they informed us of their earnest desire that conversations should start as soon as possible, and it was upon the expression of that desire that the conversation between the Italian Ambassador, the Foreign Secretary and me took place. The Foreign Secretary concurred in my suggestion, but later in the day sent me a note asking me not to commit the Government to anything specific during the conversation. As a matter of fact, I did abstain from anything of the kind.

"When the conversation was over the Foreign Secretary and I discussed what were the conclusions that should be drawn from it. It was then, as it seemed to me, that for the first time our differences became acute. This was on Friday. I was convinced that a rebuff to the Italian expression of their desire that conversations should start at once would be taken by them as a confirmation of those suspicions which I have described, suspicions that we had never really been in earnest about the conversations at all. I thought that if that were the effect, the result would be disastrous. It would be followed by an intensification of anti-British feeling in Italy, rising to a point at which ultimately war between us might become inevitable. Moreover, I was equally convinced that once the conversations had started we should find good effects of the new atmosphere in many places, and notably in Spain, where the chief difficulty between us had lain for so long.

" The Foreign Secretary, on the other hand, was unable to agree to any immediate decision. He wished to say in reply that, in the opinion of His Majesty's Government, the moment for the official opening of conversations had not arisen, and that we wished to wait until a substantial withdrawal of volunteers had taken place. In particular, he insisted that we ought to have had some indication from the Italian Government, such as their acceptance of the British formula for the withdrawal of volunteers from Spain, which, he pointed out, had been waiting for Italian acceptance for some considerable time, before we committed ourselves even to conversations. But when I asked him whether, if such an acceptance could be obtained from the Italians, he would then be able to agree to the commencement of the conversations, he made it clear that his objections would still remain. In these circumstances, with the full concurrence and at the desire of the Foreign Secretary, I decided to summon the Cabinet for Saturday afternoon, the next day. I informed Count Grandi that I could not give him our final decision until to-day, but that, in the meantime, it would be helpful if he could obtain from his Government such an assurance as the Foreign Secretary had spoken of.

" I need not recite in detail the subsequent events of Saturday and Sunday. I think the House already knows that when the Cabinet had heard the views of my right hon. Friend and myself, their views leaned to my side rather than to his, but it was a very great shock to many of my colleagues that they learned that a final decision in this sense would involve the resignation of my right hon. Friend. Prolonged and persistent efforts were made to induce him to change his decision, but it was all in vain, and in the course of the evening I received from him a letter of resignation which has been published this morning in the Press. That is the end of my account of the differences between my right hon. Friend, on the one hand, and my colleagues and me, on the other, on this particular issue.

" There remains a further brief chapter of the history which I must now relate. This morning I received a call from the Italian Ambassador in accordance with the arrangements made when we parted on Friday last. He had been in communication with his Government over the week-end, and he began by informing me that he had received from them a communication, which I think I had better read to the House. It is as follows :

" ' The Italian Ambassador informs the Prime Minister that he has submitted to the Italian Government the proposals suggested at their meeting of last Friday, and is glad to convey to him the Italian Government's acceptance of the British formula concerning the withdrawal of foreign volunteers and granting of belligerent rights.'

I have not the formula with me, but I think the House is familiar with it. It is that when a certain proportion of volunteers on both sides has been withdrawn there should be granted belligerent rights. I think I can say that in handing me this communication the Italian Ambassador intimated that I was to regard it as a gesture on the part of his Government——"

MR. THORNE : " When they knew that the Foreign Secretary had gone."

THE PRIME MINISTER : "——indicating the spirit of good will and good feeling in which they would wish to begin our conversations. The hon. Member for Plaistow (Mr. Thorne) says : ' When they knew that the Foreign Secretary had gone.' I asked the Italian Ambassador when he had received this communication, and he informed me that he had received it early on Sunday morning. I then informed the Ambassador, following on the meeting of the Cabinet, that I was happy to say we were ready to begin conversations, and that the Italian Government would be so informed at once. It would, however, be necessary, as a preliminary, as the conversations would take place in Rome, that our Ambassador, who would conduct them on our behalf, would have to return to London to receive his instructions and to make sure that he understood the mind of the Government in the matter. At the same time I told the Ambassador that I wished to impress upon him certain points. First of all I told him that the British Government regarded a settlement of the Spanish question as an essential feature of any agreement at which we might arrive. No agreement could be considered complete unless it contained a settlement of the Spanish question.

" Secondly, I repeated that, as he had been already told by my right hon. Friend (Mr. Eden), we were loyal members of the League, and that if we came to an agreement we should desire to obtain the approval of the League for it. I said it was essential that it should not be possible, if we went to the League to recommend the approval of the agreement, for it to be said that the situation in Spain during the conversations had been materially altered by Italy, either by sending fresh reinforcements to Franco or by failing to implement the arrangements contemplated by the British formula. I added that I did not believe these intimations would occasion his Government a moment's anxiety, since I was confident that his Government would approach the negotiations in the same spirit as we should do, namely, in perfect good faith and with a sincere desire to reach agreement.

" Perhaps in that last sentence I have expressed that difference in outlook between my right hon. Friend and myself of which he has told us of his consciousness. I am not here to say that the actions of the Italian Government in the past have been satisfactory to me, but I am concerned with the future, not the past. I believe that if these negotiations are approached in a spirit of mutual confidence there is a good hope that they may be brought to a successful conclusion, but if you are going beforehand to enter upon them in a spirit of suspicion, then none of those conditions that you can think of, the initial withdrawal of troops or anything else that my right hon. Friend suggests, is going to save you. If there is going to be bad faith there will be bad faith, and no assurances beforehand are going to alter it.

" I know very well that the decision of the Government is

going to be misrepresented; it has been misrepresented already. The right hon. Member for South Hackney (Mr. H. Morrison), who carries his partisanship to what I might call old-fashioned lengths, is already suggesting to his audiences terms of an agreement which has not yet even begun to be discussed. Let me make it plain that there is no question at this moment of what the terms of the agreement are to be. The question is whether we are to enter upon negotiations or to refuse even to contemplate them, and if there be any here who really wish to obtain peace, do they think they can ever obtain peace by continuing a vendetta and refusing even to talk about their differences? I have never been more completely convinced of the rightness of any course that I have had to take than I am to-day of the rightness of the decision to which the Cabinet came yesterday. What we are seeking to do is to get a general appeasement throughout Europe which will give us peace.

" The peace of Europe must depend upon the attitude of the four major Powers—Germany, Italy, France and ourselves. For ourselves, we are linked to France by common ideals of democracy, of liberty and Parliamentary government. France need not fear that the resignation of my right hon. Friend upon this issue signifies any departure from the policy of the closest friendship with France of which he has been such a distinguished exponent. I count myself as firm a friend of France as my right hon. Friend. The difference between him and me will never mean that there is any difference between us about our relations with France. On the other side we find Italy and Germany linked by affinities of outlook and in the forms of their government. The question that we have to think of is this: Are we to allow these two pairs of nations to go on glowering at one another across the frontier, allowing the feeling between the two sides to become more and more embittered, until at last the barriers are broken down and the conflict begins which many think would mark the end of civilisation? Or can we bring them to an understanding of one another's aims and objects, and to such discussion as may lead to a final settlement? If we can do that, if we can bring these four nations into friendly discussion, into a settling of their differences, we shall have saved the peace of Europe for a generation. My right hon. Friend and I have differed not upon these general aims, which we share with equal earnestness and conviction, but in my judgment—and I hope that the House will agree with me and my colleagues in this—the response made this morning, the desire which was expressed by the Italian Government for a frank discussion, constitute an important step towards the accomplishment of our purpose."

In the Debate that followed, the Opposition attacked the Prime Minister with great bitterness, affecting a profound sympathy with the former Foreign Secretary whose policy and principles they had hitherto treated with contempt. " It stood out a mile," said Mr. Attlee, Leader of the Socialist Parliamentary Party, " that the late Foreign Secretary was standing for principles, certain definite principles in the government of the world, and that the Prime Minister was rejecting them all."

" Just at this time, the Prime Minister goes whining to him for an agreement on Anglo-Italian relations, Signor Mussolini has been insulting the Prime Minister's colleagues for months and months, is fomenting discontent all through the Near East, including Palestine and Egypt and everywhere else, is carrying on an abusive campaign against this country, and his friends, with weapons which he supplies, attack our ships and kill our sailors. This is the moment chosen by the Prime Minister to go cap in hand to Mussolini and say : ' Will you please give me an agreement ? Everything is to be forgiven and everything is to be forgotten. There are no conditions.'

" Anything more like a surrender to dictatorship than the line which the Prime Minister took to-day I have never heard," Mr. Attlee said at the conclusion of his speech. " Apparently he must come to terms with Signor Mussolini and he must not mention any prerequisites on his side." Mr. J. Griffiths, Socialist member for Llanelly, spoke of " a definite lining up by this Government beside the Fascist Powers," and stated that it was " shaking hands with murder to shake hands with Mussolini." At twenty-five minutes to eleven at night, the Prime Minister rose again after a speech by Mr. David Grenfell, member for Gower, who after declaring that there were 200,000 foreign troops in Spain under the direction of Italy, advanced the view

*that the only proper course was " to refuse to deal singly with
these nations who have no political morality ; who do not
acknowledge ordinary values in human conduct ; who play the
part of the bully in a public house, who shouts and thumps the
table and makes his impossible demands upon his associates."*

" The hon. Member for Gower (Mr. Grenfell) informed the
House that his party intend to-morrow to move a Vote of
Censure on the Government. I deem it, therefore, my duty
to speak to-morrow on that Vote of Censure ; and, in those
circumstances, I do not think it would be reasonable to expect
me to say very much more to-night. Indeed, at this point,
I have very little I should wish to add to what I have already
said. I must make one or two observations upon the attitude
of the party opposite as illustrated, I think, very clearly by the
speech to which we have just listened. I said in my speech
that I was quite sure that the attitude of the Government
would be misrepresented. The whole speech of the hon.
Member was a misrepresentation of the attitude of the Government. It was a travesty of the situation. He brought out of
his own fancy a highly imaginative account of the terms that
we were prepared to accept. He said that we were proposing
to make peace on Signor Mussolini's own terms, and he contemplated that this would include the setting up of a Fascist
State in Spain, and, if necessary, other Fascist States elsewhere,
and he did not even exclude this country from the range of
Signor Mussolini's ambitions.

" It was curious to me, remembering how, in his speech,
the Leader of the Opposition drew for us a picture of the
weakness of the Italian position, how they had distributed
their armies in different countries, how their economic condition was rapidly going downhill, and how they were on the
verge of collapse ; and yet this wretched country, supposed
to be almost at the last extremity of exhaustion, is the one, we
are told, that would impose terms upon this great country
with all its wealth. It is neither reason nor common sense."

MR. STEPHEN : " Why did you let Eden go ? "

THE PRIME MINISTER : " The hon. Member asks, why did
we let him go ? We have done our best to persuade the late
Foreign Secretary to stay. It is not by our desire that he has

left us. I repeat what I said before, that, in our view, there was no necessity for my right hon. Friend to leave the Government. As he himself has justly said, it is for each man to decide for himself what his duty and his conscience enjoin upon him to do.

" Do not let us proceed upon the assumption that the moment we enter upon conversations we are committed to do whatever the other party to the conversations asks us to do. I really think that the hon. Member opposite must have forgotten that part of my previous observations when I was recounting my interview with Count Grandi this morning. I said then, and I said it quite deliberately, that I had given certain intimations to Count Grandi as to what were the essentials of any subsequent agreement between us, and he will remember that I said to Count Grandi that we could conclude no agreement which did not include a settlement in Spain. My hon. and gallant Friend the Member for Carlisle (Brigadier-General Spears) made some observations a little while ago in which he suggested that the assurances given to us by the Italian Government were inconsistent with some words which had been used by Herr Hitler in his speech yesterday. It is not for me to say what is the explanation of the inconsistency, if inconsistency there be. But my hon. and gallant Friend drew the conclusion that this inconsistency proved that the Italian assurances given to us were not to be depended upon. [HON. MEMBERS : ' Hear, hear ! '] That reflects the whole attitude of the party opposite, and I shall have some further remarks to make later upon that attitude.

" I would point out to my hon. and gallant Friend that, assuming for the sake of argument he is correct that the assurances given to us by the Italian Government are not to be depended upon and will not be fulfilled, then there will be no agreement. Not only did I tell Count Grandi that a settlement in Spain was a necessary and essential element in any agreement that we might make, but I pointed out to him that if we made an agreement we could not ourselves go to the League and ask the League to approve that agreement if in the meantime anything had been done by the Italian Government in regard to Spain which had altered the situation in favour of General Franco, either by sending reinforcements to Spain or by failing to implement the assurances and the undertakings that they had given when they accepted the British formula. No intimation could be plainer than that. I expressed my personal opinion that I believed the assurances given by the Italian Government would be fulfilled and carried out, but I made it perfectly plain that if they were not, then the chances of agreement were nil.

" The position of the party opposite is, I think, perfectly plain from the discussion to-day. Indeed, if it was not plain before, it was made plain by what the hon. Member for Gower has just told us. He would not negotiate either with Germany or Italy. He would not even enter into conversations with them to see whether there were any grounds for negotiations."

MR. GRENFELL : " Separately."

THE PRIME MINISTER : " He would stand on a platform and tell a straight story and invite them to make peace with us on terms which would be satisfactory to ourselves. I wonder whether he is ingenuous enough to think that that would be a practical step towards a solution of the difficulties."

MR. GRENFELL : " Hitler does it. He tells the world, and he has had great success."

THE PRIME MINISTER : " He has not made peace. One has only to look at the situation in Europe as it is to-day and consider whether it has improved or whether it has got worse during the last twelve months, to see whether we have any chance of ameliorating the situation unless we ourselves are ready to take some practical step, at least, to find out whether there is any possibility of making terms—not terms which are satisfactory to us alone but terms which are mutually satisfactory to the countries which enter into negotiations with us. How unreasonable we should be if some other country were to propose that we should enter into conversations with a view to making an agreement—it might be a political agreement or a commercial agreement—if before entering into the conversations we made a demand that they should concede a large proportion of the most important things we wanted to get. That is the process suggested by the hon. Member."

MR. GRENFELL : " The right hon. Gentleman is reading

into my mind things which I have never uttered, and which I have never contemplated. He knows that the parallel he has offered to the House exists. He and his party refused to consider an agreement with Russia until they had complied with the British Government's conditions."

THE PRIME MINISTER : " Did that result in an agreement ? I do not know the particular occasion to which the hon. Member refers——"

MR. GRENFELL : " The Debt settlement."

THE PRIME MINISTER : " It may be reasonable to say that if a country owes money there should be some indication that it is going to pay that money. The hon. Member is making this error again, in confusing the entering into conversations with the making of an agreement. It would not be unreasonable to demand that certain things should be done before an agreement is made. We are not prepared to make peace at any price. We have essentials that must be conceded to us before we can make an agreement. The hon. Member asked what sort of a settlement I had in mind when speaking of a settlement in Spain being an essential part of an agreement. The ex-Foreign Secretary has stated more than once what we had in mind when we talked about a settlement in Spain. Provided there is no foreign interference, we desire to let the Spaniards make their own settlement. We do not consider that it is part of our duty or part of our aim to dictate to the Spaniards what settlement they shall make. The settlement we want is a settlement of Spanish questions by Spaniards free from foreign interference. The party opposite profess to be super-pacifists. They have often in the past accused the National Government of a policy tending towards war, but I wonder whether those who are constantly seeking peace are prepared to do anything to ensue it ? The hon. Member opposite said that I had spoken of a four-Power pact. I never used those words."

MR. GRENFELL : " An agreement between four Powers."

THE PRIME MINISTER : " The word ' pact ' might perhaps carry implications that I did not intend. Surely it cannot be disputed that those four Powers I named are the most powerful in Europe. After all, Russia is partly European but partly Asiatic. Surely it cannot be denied that if the most powerful countries in Europe can settle their differences it would be the greatest step that could possibly be taken for the establishment of European peace. Why should the hon. Gentleman assume that when I talk of a better understanding between these four Powers I am contemplating that they should set themselves up as a sort of Soviet dictatorship which is going to determine the constitution and the destinies of all the small Powers ? I have not suggested anything of the kind. I never had anything of the kind in my mind. I was suggesting better relations between them, but that does not mean of course that other countries are not to have their say, or that the interests of other countries are not to be considered.

" I shall say no more to-night. I hope at any rate that I have made two things clear: first of all that it is conversations that we are proposing, and not at this stage agreement; and, secondly, that the agreement, if agreement there is to be at a later stage, does not mean agreement upon any terms that any other country may impose upon us. It has to be agreement that must be acceptable to us, and it must at least include those things which I have named."

MR. GRENFELL: "The right hon. Gentleman has not answered my questions. Will he answer some of those questions before the Debate finally closes to-morrow ?"

THE PRIME MINISTER *indicated assent*.

THE SUPREME RESPONSIBILITY

On the resumption of the Debate next day, Mr. Arthur Greenwood moved:

" That this House deplores the circumstances in which the late Foreign Secretary has been obliged to resign his office and has no confidence in His Majesty's present advisers in their conduct of foreign affairs."

In the course of his speech, Mr. Greenwood made many contemptuous references to the Prime Minister's alleged " cowardice." " Instead of doing anything on a broad international basis, the Prime Minister has sneaked round to the pirates' lair to come to terms with them." " The right hon. Gentleman talked about a vendetta. We have no vendetta against Italy. [Hon. Members: ' Oh! '] We are implacably opposed to dictators who deny the people their freedom. [Hon. Members: ' What about Stalin? '] The Yorkshire Post goes on to remind the Prime Minister that a vendetta is not an English institution. I believe the right hon. Gentleman is being Italianised." Mr. Greenwood also made the taunt, since familiar, that everything that occurred that caused satisfaction to Germans and Italians must necessarily be dictated by them: Mr. Eden's resignation was one of them. " And the dictators, no doubt, will have to be consulted when the next Foreign Secretary is appointed." The general attitude of the Socialist Opposition to the Government's readiness to meet Italy half-way and to put an end to the bickerings and accusations that were passing between the two countries to their mutual detriment was summed up by Mr. Greenwood's closing sentences.

" Liberty cannot be maintained and strengthened by a relapse to the standards of the jungle. Liberty cannot be kept by a base subservience to the ruthless will of the dictators. The Prime Minister's new attitude, because he is bound by the pledges of 1935, is really a renunciation of all that is best in modern political thought.

His statement yesterday—and we shall see this gathering as the days go by—has shocked the moral conscience of the world, it has hardened the forces of dictatorship and militarism everywhere, it has humbled the people of this land, who gave their allegiance a little over two years ago to political leaders who stood for a new way of dealing with this centuries-old problem of international difficulties. It is because of that that we have put down this Vote of Censure. It is a challenge to the Government, a challenge to explain to the people why the election manifesto of 1935 has been torn up and trampled upon. It is a challenge to meet the people and to ask them for a mandate for this new, contradictory policy."

The Prime Minister rose to reply at half-past four.

"THE right hon. Gentleman the Member for Wakefield
(Mr. Greenwood) has just said that this is a challenge
to the Government. It is a Vote of Censure put down
by the Opposition, and therefore the issue that will have
to be decided to-night is a party issue. I shall desire to devote
the most part of what I have to say on that aspect of affairs,
to the difference between the supporters of the National
Government and the party opposite, but since this Vote of
Censure is linked with the circumstances in which the late
Foreign Secretary has resigned his office, there is one point
on which I think I must just say a word to begin with. It is
this : What is the issue which divided my right hon. Friend
and myself, and with myself my colleagues ? Because a good
deal of the criticism which was directed against me or my
colleagues yesterday appeared to me to be based upon assumptions which were not warranted by the speech of my right hon.
Friend. Therefore I ask, Was the issue that divided us, as
was stated by my right hon. Friend, the time and place of
negotiations, or was it, as was stated on his own behalf by
my Noble Friend the Member for South Dorset (Viscount
Cranborne), a great principle of international good faith ?

"Let us be quite clear about this. If it be a great principle
of international good faith, I think the conclusion is that
conversations could not be held with countries whose record
is not, like our own, completely clean. [HON. MEMBERS :
' Oh ! '] I assume that our record is completely clean, but
perhaps some hon. Members do not take that view. I say
that that is a position which I can understand ; it is the position
which was taken up last night by the hon. Member for Gower
(Mr. Grenfell), it really is the position which has been taken
up to-day by the right hon. Gentleman opposite, but it is not
the position of my right hon. Friend. It will be remembered
that at the beginning of his speech he said that the Government
had long been committed to consultations with Italy, and, of
course, if we had been relying upon a great principle of inter-

national good faith as precluding conversations with those who were not considered to have supported that principle, he must have protested against those conversations, and he must have resigned at that time."

MR. R. TAYLOR : " In boxing, you would have been disqualified."

MR. KIRKWOOD : " The right hon. Gentleman is listening to you."

THE PRIME MINISTER : " I know he is listening."

MR. KIRKWOOD : " And he is not agreeing with you."

THE PRIME MINISTER : " I am endeavouring, and shall endeavour, to be scrupulously fair to my right hon. Friend, for whom I continue to have the highest regard. All the same, we must not have misunderstanding upon this subject, and I wish to say here, in the presence of my right hon. Friend, that I have no recollection that at any time he ever said to me that this question of international good faith constituted an embargo upon conversations either with Italy or with Germany. That is one view. The view has been put by the right hon. Gentleman opposite—no truck with the dictators—is another variant of it, not perhaps put on quite such a high moral principle, but intelligible as coming from the Opposition. But there are others who do not go quite so far as that. They say : ' We do not refuse ever to talk with them, but in view of their past record, let them first say that they are sorry for what they have done—[HON. MEMBERS: ' No ']—and show that they are conscious of what they have done, and show by some penitent act that they have changed their heart.' "

SIR ARCHIBALD SINCLAIR : " Who said that ? "

THE PRIME MINISTER : " The right hon. Gentleman need not get so indignant. I am not professing to quote. I am paraphrasing in my own words what I conceive to be the effect of the suggestion that has been made. What is it that this section of opinion says should be done before we enter into these conversations ? I want to know what it is ? "

SIR A. SINCLAIR : " Before we enter upon a new agreement the agreement which was negotiated nearly a year ago should first be carried out."

THE PRIME MINISTER : " Agreement to do what ? "

Sir A. Sinclair: "To stop propaganda abroad and to evacuate the volunteers from Spain."

The Prime Minister: "To evacuate volunteers from Spain. That, of course, is what I have described as indicating that they are conscious of the wrong they have done. I wonder why the right hon. Gentleman stops at Spain. Why does he not add that they should come out of Abyssinia, too? It seems to me that, according to his principles, we ought to ask them that. The right hon. Gentleman would ask it. That exactly demonstrates the point that I am endeavouring to make, that really this suggestion that we would enter into conversations, providing these things were done first, is humbug. (Interruption.) "

Mr. Speaker: "Attacks have been made on the Government. Surely, the Leader of the Government has a right to reply."

Mr. Shinwell: "On a point of Order. May I ask whether it is not perfectly appropriate that hon. Members on this side should interject, when interjections were common during the speech of my right hon. Friend? "

Mr. Speaker: "I watched very closely when the right hon. Member for Wakefield (Mr. Greenwood) was speaking, and I found that most of the interjections came from hon. Members behind him."

The Prime Minister: "I am not complaining of interjections, as long as I am allowed to develop my argument. What my argument is leading to is this, that no business is ever possible on the lines which I have just been describing. No nation with any self-respect would accept conditions of that kind before entering into conversations. If you really mean to have conversations, you cannot lay down such conditions beforehand. This is merely another aspect of the perfectly logical attitude which seems to be taken up by the Opposition, that there are certain nations whose behaviour has been such that they are not prepared to enter into conversations with them. The choice, then, simply comes down to this: Are we prepared, do we desire to have conversations, or not? If we do, then it seems to me that the sooner we have them the better.

"There is another argument which has been prominent in

D

the discussion, an argument certainly well calculated to arouse strong feelings in this House and in the country. It is suggested that to enter into conversations is a humiliation for us. There has been talk about paying sacrifices to the dictators. The right hon. Gentleman the Leader of the Opposition said that I was going whining to Signor Mussolini. Gibes and taunts of that kind leave me absolutely unmoved. They convince me only of one thing, and that is that those who make them do not realise the greatness of this country. It is a great country, a strong country, a country that is the head and centre of a great Empire. It is a country to which countless millions of people look up for leadership, because they respect her. It is for a great country to do what a small or a weak country cannot always afford to do—to show magnanimity, and whoever aspires to lead her must be ready to ignore abuse.

" Once upon a time there were Liberals who held fast to that view. Once upon a time there were Liberals who after the Boer War did not say that we must have performance first; they took the view that faith and trust in honour and good faith were sufficient to fix a standard to which men would find it easier to conform. They knew that risks were being taken in reliance upon, and their acceptance of, those principles. That is the kind of Liberalism about which in my youth I used to hear so much, and which in later times has shown its belief in the same principles in its dealings a dozen times with the Dominions, with Ireland and with India. How shabbily does the attitude of the right hon. Member for Caithness and Sutherland (Sir A. Sinclair) compare with that of his great predecessors—John Morley, Campbell-Bannerman, Asquith ! Do not let hon. Members trouble themselves because others try to belittle their country by talking of surrender and running away. Let us rather ask ourselves whether what we are doing is right, and whether it will contribute to the end we have in view.

" It is suggested that in what we have done we have had to go behind the backs of our friends. [HON. MEMBERS : ' Hear, hear.'] Who speaks with knowledge of what we have done and whether we have gone behind the backs of our friends ? [HON. MEMBERS : ' Eden.'] My right hon. Friend never said anything of the kind. On the 25th of last month my right hon. Friend had a conversation with the French Ministers, including the French Prime Minister, in which he informed them that we contemplated opening conversations with Italy."

MR. GREENWOOD : " They were informed, but they were not consulted."

THE PRIME MINISTER : " I put it to the House. The right hon. Gentleman says that we went behind the backs of our friends and took isolated action. I tell him that we did tell our friends what we intended to do, and he now says that we informed them but did not consult them. The conversations went further than that. Not only were the French informed of our intentions, or of our contemplated opening of conversations with the Italians, but there was considerable discussion on the subjects which might be discussed when we came to open those conversations. Without going into details, which perhaps it would be going too far to enter upon now, I think I may say that there appeared to be a complete agreement between the French and ourselves upon the subjects which would then be discussed. I remember one thing in particular which was reported as having been specially insisted upon by the French, and that was that the discussions should include a settlement of the Spanish question. That bears out what I said last night and yesterday afternoon upon that question. A settlement of the Spanish question is to be included. I have told the Italians that it is to be included if we are to have an agreement later on. I altogether repudiate any suggestion on the part of hon. and right hon. Members opposite that we have done anything behind the backs of our friends, or that we have not acted in full consultation with them.

" The important point is not entering upon the conversations, but what is to be discussed at those conversations and what is to be the agreement, if there be an agreement, at the end of them. Bound as we are to our French friends by constant communications and by constant sympathy in the past, does the House suppose that we had it in our mind to conduct these discussions without keeping in close touch with our French friends the whole way through ? It seems to me obvious, or perhaps hon. Members have not realised what we had in mind, that if these conversations are to lead, as we desire them to lead, not merely to an improvement of the relations between ourselves and Italy but to general appeasement all round the Mediterranean, in which the French are particularly interested, we could not possibly achieve that end unless the French were entirely with us from the beginning to the end."

MR. ATTLEE : " If that is so, why when I put this specific point to the right hon. Gentleman yesterday did he give me no reply ? When I made the statement about consultations with the French, why did the right hon. Gentleman not take the opportunity of telling us what he has told us now ? He made no statement."

THE PRIME MINISTER : " The right hon. Gentleman must be alluding to the speech that I made in the evening, because he spoke after me in the afternoon."

MR. ATTLEE : " I put a specific point to the right hon. Gentleman. I said that there had been no mention of France."

THE PRIME MINISTER : " I think the right hon. Gentleman is mistaken."

MR. ATTLEE : " I asked whether there had been consultations and I got no reply."

THE PRIME MINISTER : " I am sorry if the right hon. Gentleman thought that I was discourteous to him in not replying to his question. I can assure him that I did not intend deliberately to avoid his question. If I did not mention it last night—and I think he will find if he reads the OFFICIAL REPORT that was the only opportunity I had—he will remember that I got up very late, and that I had not intended to say more than a few words. I hope what I have said to-day will make amends to him for my not having mentioned it last night."

MR. ATTLEE : " While thanking the right hon. Gentleman for meeting that specific point, he will realise why my right hon. Friend referred to the matter. As the Prime Minister had not answered on a very vital question as to whether we were acting with France, we naturally assumed that he had not an answer."

THE PRIME MINISTER : " I hope that the right hon. Gentleman and his Friends will not assume again that because I do

not answer every specific point, I have no answer to give.
I now want to go to another point which was mentioned by
the hon. Member for Gower (Mr. David Grenfell) last night,
and to which I am afraid I did not reply then. It was brought
up to-day with greater emphasis by the right hon. Gentleman the Member for Wakefield (Mr. Greenwood). He
said that I had shocked the moral conscience of the world
yesterday by my speech. He said that some passages which
he was about to read out—I will not attempt to repeat his
words from memory, but they were to the effect that those
passages were such as he would never have expected any
British Prime Minister to utter. I wondered what it was that
I had said, but when he came to read out the three principles on which I had, on a former occasion, stated that our
foreign policy was based, it did not seem to me that there was
anything in those principles, which as the right hon. Gentleman said had been uttered by Tory Prime Ministers for 100
years, of which I need be ashamed or which need shock anybody's conscience, not even that of the right hon. Gentleman
himself. But I rather gathered that what had so shocked him
was not what I said but what I had omitted to say.

" He went on to observe that I had said nothing about the
League or about collective security. I will say something
about them now. I have often expressed the view that the
party opposite allow themselves to be governed by phrases,
the actual meaning of which they never take the trouble to
think out. Among those phrases is ' collective security.'
What do they mean by collective security ? [HON. MEMBERS :
' What do you mean ? '] I mean by collective security a
system under which the collective action of a number of
States is assured to prevent aggression, or if aggression is
undertaken, to put a stop to it and punish the aggressor.
I wonder whether anybody differs from that definition.
[HON. MEMBERS : ' No ! '] I am glad that we are agreed so
far. Does anybody here believe that the League, as it is
constituted to-day, can afford collective security ? "

MR. GALLACHER : " Emphatically yes."

HON. MEMBERS : "What did you mean at the last Election ? "

THE PRIME MINISTER : " I was coming to that. What did
we mean at the last Election ? I say that the situation has

completely changed since the last Election. At the last Election it was still possible to hope that the League might afford collective security. I believed it myself. I do not believe it now. I would say more. If I am right, as I am confident I am, in saying that the League as constituted to-day is unable to provide collective security for anybody, then I say we must not try to delude ourselves, and, still more, we must not try to delude small weak nations, into thinking that they will be protected by the League against aggression and acting accordingly, when we know that nothing of the kind can be expected.

"The party opposite seem to me to be the worse kind of diehards. They keep on repeating clichés and phrases and tags which once may have had some significance but have none to-day. You cannot expect a motor car to win a race if half its cylinders are out of action. You cannot expect a League constituted originally to perform certain functions, on the assumption that if it did not embrace every nation in the world, it embraced practically all the powerful nations of the world—you cannot expect a League which has been given a function corresponding with that state of things, to be able to exercise that same function if nearly all the great Powers have left it."

MR. NOEL-BAKER : " Is it not a fact that membership of the League is the same as it was at the time of the last General Election, except for Italy, which had then been declared an aggressor ? "

THE PRIME MINISTER : " The hon. Member might just as well have put that interruption into his own speech. I say that the power of the League does not depend upon its nominal membership. It depends upon the conviction of its members that it can carry out its functions. At the time of the last Election the conviction that it could not carry out its functions was not universal, even if some suspicion had entered into the minds of some members of the League. I say that to-day you will not find anywhere in the League any conviction that collective security can be provided by the League as now constituted. What is the conclusion to be drawn from that ? [HON. MEMBERS : ' Why do you stay in ? '] I am staying in because I still have faith that the

League may be reconstituted, because I still believe that there is important and valuable work for the League to do. But I doubt very much whether the League will ever do its best work as long as its members are nominally bound to impose sanctions or to use force in support of obligations.

" I would not change an article in the Covenant. (Interruption.) I am trying to say something which has a serious meaning, and if hon. Members will not listen to me now, I hope they will read what I am saying. I am saying what I would do about the League and I say I would leave the Covenant as it is. I would not tear up a single article of it, not even Article 16, in the hope that some day it might be reconstituted in such a form that we might rely upon being able to use those powers for the function for which they were originally intended. But I would have it clearly understood, to-day, that the League cannot use them and cannot be expected to use them and that the nations which remain in the League must not be saddled with liabilities or risks which they are not prepared to undertake. Nor must other nations expect that the League will provide that security which it was once hoped it would provide. I believe that if the League would throw off shams and pretences which everyone sees through, if it would come out with the declaration of what it is prepared to do and can do as a moral force to focus public opinion throughout the world, it would justify itself. It would be a real thing ; it might draw unto itself again some of those who have lost faith in it in the past, and the future of the League might be assured for the benefit and salvation of mankind.

" The party opposite have been asked what they would do in these circumstances. You may take the view that you are not prepared even to talk with those who differ from you or whose standards of public conduct you do not approve. That has been, I will not say our intention, but actually what has happened up to now. Can anybody say that we have approached nearer to peace by pursuing a policy of that kind ? Can anybody say that we have taken fear out of the hearts of men ? Can anybody say that we have lightened the menace that has been hanging over us ? Must not everybody admit that month after month we have seemed to be getting nearer and nearer to war ? I believe that the policy of the party opposite, if persisted in, this policy of holding their hands and turning their backs, of making speeches and of doing nothing, is a policy which must presently lead us to war."

MR. GALLACHER : " Go to the country."

THE PRIME MINISTER : " There may come a time again, as there have been times in the past, when someone who occupies the position that I hold to-day will have to face again the awful responsibility of answering that question : ' Will you plunge your country into war ? ' I pray that that responsibility may not fall upon me, but does not an almost equally heavy responsibility lie upon a man who feels, as I do, that if we do not take action, we may presently be faced with that frightful question, and who feels that by taking action he may do something to avert it ?[1] I feel that I should fail in my duty if I failed to take that action now, as I have done."

[1] It is impossible now to avoid the conclusion that had the Prime Minister not taken the action he did in opening conversations with Italy, world war could not have been averted seven months later. It was Signor Mussolini's immediate response to Mr. Chamberlain's appeal for mediation on 29th September that alone saved peace at that time.

"OUT OF STRENGTH . . ."

Meanwhile the Government pressed forward with its plans for national rearmament—a policy made essential by the popular crusade for unilateral disarmament so long and successfully conducted by the Socialist Party and the consequent position of weakness in dealing with strong and armed powers in which the country found itself. To substitute a policy based on conciliation and physical strength for one based on provocation and physical weakness was the Prime Minister's consistent object. On the afternoon of Monday, 7th March, he spoke in support of the proposals contained in the Government's White Paper on Defence.

" THE White Paper which we are discussing this
afternoon is the fourth of its kind. It is significant
of the state of international affairs and international relations that for four successive years we have been discussing
these subjects and turning our attention to figures of such
magnitude. I think it is no less significant that, generally
speaking, throughout the country there is a conviction that the
course we embarked upon when we began our rearmament
was one which could not have been avoided, and one which
must now be carried through to the end. The White Papers
of 1935 and 1936 were devoted largely to explaining the
circumstances which had led His Majesty's Government to
the conclusion that the deficiencies in our armaments must be
made good, and they also defined in broad terms the objectives
which were aimed at in the plans which we were putting forward for the reconditioning and the modernising of our Forces.
The White Paper of 1937 gave some indication of the extent
of the field to be covered, and pointed to the total sum
which we might expect to have to spend in the course of the
next five years.

" The White Paper of to-day is in the nature of a survey
of the progress made, and it contains also some account of the
measures taken by the Government for the protection of
civilians against the effects of air raids. A statement of this
kind must necessarily, for purposes of preserving the public
interest, be on somewhat broad lines. On the Estimates
which will presently come before the House, it will be possible
and desirable to go much further into details; but this
afternoon I propose to avoid details as much as possible,
and confine myself to more general observations. I would
like to begin by saying a few words about the work of the
Minister for the Co-ordination of Defence. I remember that
when he was appointed, a good many doubts were expressed
as to whether, in fact, any such Minister could have the

authority which was requisite for the purposes which the House had in mind when the appointment was called for. Even after my right hon. Friend's appointment, doubts as to the capacity, not of my right hon. Friend personally, but of any Minister in his position, to carry out those duties still persisted. Some hon. Members appeared to think that, in fact, he was to act more like a Minister of Munitions than like a Minister whose duty it was to see that plans were prepared for contingencies, and to see that the Services were so co-ordinated as to allow each Service to play its appropriate part. My right hon. Friend the Member for Epping (Mr. Churchill) has played merrily on more than one occasion on the meagreness of my right hon. Friend's staff, which he alleges consists only of a typist and an office boy."

MR. CHURCHILL : " I was quoting the Minister himself."

THE PRIME MINISTER : " My right hon. Friend does not deny that he made merry. The Minister for the Co-ordination of Defence is not, of course, an executive officer, but a co-ordinating officer, and, in fact, his staff does not consist merely of his personal assistants, but it is to be found in the whole machinery of the Committee of Imperial Defence. I think probably most hon. Members are of opinion that my right hon. Friend has performed invaluable services in the work of supply. He is not, of course, the Minister who places contracts, but he has a great work to do in allotting priority of orders among the three Services, and of making sure that their programmes are kept in proper balance and not thrown out by deficiencies in one section or another. He has, then, in that direction performed invaluable services. But after watching his activities closely, I feel that I can with complete confidence give the House an assurance that the original object which we had in mind in appointing him has been achieved. Co-ordination, which already even before his appointment did exist, has been greatly strengthened and improved. The system of control, which has been described on a previous occasion, is working smoothly and efficiently. As hon. Members know, it is based upon the Committee of Imperial Defence, of which the Prime Minister is Chairman, and the Minister for the Co-ordination of Defence is Vice-Chairman. He is responsible, on behalf of the Prime Minister, for the supervision and control of the whole of the organisation and activities of the Committee of Imperial Defence.

" On matters of Defence policy and strategy the Committee is advised by the Chiefs of Staff, who are themselves advised by a Joint Planning Committee. The Joint Planning Committee consists of the Directors of Plans in each of the three Services, and that Committee, in turn, is assisted by three further officers drawn from the Army, Navy and Air Force, each of whom is a graduate of the Imperial Defence College. As a result of this strengthening of the machinery of planning, there has been an enormous speeding up of the process of planning and of strategical appreciations, both those that are designed to meet emergencies and those which take account of long-range policy. In a word, I can say that never has planning for strategical purposes been brought to so complete a state as it is at present, and never has any Government been so well served with co-ordinated advice and information on strategy as is the case at present. But there is another phase of the work to which I would like to refer in which an important part has been played by my right hon. Friend. At this time of the year, it is customary, and indeed necessary, to make a review of the requirements of the Services before the Estimates are prepared and laid before the House ; but recently a more intensive survey than usual has been carried through by my right hon. Friend, in conjunction with the heads of the several Services. This inquiry was originally initiated last Summer by myself when I was Chancellor of the Exchequer, in consultation with the Minister, and the purpose of it was to establish the relations of our Defence programme with the total resources available to us—resources of man power, of productive capacity and of finance.

" All those three factors are closely connected with the credit of the country and the general balance of trade. All of them are important, but all of them are especially important and need to be weighed with particular care in times of peace, when we are trying to avoid any undue interference with ordinary trade and commerce. I know that there are some who have thought that perhaps it would be better that we should devote the whole of our resources to the production of munitions. That is a course which any Government would hesitate to take in peace time, unless they were convinced that matters had become so critical that it could not any longer be avoided ; but, of course, to do that would be to deal a terrible blow at industry. It would not merely mean the loss of orders on hand or immediately in prospect ; it would mean the loss of the good will which, if it once disappeared, it might take a very long time to recover, if indeed it ever were recoverable. The fact is that wars are not only won with arms and men ; they are won with the reserves of resources and credit. That is what we mean when we speak of the staying power of a nation. Staying power depends upon the maintenance of those commercial and industrial activities. When we glance over our past history we see that our staying power has made important contributions to victory.

" There is another point, too. The economic stability of a country, its possession of staying power, is recognised to be a powerful deterrent against attack, because unless a nation can feel that it is possible to knock out its opponent by a sudden blow—and recent experience is not encouraging to that theory—then the strongest people may hesitate to risk a struggle with a country whose staying power may be able indefinitely to prolong their resistance. From these considerations I draw the conclusion that in a period of protracted and heavy expenditure, such as we are passing through now, we must be careful to preserve our economic and industrial stability. So in making this investigation to which I have referred, we thought that it should embrace all the factors that were relevant to its consideration—the international situation, the policy for which the programmes were designed, the productive capacity of the country, our resources in labour and especially in skilled labour, the armaments of other countries, and, finally, financial considerations. After weighing up all these factors the results of this investigation have been translated into a balanced plan of Defence preparation and expenditure, based upon the full consideration of all factors, strategic and otherwise. These results are shown in the White Paper and in the memoranda which accompany the Estimates. Knowing, as I do, the careful and thorough work which has been put in upon that inquiry, I can assure the House that the money which we are asking them to spend is being spent wisely, and that we are, I believe, obtaining full value for it.

" In this connection perhaps I might take the opportunity of assuring the House that the effort of the Defence Departments to secure their needs as cheaply as possible and to avoid the possibility that excessive profits may be left in the hands of manufacturers, has not in any way been relaxed. In earlier debates the House has been informed of the general nature of the arrangements that have been made for this purpose. The Treasury Inter-Services Committee meets at frequent intervals, and of course Treasury control has been fully maintained. The House may remember that last year the Estimates Committee went fully into the question, and they reported that they were satisfied that the methods followed were soundly conceived and fair both to the taxpayer and to the contractor. They also recorded their opinion that, so far as an estimate could be formed, the methods have been effective in preventing profiteering at the taxpayers' expense.

" I said a little while ago that I wanted this afternoon to avoid going into detail, but without doing that there is one point in connection with the Air Estimates on which I would like to take the opportunity of saying a word in fulfilment of a promise which I made the other day to my hon. and gallant Friend the Member for the Isle of Thanet (Captain Balfour). The question which my hon. and gallant Friend asked was :

" ' Whether the present Royal Air Force expansion programme for completion by March, 1939, is still anticipated to provide parity in first line strength with any European Air Force within striking distance of our shores ? '

" In so framing his question I imagine that my hon. and gallant Friend had in mind a statement which was made by my predecessor, Mr. Baldwin as he then was, on 8th March, 1934. This is what Mr. Baldwin said :

" ' This Government will see to it that in air strength and air power this country shall no longer be in a position inferior to any country within striking distance of our shores.'

" The House will see that my hon. and gallant Friend, in confining himself to first line strength, has taken a much narrower view of parity than Mr. Baldwin took in the phrase that he used of 'air power and air strength.' Although I am aware that first line strength has on many occasions been taken as a yardstick of parity, I am bound to say that the more I examine into the conditions the more I am forced inevitably to the conclusion that first line strength is only one of a number of factors which go to make up the air power and air strength of which Lord Baldwin spoke. Apart from the difficulties of deciding what machines or what squadrons you should include in the first line, there are also to be considered the reserves of aircraft, the reserves of bombs and equipment, the war potential which could be used in aircraft or bombs, the access to raw materials which will be required in their manufacture; and also I do not think we can leave out the value of an anti-aircraft defence, including any special devices which may have been developed by one country or another.

"Then, of course, we must take account of personnel and the moral of the force. I believe Napoleon once said that in war the moral was to the physical as three to one. We have to take into account the training of air pilots and their racial temperament and characteristics. And of course we must also include the quality of the aircraft, as measured by their speed, their range and the nature of their equipment. I do not think we can stop there. Even in the case of capital ships parity of tonnage and parity of gun power do not represent any complete measure of equality, but in the case of aircraft we cannot set one aeroplane against another as you can set one capital ship against another. In examining the problems of war the Committee of Imperial Defence must take into account all the elements that come into play, of which air power, though it is of the first importance, is after all only one, and one which cannot be considered in isolation. I think, therefore, that to attempt to measure air power and air strength simply by first line strength is a delusion and a snare, that we have to look at our Defence problems as a whole from a wider aspect. We must take account of the aggregate and effectiveness of our resources, and in the various programmes which we have put forward I can tell the House that we are satisfied that we are making the best and most effective use of these resources."

Mr. Garro Jones : " It is a very important matter and one which the Prime Minister ought not to be allowed to pass. However small a part of the whole programme the right hon. Gentleman may consider first line strength to be, I think it is vital, before the House can assess the value of the point he has made, that he should tell the House what is his information with regard to the first line strength of the German and British air forces."

The Prime Minister : " I do not propose to enter into details in this opening statement. I have no doubt that in the course of the Debate a great number of questions will be asked by right hon. and hon. Gentlemen, and there will be an opportunity, before the Debate closes, for a reply by my right hon. Friend the Minister for the Co-ordination of Defence. That will be the time for the hon. Gentleman to get answers to such questions as should be answered, and it is not now desirable that I should interrupt the general statement I was going to make by going into matters of detail.

" The question arises now, what is the policy for which these programmes are designed ? I will try to put that in the form of a general statement. The corner-stone of our defence policy must be the security of the United Kingdom. Our main strength lies in the resources of man power, productive capacity and endurance of this country, and unless these can be maintained not only in peace but in the early stages of war, when they will be the subject of continuous attack, our defeat will be certain whatever might be the fate in secondary spheres elsewhere. Therefore, our first main efforts must have two main objectives : we must protect this country and we must preserve the trade routes upon which we depend for our food and raw materials.

" Our third objective is the defence of British territories overseas from attack, whether by sea, land or air. I would remind the House that our position is different from that of many Continental countries in that we have the necessity at all times of maintaining garrisons overseas in naval bases and strategic points in different parts of the world. That makes it necessary for us to have available forces which can be despatched on what may be called Imperial police duty. In war time there would undoubtedly be substantial demands for reinforcements to be sent to these strategic points, but, taking them in order or priority, they are not as vital as the defence of our own country, because as long as we are undefeated at home, although we sustained losses overseas we might have an opportunity of making them good hereafter. The fourth and last objective which I will mention can be stated quite shortly, namely, co-operation in the defence of the territories of any allies we might have in case of war. These objectives have been before us in the preparation of each of the Service programmes. We have endeavoured to give to each Service means adequate to the role it is expected to play. Taken as a whole the programmes represent a careful balance struck after due account has been taken of the considerations I have mentioned, and when they are added together I think they form an impressive picture of the armed power and economic might of this country.

" I think I must here interpolate something about the cost. In February, 1937, when I was still at the Treasury, I said to the House that the expenditure before us could not, in my opinion, be met entirely from revenue, and afterwards a Memorandum of the proposals of the Government was circulated to the House and subsequently received Parliamentary sanction in the shape of the Defence Loans Act, 1937. I should like now to repeat one or two of the outstanding points which were put before the House on that occasion. In the first place, we said that expenditure on Defence in future years would undoubtedly be very much higher than the £188,000,000 which was provided in 1936-37. It was not at that time possible to say which year would see the peak of the expenditure, but we indicated that it would be very imprudent to anticipate that the total sum required over five years would be much less than £1,500,000,000. We said then that neither the amount nor the period of any borrowing could at the moment be predicted. All that we could do was to put a limit to the amount which might be borrowed, and in the Defence Loans Act that limit was fixed at £400,000,000.

" In connection with that we laid down certain important principles : First, that the Estimates should show the total expenditure of the amount of money to be borrowed as well as the net amount which would be required to be found by the Budget. Secondly, we declared that the loans should not be used to relieve current expenditure on the maintenance of the Forces, and, in the third place, the Act provided for a fixed rate of interest to be charged to Defence expenditure upon the money borrowed, and that after five years arrangements should be made to repay the capital at such a rate as would result in the entire redemption in the course of 30 years. The time has now come to review these arrangements, but the Government, having reviewed them, see nothing to change except such necessary modifications of the total figures as have arisen out of further developments since they were first announced. In 1938 the Defence Estimates amounted to £343,500,000; in 1939-40 they must inevitably be more than that. That year may see the peak of our expenditure, but it is too soon yet to speak with certainty, and further increases or diminutions must depend on the circumstances of the time. One thing we can say with certainty is that the £1,500,000,000 which we contemplated only a little time ago is now not sufficient for our purpose. It is too soon to say what figure will be substituted for that £1,500,000,000, but I am afraid the House must expect a substantial advance upon it.

" I need not impress upon hon. Members the gravity of these figures or of the prospect which lies before us if no alleviation of the situation takes place. Hitherto we have endeavoured to avoid undue interference with trade, and I think that, on the whole, we may congratulate ourselves upon a very considerable measure of success. It is interesting to observe that while in 1935 our exports amounted in value to £426,000,000, in 1936 they had gone up to £441,000,000 and in 1937 to £522,000,000—nearly £100,000,000 more than in 1935. I trust we may be able to maintain that attitude, and that we may be able to pursue the course of our rearmament without undue acceleration, though we fully realise the burdens that must mean for the people of this country. Although we shall not cease our efforts for an amelioration of the position, we ought to make it known that our desire for peace does not signify a willingness to purchase peace to-day at the price of peace hereafter.

" Nor can we abrogate our moral responsibilities to our own people or to humanity in general. We cannot divest ourselves of interest in world peace. Quarrels which begin in a limited area may be a deep concern to us if they prove to be the starting point of a general conflagration, and, therefore, while we have neither the desire nor the intention of embarking on meddlesome interference with other people's affairs, we shall from time to time think it is our duty to raise our voice on behalf of peaceful discussion and negotiation rather than the use of force, or the threat of force, and we shall have the more confidence in doing that because we are convinced that our aims command the sympathy of the most part of the world. In conclusion, let me repeat my earnest hope of the success of our efforts for European appeasement, to be followed in due course by disarmament. In the meantime we cannot afford any relaxation of our exertions, but if in the end we should fail to re-establish confidence and peace we shall not hesitate to revise our programmes or the rate of their acceleration, and we are confident that in doing so we shall have the support of the country whatever may be the sacrifices demanded of it.

"Let me turn for a moment to a consideration of the Amendment put on the Paper by the party opposite. I could not help wondering when I read it whether it was really necessary to use 100 words to try to conceal a meaning which, after all, has not been concealed. We can paraphrase the Amendment in one or two short sentences. What it means is this. 'We want to vote against Defence, but we do not think it prudent to go to the electors and say so. We will, therefore, tell them that we should be delighted to vote for the Estimates if only we could be convinced that the motives of the Government were pure and honourable like our own. Since, instead of coming out in favour of the side that we favour in Spain, they will persist in pursuing the detestable policy of neutrality, we are going to do the best we can to prevent the country from having any arms at all.' I think I see also in this Amendment some evidence that it is to be used as part of a campaign of misrepresentation."

MR. GEORGE GRIFFITHS: "What about the 1935 election?"

THE PRIME MINISTER: "It proceeds on the assumption that the Government have changed their policy, and, in particular, have abandoned the League of Nations. I, on the contrary, claim that I am a better friend of the League than some of those who speak of it. The League to-day is mutilated; it is halt and maimed; and those who, like myself, do their best to build it up afresh to be a real world League——"

Colonel Wedgwood : " A League of dictators."

The Prime Minister : "——which could protect the weak and limit the powers of the strong, serve it better than those who would attempt to put on it in its present state tasks which are manifestly beyond its strength. What is, in fact, meant by this phrase that peace can be attained only through collective security under the League of Nations ? We have never said that in no conceivable circumstances could collective security under the Covenant be provided, but I ask what small country in Europe to-day, if it be threatened by a larger one, can safely rely on the League alone to protect it against invasion ? I challenge hon. Members opposite to answer that question. There can be only one honest answer to it, and that is 'none,' although a small nation may have powerful friends who will act as its guardians and protectors, and so preserve the peace. If that be so, why should we try to persuade small nations that they can rely on peace where there is no peace ? Why should we mislead them by giving them an assurance of security when any such security can be only a delusion ?

" The ideals of the League are grand and magnificent, and I will never believe that they are not ultimately attainable. We shall not bring them nearer by pretending to ourselves that they are within our grasp, because it will require prolonged and sustained effort before that can be achieved. In all such efforts the Government will take their full share just because we believe in the possibility that the League may some day be the salvation of the world. Since we must recognise that that day is still far away, we shall do well to take thought for the perplexities of the hour, which will not wait.

" A study of the White Paper, and perhaps much more, any observation of what is going on in the country to-day, will convince people of the enormous progress that we have made in the building up of our defensive forces. It has made a deep impression upon foreign nations. I remember that in 1935 the Leader of the Opposition said that our armaments programme was rattling us back to war. It has had exactly the opposite effect. The sight of this enormous, this almost terrifying, power which Britain is building up has a sobering effect, a steadying effect, on the opinion of the world. Everyone knows that these forces, great and powerful as they are, are not going to be used for aggression. We cannot regard the prospect before us with satisfaction or even with equanimity. We have glimpses revealed to us from time to time of vast expenditures going on into the dim spaces of the future. This is no time to sit idle while the boat drifts on to the cataract, and I desire to see our country strong, because I believe that in her strength lies the best hope of peace. Side by side with a process of building up her strength I will lose no opportunity of trying to remove the causes of strife or war. Neither past memories nor present misrepresentations will deter me from doing what I can to restore confidence and tranquillity of mind in Europe. This is no change of policy. These are the views I have expressed both in private and public at any time during the last three or four years. They were well known to all my colleagues when I became Prime Minister, and they have not changed since.

" Because I do not share the views of the Opposition that one has to take sides with the party they favour in Spain, they charge me with having a bias towards dictators."

MR. COCKS : " Absolutely true."

THE PRIME MINISTER : " There is no foundation for the charge. But I have to deal with a world in which dictatorships exist. I have no interest in other forms of government, except in so far as they react on other countries. I have no bias in favour of Nazism, Fascism or Bolshevism, because all of them seem to me to be inconsistent with what is all-important to me, because it is the root of my political creed, and that is individual liberty. No sensible man will ask that liberty, even the liberty of the individual, should be completely unfettered. That would merely be to allow one individual to gratify his own selfishness at the expense of others. But subject to reasonable restrictions, I believe in liberty of thought, of speech, of action. Without that there can be no true democracy. I do not believe that a democracy need necessarily be less efficient than other systems of government. It may, indeed, sometimes lag behind in time in making its decisions, but, at any rate, democracy can do what no dictator can permit himself; democracy can afford to make mistakes. For the preservation of democracy, which means the preservation of our liberty, I myself would fight, and I believe that the people of this country would fight. I am convinced in the innermost core of my mind that the course we are pursuing in putting forward our present programme for Defence is the surest way of avoiding the grave necessity of fighting at all."

THE ANSCHLUSS

How necessary was the rearmament of this country, was shown a week later when a Germany armed to the teeth was able to secure, in face of those Powers which had wished to preserve the independence of Austria, and without the firing of a single shot, that Anschluss or union with Austria which she and her fellow Germans in that country had been denied, even in the form of an economic treaty, when it had been demanded seven years before without power to enforce it. The evil of this act of force, even if desired by the overwhelming majority of the Austrian people who had had little other economic hope since the dismemberment of the Austrian Empire in 1918 save in union with Germany, was not so much that it deprived Austria—" a political and economic entity," as Mr. Boothby put it, " which it was impossible to sustain"—of its independence and strengthened the power of Germany, as that it strengthened the claims of might, as opposed to those of right, to decide international issues. It threatened by a violent shock to the complicated fabric of European relationships to involve the whole world, including this country, in the untold evil of another Great War. At 3.37 on the afternoon of Monday, 14th March, the Prime Minister made an official statement in the House of Commons on the events that had just occurred.

" THE main sequence of events of the last few days
will be familiar to hon. Members, but no doubt
the House will desire that I should make a statement on
the subject. The result of the meeting at Berchtesgaden
on 12th February between the German and Austrian Chancellors was stated by the former to be an extension of the framework of the July, 1936, Agreement. Hon. and right hon.
Gentlemen will recollect that that Agreement provided,
among other things, for the recognition of the independence
of Austria by Germany and the recognition by Austria of
the fact that she was a German State. Therefore, whatever
the results of the Berchtesgaden meeting were, it is clear
that the agreement reached was on the basis of the independence of Austria.

" On Wednesday of last week Herr von Schuschnigg
decided that the best way to put an end to the uncertainties of
the internal situation in his country was to hold a plebiscite
under which the people could decide the future of their
country. Provision for that plebiscite is made in the Austrian
Constitution of 1934. This decision on the part of the Austrian
Chancellor was unwelcome to the German Government,
as it was also unwelcome to the Austrian National Socialists
themselves. Matters appear to have come to a head on the
morning of 11th March when Herr von Seyss-Inquart,
who had been appointed Minister of the Interior as a result
of the Berchtesgaden meeting, together with his colleague,
Dr. Glaise-Horstenau, presented an ultimatum to the Chancellor. They demanded the abandonment of the plebiscite and
threatened that if this was refused, the Nazis would abstain
from voting and could not be restrained from causing serious
disturbances during the poll. The two Ministers also demanded
changes in the provincial Governments and other bodies.
They required, so I am informed, an answer from the Chancellor, before one o'clock in the afternoon. The Chancellor
declined to accept this ultimatum, but offered a compromise

under which a second plebiscite should be held later, with regular voting lists. In the meantime, he said, he would be prepared to make it clear that voters might vote for his policy but against him personally, in order to prove that the plebiscite was not a personal question of his remaining in office. Later that day, feeling himself to be under threat of civil war and a possible military invasion, the Chancellor gave way to the two Ministers and agreed to cancel the plebiscite on condition that the tranquillity of the country was not disturbed by the Nazis. There seems to be little doubt that this offer was referred to Germany. In any event, the reply which the Ministers returned was that this offer was insufficient and that Herr Schuschnigg must resign in order to be replaced by Herr Seyss-Inquart. It appears that the Austrian Chancellor was given until 4.30 p.m., Greenwich time, in which to reply and was informed that if his reply was not satisfactory, German troops would be ordered to move at 5 o'clock. This fact seems to show that Germany was behind the ultimatum.

" Later in the day a fresh ultimatum was delivered, which appears to have been brought from Germany by aeroplane. The demands made were the resignation of the Chancellor and his replacement by the Minister of the Interior, a new Cabinet of which two-thirds were to be National Socialists, the Austrian Legion to be readmitted to the country and given the duty of keeping order in Vienna, and the total readmission of the Nazi party. A reply was required before 6.30 p.m., Greenwich time. To these demands the Austrian Chancellor announced, a little later on the wireless, that he had, in view of the German threatened invasion, yielded in order to avoid the shedding of German blood. He said that he wished the world to know that the President and he had yielded to force and that Austrian troops had been instructed to oppose no resistance to German troops if and when the latter crossed the frontier. The subsequent entry of German troops into Austria and the visit of the German Chancellor to Linz will be known to hon. Members.

" His Majesty's Government have throughout been in the closest touch with the situation. The Foreign Secretary saw the German Foreign Minister on 10th March and addressed

to him a grave warning on the Austrian situation and upon
what appeared to be the policy of the German Government
in regard to it. In particular Lord Halifax told him that
His Majesty's Government attached the greatest importance
to all measures being taken to ensure that the plebiscite was
carried out without interference or intimidation. Late on
11th March our Ambassador in Berlin registered a protest
in strong terms with the German Government against such
use of coercion, backed by force, against an independent State
in order to create a situation incompatible with its national
independence. Such action, Sir Nevile Henderson pointed
out, was bound to produce the gravest reactions, of which it
would be impossible to foretell the issue. Earlier that day I
made earnest representations in the same sense to the German
Minister of Foreign Affairs, with whom my Noble Friend also
had two further conversations on that day.

"To these protests the German Government replied in a
letter addressed to His Majesty's Ambassador in Berlin by
Baron von Neurath. I think I should read the terms of that
communication in full. They are as follow:

"'MONSIEUR L'AMBASSADEUR,

"'In your letter of March 11th your Excellency
stated that news had reached the British Government that a
German ultimatum had been delivered in Vienna demanding
the resignation of the Austrian Chancellor, his substitution
by the Minister of the Interior, the formation of a new Cabinet
with a two-third majority of National Socialist members and
the readmission of the Austrian Legion. Should this news be
correct the British Government protested against such coercion
by force against an independent State in order to create a
situation incompatible with its national independence.

"'In the name of the German Government, I must state in
reply that the British Government is not within its right in
claiming the role of a protector of the independence of Austria.
In the course of the diplomatic conversations regarding the
Austrian question the German Government have never left
the British Government in doubt that the form of the relations
between the Reich and Austria can only be regarded as an
internal affair of the German people which is no concern of

third Powers. It is superfluous to recapitulate the historical and political bases of this standpoint.

" ' For this reason the German Government must from the outset reject as inadmissible the protest lodged by the British Government, even though only conditional. At the same time, in view of the information quoted in your letter that the Reich Government had made demands of the character of an ultimatum in Vienna, the German Government does not desire to omit, in the interests of truth, to make the following statement respecting the events of the last few days.

" ' A few weeks ago the German Chancellor, recognising the dangers resulting from the intolerable position which had risen in Austria, initiated a conversation with the then Austrian Chancellor. The aim was to make yet another attempt to meet these dangers by agreement upon measures which should ensure a calm and peaceful development in consonance with the interests of both countries and with those of the whole German people. The Berchtesgaden agreement, had it been loyally carried out on the Austrian side in the spirit of the conversation of 12th February, would in fact have guaranteed such a development.

" ' Instead of this, the former Austrian Federal Chancellor, on the evening of 9th March, announced the surprising decision, taken on his own sole authority, to hold within a period of a few days a plebiscite, which having regard to the surrounding circumstances and in particular the detailed plans for the carrying out of the plebiscite, was intended to have, as it could only have, as its purpose the political repression of the overwhelming majority of the population of Austria. This proceeding, standing as it did in flagrant contradiction to the Berchtesgaden agreement, led as might have been foreseen to an extremely critical development of the internal situation in Austria. It was only natural that those members of the Austrian Government who had taken no part in the decision to hold a plebiscite should raise the strongest protest against it. In consequence there ensued a Cabinet crisis in Vienna, which in the course of the 11th of March led to the resignation of the former Federal Chancellor and the formation of a new Government. It is not true that forcible pressure on the course of these developments was exercised by the Reich. In particular the statement subsequently spread by the former Federal Chancellor—to the effect that the German Government had delivered an ultimatum with a time-limit to the Federal President, in accordance with which he was to appoint as Federal Chancellor one of certain proposed candidates and construct the Government in conformity with the proposals of the German Government, failing which the entry of German troops into Austria would have to be contemplated—is pure imagination. As a matter of fact the question of the despatch of military and police forces from the Reich was first raised by the fact that the newly formed Austrian Government addressed to the Government of the Reich, in a telegram which has already been published in the Press, an urgent request that, for the re-establishment of peace and order and for the prevention of bloodshed, German troops should be despatched as soon as possible. Faced with the directly threatening danger of a bloody civil war in Austria, the Government of the Reich decided to meet the appeal then addressed to it.

" ' Such being the case it is completely inconceivable that the conduct of the German Government, as it stated in your letter, could lead to unforeseeable consequences. A general review of the political situation is given in the Proclamation which the Chancellor of the German Reich addressed at noon to-day to the German people. In this situation dangerous consequences could only come into play if an attempt should be made by any third party, in contradiction to the peaceful intentions and legitimate aims of the Reich, to exercise on the development of the situation in Austria an influence inconsistent with the right of the German people to self determination.

" ' Accept, etc.,

" ' FREIHERR VON NEURATH.'

" That concludes the letter by Freiherr von Neurath in reply to the protest of the British Government. I do not wish to enter into any long argument about the historical narrative of events as described by Baron von Neurath, but I am bound at once to refute his statement to the effect that His Majesty's Government were not within their rights in interesting themselves in the independence of Austria, and that, as in the opinion of the German Government relations between Austria and Germany are a purely internal affair, His Majesty's Government, as a third party, have no concern in them. The interests of His Majesty's Government in this question cannot, however, on any tenable ground be denied. In the first place, Great Britain and Austria are both members of the League, and both were signatories, as was also the German Government, of treaties which provided that the independence of Austria was inalienable except with the consent of the Council of the League of Nations.

" Quite apart from this, His Majesty's Government are, and always must be, interested in developments in Central Europe, particularly events such as those which have just taken place, if only for the reason, as I stated in the House only a fortnight ago, that the object of all their policy has been to assist in the establishment of a sense of greater security and confidence in Europe, and that that object, as I said then, must inevitably be helped or hindered by events in Central Europe. Throughout these events His Majesty's Government have remained in the closest touch with the French Government, and the French Government have, I understand, also entered a strong protest in Berlin on similar lines to that lodged by His Majesty's Government. It seems to us that the methods adopted throughout these events call for the severest condemnation, and have administered a profound shock to all who are interested in the preservation of European peace. It follows that what has passed cannot fail to have prejudiced the hope of His Majesty's Government of removing misunderstandings between nations and promoting international co-operation.

" It might seem unnecessary to refute rumours that His Majesty's Government had given consent if not encouragement to the idea of the absorption of Austria by Germany, were there not evidence that these are being sedulously being put about in many quarters. There is, of course, no foundation whatever for any of these rumours. The statement which I have already made shows clearly that His Majesty's Government emphatically disapprove, as they have always disapproved, actions such as those of which Austria has been made the scene.

" The attitude of Czechoslovakia to these events is a matter of general interest, and in this connection I can give the House the following information. The Czech Government have officially informed His Majesty's Government that though it is their earnest desire to live on the best possible neighbourly relations with the German Reich, they have followed with the greatest attention the development of events in Austria between the date of the Austro-German Agreement of July, 1936, up to the present day. I am informed that Field-Marshal Goering on 11th March gave a general assurance to the Czech Minister in Berlin—an assurance which he expressly renewed later on behalf of Herr Hitler—that it would be the earnest endeavour of the German Government to improve German-Czech relations. In particular, on 12th March, Field-Marshal Goering informed the Czech Minister that German troops marching into Austria had received the strictest orders to keep at least 15 kilometres from the Czech frontier. On the same day the Czechoslovak Minister in Berlin was assured by Baron von Neurath that Germany considered herself bound by the German-Czechoslovak Arbitration Convention of October, 1925.

" The House may desire me to repeat what our position in regard to Austria was. We were under no commitment to take action *vis-à-vis* Austria, but we were pledged to consultation with the French and Italian Governments in the event of action being taken which affected Austrian independence and integrity, for which provision was made by the relevant articles of the Peace Treaties. This pledge arises from agreements reached between the French, Italian and United Kingdom Governments, first in February, 1934, then in September of the same year, and finally at the Stresa Conference in April, 1935, in which the position was reaffirmed, to consult together in any measures to be taken in the case of threats to the integrity and independence of Austria. We have fully discharged the pledge of consultation with both the French Government and the Italian Government, to whom we made an immediate approach when Austrian independence seemed to be threatened by recent events. As a result of that consultation with the French Government, His Majesty's Government and the French Government addressed similar

E

protests to the German Government on the action that had been taken. From the Italian Government we received no full exposition of their views, but their attitude has been defined with great precision in the statement issued on behalf of the Italian Government which appears in the Press to-day.

" It is quite untrue to suggest that we have ever given Germany our assent or our encouragement to the effective absorption of Austria into the German Reich. We had, indeed, never refused to recognise the special interest that Germany had in the development of relations between Austria and herself, having regard to the close affinities existing between the two countries. But on every occasion on which any representative of His Majesty's Government has had opportunities to discuss these matters with representatives of the German Government, it has always been made plain that His Majesty's Government would strongly disapprove of the application to the solution of these problems of violent methods. It must have, as I have constantly pointed out to the House, a damaging influence upon general confidence in Europe.

" In appraising recent events it is necessary to face facts, however we may judge them, however we may anticipate that they will react upon the international position as it exists to-day. The hard fact is—and of its truth every hon. Member can judge for himself—that nothing could have arrested this action by Germany unless we and others with us had been prepared to use force to prevent it. I imagine that according to the temperament of the individual the events which are in our minds to-day will be the cause of regret, of sorrow, perhaps of indignation. They cannot be regarded by His Majesty's Government with indifference or equanimity. They are bound to have effects which cannot yet be measured. The immediate result must be to intensify the sense of uncertainty and insecurity in Europe. Unfortunately, while the policy of appeasement would lead to a relaxation of the economic pressure under which many countries are suffering to-day, what has just occurred must inevitably retard economic recovery, and, indeed, increased care will be required to ensure that marked deterioration does not set in.

" This is not a moment for hasty decisions or for careless

words. We must consider the new situation quickly, but with cool judgment. I am confident that we shall be supported in asking that no one, whatever his preconceived notions may be, will regard himself as excluded from any extension of the national effort which may be called for. As regards our defence programmes, we have always made it clear that they were flexible, and that they would have to be reviewed from time to time in the light of any development in the international situation. It would be idle to pretend that recent events do not constitute a change of the kind that we had in mind. Accordingly we have decided to make a fresh review, and in due course we shall announce what further steps we may think it necessary to take."

THE SPANISH IMBROGLIO

Two days later, on the evening of 16th March, the Prime Minister spoke again on the foreign situation, this time arising out of the affairs of Spain, where as a result of a great and unexpectedly sudden victory the Nationalist Forces under General Franco were threatening by a march to the Mediterranean to cut off the Republicans in Catalonia from those in central and southern Spain. The Opposition, in its anxiety to assist the Spanish Socialists and Communists in their hour of adversity, attributed this victory entirely to Italian and (according to Sir Archibald Sinclair) German troops, whereas it now appears from the number of foreign prisoners and material captured in that action by the Nationalists that the foreign help given at that time to the Republicans was very substantial. This, however, the Opposition almost entirely ignored. Mr. Greenwood said that the Prime Minister by his inaction was by implication selling Spain to Mussolini as he had sold Austria to Hitler. Mr. Attlee, moving the adjournment, urged a " craven government" to end non-intervention and to take a firm stand, regardless of consequences, on behalf of his friends in Spain by supplying them with arms and ammunition. " I give the Government this warning. They have had many chances lately of taking a stand on the side of freedom, a stand for collective security and a stand on the side of international law, and of preventing things from going down the abyss. Those chances have been neglected. They have another chance now by joining with France and concerting with them measures to help the people of Spain, and if they reject it, it may be a case of now or never."

"IN the speech to which we have just listened the right hon. Gentleman has used some hard and provocative words. It is tempting to reply in kind, but for my part I feel that the international situation to-day is so grave that I have no heart for interchanges across this Table of reproaches and accusations of betrayal. I want, therefore, to address myself to the right hon. Gentleman's Motion, and in a spirit of greater gravity than might be perhaps employed on a less grave occasion. The right hon. Gentleman (Mr. Attlee) has asked leave to move the Adjournment of the House

' to call attention to a definite matter of urgent public importance, namely, the lack of Ministerial policy to counter the grave menace to British interests arising out of the armed intervention in Spain by certain foreign Powers.'

I wish to point out that leave was asked and obtained on a definite matter—the situation in Spain. In the concluding words of the right hon. Gentleman in which he called for a declaration of Government policy on matters going far beyond Spain, it seemed to me that he was attempting to take this matter rather out of the narrow limits within the terms of the Motion. What we have to deal with in connection with this Motion is the grave menace—to use the words of the Motion—to British interests arising out of the armed intervention in Spain by certain foreign Powers. From what does this menace arise? Apparently, the right hon. Gentleman thinks that it is something which has grown up suddenly, in the night. [Hon. Members : ' No.'] He must think so, or he would not have moved this Motion. I assume that what he means is that a victory by General Franco is the menace in question."

Mr. Neil Maclean : " Intervention by foreign Powers."

The Prime Minister : " Why, then, is the matter urgent? I can only assume it is because the right hon. Gentleman thinks that this victory is imminent. He went on to make what seemed to me to be a number of assumptions which were hardly justified by the evidence before us. Why does he think a victory is imminent? It may be, I am not saying it is not; but we have heard on a good many occasions that victory was imminent on one side or the other. I remember the right hon. Gentleman coming back from Spain and saying that the other side were on the point of victory. There have been successive disappointments, first on one side and then on the other for quite a long time.[1] I ask myself, supposing it be true that that which suddenly seems to have altered the situation in favour of General Franco's forces, does presage what I may call a complete victory, can it be said that that is due to the accession of fresh forces and munitions to his side? [HON. MEMBERS: 'Yes.'] Of course, it can be said, but can it be supported? After all, there are foreign forces on both sides. There are rumours of additions to the foreign forces on both sides, but as far as I am concerned I am bound to say that I have not yet seen evidence which I can feel was convincing and reliable as to the numbers or quantities of the forces or munitions on either side.

" Hon. Members opposite admit that they are partisans in this matter. They believe every story against the other side and disbelieve all the stories which they think are not favourable to their own side. I cannot take up that line. I have to weigh the evidence before I found upon it action which may involve His Majesty's Government first, and then the people of this country, in serious consequences. I say that so far the rumours, although they may be considered to be more or less probable, are still only rumours, and I have no definite evidence of these fresh accessions of forces which hon. Members opposite appear to take for granted. As far as I can see, there is no reliable evidence that, whatever may be the effect of this recent advance of General Franco, he has not been able to carry it through with the forces which were at his disposal and have been at his disposal for some time.

" I ask myself, in the second place, what is this Ministerial policy for which the right hon. Gentleman has called, and

---

[1] Mr. Chamberlain was right in his forecast of the Spanish military situation: the Opposition wrong. After General Franco's victory in March and the arrival of his armies on the Mediterranean coast, a long period of deadlock set in on all fronts.

which he says would counter the menace to British interests ? Perhaps I may say once again what our policy has been. Our policy has been the policy of non-intervention. Some countries have intervened, but certainly this country has not. The civil war in Spain started in July, 1936. It was in August of the same year that the Non-Intervention Committee was set up. It has been the custom of hon. Members opposite to jeer at the non-success, as they say, of the Non-Intervention Committee. Of course, no one can pretend for one moment that the setting up of the Non-Intervention Committee and the working of it have been successful in stopping intervention. We do not pretend—it would be ridiculous to do so —that there has been no intervention since then. I say that it has restricted intervention; that if there had been no Non-Intervention Committee, intervention would have undoubtedly taken place on a far larger scale.

" In the second place, it has averted international war being carried on first on Spanish soil and probably spreading to all Europe. The fact that the war has been confined to Spanish territory and for the most part to the Spanish people, is a remarkable tribute to the success of the British policy of non-intervention. We have ourselves scrupulously observed our obligation of impartiality under the Non-Intervention Agreement, and we have made every endeavour to persuade other parties to that agreement to follow our example. Perhaps one might cite again as a testimony to the impartiality we have shown the fact that we have been so freely criticised by both sides. The right hon. Gentleman has assumed that the success of General Franco will mean handing over Spain to what he calls the Fascist Powers. He has assumed that victory for that side will mean that Spain will pass under the complete control of Germany and Italy. He has assumed that this has long been the intention of those two Powers and, apparently, he thinks that their objective is now in sight. The Government have never taken that view. The House will remember some words spoken by the late Foreign Secretary on the 1st November :

" ' There are those who are convinced that, supposing the insurgent forces are victorious, the result will be a Spain in

E *

active alliance with a foreign policy directed against this country. I do not accept that. We are just as alive to the dangers as hon. Members opposite, but there are strong forces working in another direction, forces of trade and commerce, forces of geography. This country is still and will continue to be, I trust, the greatest naval power in Europe. That is not without its effect when it is known that we have no intention, no kind of afterthought, either direct or indirect, about the territorial integrity and the political independence of Spain. Spaniards know that very well. They know very well too that no British war material has killed any Spaniards on either side. These factors will I believe be important in the future. . . . We have every desire to live on friendly terms with Spain, and I believe that Spain . . . whatever the outcome will share that sentiment.'

" Then again on the 21st December my right hon. Friend said :

" ' I have been convinced from the first that no one who intervened in this strife in Spain was going to benefit by that intervention. I see no reason to alter that opinion in any way, and if other nations insist upon burning their fingers in the Spanish furnace that is no reason why we should do so.'

" We intend to continue in the future, as we have in the past, to be in close touch with the French Government. I believe to-day, as I have believed hitherto, that we shall best serve British interests, we shall best serve peace, and best serve the cause of freedom, if we keep out of Spain and make our policy one of non-intervention, and do not, as the late Foreign Secretary said, attempt to burn our fingers as other nations may still do."

THE VITAL INTERESTS OF BRITAIN

Meanwhile the Opposition continued its attack on the Government's more general measures of appeasement. It appeared to regard the Anschluss, not so much as a warning of what must inevitably come of trying to secure an international order without either the co-operation of half the Powers of Europe or any programme for peaceful (as opposed to arbitrary) treaty revision, but rather as a kind of judgment on the Prime Minister for his attempts to re-establish contact with the " have-not" powers that had abandoned the " League." " It seems to me," Mr. Attlee had said on 14th March, " that this event knocks down the house of cards which the Prime Minister has been building. It shows the futility of thinking you can deal with dictator states." The alternative recommended was a military alliance with France and Soviet Russia and such of the smaller League members as could be induced to join in such a crusade and a challenging intimation to Germany and Italy—the " aggressor States"—that any interference with the status quo would be met by their joint arms. In particular it was urged that Britain should join with France and the Soviet in giving an undertaking to afford military assistance to Czechslovakia in the event of unprovoked aggression. As the German minority in that country, amounting to three and a half millions or nearly a third of the total population, was growing increasingly restless under the Czech rule which had been imposed upon them by the Versailles treaties, this might easily come to mean that any change in the existing situation could only be brought about by another world war. At ten minutes to four on Thursday, 24th March, the Prime Minister therefore rose to make an anxiously awaited declaration on British foreign policy.

" I BELIEVE it will be the general wish of the House that I should initiate a Debate on Foreign Affairs this afternoon by making a statement as to the attitude of His Majesty's Government as affected by recent events in Europe. I deliberately choose the word 'attitude' rather than 'policy,' because I cannot imagine that any events would change the fundamental basis of British foreign policy which is the maintenance and preservation of peace and the establishment of a sense of confidence that peace will, in fact, be maintained. That must, I think, always be the aim of any Government of this country, because, as has so often been said, peace is the greatest interest of the British Empire. But that does not mean that nothing would make us fight. We are bound by certain Treaty obligations which would entail upon us the necessity of fighting if the occasion arose, and I hope no one doubts that we should be prepared, in such an event, to fulfil those obligations. Then there are certain vital interests of this country for which, if they were menaced, we should fight—for the defence of British territories and the communications which are vital to our national existence. There are other cases, too, in which we might fight, if we were clear that either we must fight or else abandon, once and for all, the hope of averting the destruction of those things which we hold most dear—our liberty and the right to live our lives according to the standards which our national traditions and our national character have prescribed for us.

" All the same, our object must always be to preserve these things which we consider essential without recourse to war, if that be possible, because we know that in war there are no winners. There is nothing but suffering and ruin for those who are involved, and even if we ourselves were not involved, with our world-wide ramifications of trade and finance, we could not fail to be involved in the consequences of war and the destruction of life and property which sooner or later must react upon ourselves. The problem, then, is how are we to achieve this purpose of maintaining peace in a world in which conditions are constantly changing and in which, therefore, we must from time to time change our own methods in order to meet new situations as they arise?

" For a long time a majority of the people of this country cherished the belief that in the League of Nations we had found an instrument which was capable of enforcing and maintaining peace. Some recent words of mine have, in some quarters, been taken to mean that there has been a sudden change in the attitude of His Majesty's Government, not only to that thesis that the League could give us security, but to the League itself; that we had thrown over the League and that we had abandoned it as one of the principal elements in our policy. I do not deny that my original belief in the League as an effective instrument for preserving peace has been profoundly shaken. That arises from the present condition of the League itself. But it has not arisen from any recent events. As long ago as June, 1936, speaking in London, I referred to the failure of the policy of collective security to prevent war, to stop war once it had begun, or to save the victims of aggression. I went on to say :

" ' There is no reason why, because the policy of collective security, in the circumstances in which it was tried, has failed, we should, therefore, abandon the idea of the League and give up the ideals for which the League stands. But if we have retained any vestige of common sense, surely we must admit that we have tried to impose upon the League a task which was beyond its powers to fulfil.'

I have not changed the views that I expressed nearly two years ago. I have not ceased to believe in the possibility that the League might be so revivified and so strengthened as to serve as an effective instrument for the preservation of peace. But I say that is not the position to-day. It is interesting to observe that while I have not changed my views, others, who did not share them at the time, have since come round to my way of thinking. Let me quote a few words from a journal published not many weeks ago :

" ' The League has, for the moment, ceased to be an instrument of collective security. It remains as a useful machine for international collaboration in the cause of peace, and it supplies a means of conciliation by which disputes between its members can be peacefully adjusted. But as a method of enforcing peace and restraining aggression, the League, in practice, no longer exists. It may be restored and revived, but the facts to-day have to be faced to-day.'

Do hon. Members opposite accept that statement of the position ? "

HON. MEMBERS : " No."

COLONEL WEDGWOOD : " Certainly not."

THE PRIME MINISTER : " I am sure they recognise the source from which I have drawn those words. They might, indeed, have come from a speech of my own, but, as a matter of fact, they are drawn from a leading article, and, I think in the circumstances, I should say a courageous article, in the *Daily Herald*. I hope hon. Members opposite will be prepared to accept from their own organ what, perhaps, I could hardly expect them to accept from me, and that they will be willing to face to-day these hard facts. Since I am looking now, not for differences, but for agreement, may I not hope that hon. Members opposite will also agree with me that the best thing we could do for the League would be to nurse it back to health, not only because its original aims were right, but because, if only we could make it wide enough and strong enough to fulfil the functions for which it was originally designed, it might yet become the surest and most effective guarantee for peace that the world has yet devised ?

" It may be contended that I am giving too restricted an interpretation of the phrase ' collective security.' After all, for practical purposes it is not necessary for collective security to ensure the co-operation of every one of the 58 nations which still remain members of the League, provided that we can get the co-operation of a sufficient number to present a front of overwhelming power to any potential aggressor. Indeed, it might plausibly be argued that to deal with a smaller number of nations and to dispense with the somewhat slow and cumbrous machinery of Geneva might be a way of dealing with the problem of the lightning strokes of modern warlike operations, far simpler than the older method of collective security through the League as a whole.

I think that from the practical point of view there is much to be said for a proposition of that kind.

" I would make only two observations upon it. The first is this : However completely we encase such a proposal as that in the Covenant of the League, however wholeheartedly the League may be prepared to give its sanction and approval to such a subject, as a matter of fact it does not differ from the old alliances of pre-war days, which we thought we had abandoned in favour of something better. A second observation that I would like to make is that the value of such alliances as that, as a deterrent to possible aggression, must obviously depend upon their military efficiency, upon the numbers and equipment of the forces that can be mobilised, on their distribution in relation to the area in which they might have to be employed, and on the amount of preparation and co-ordination of plans which it might be possible to achieve beforehand.

" But there is one conclusion which, I think, emerges from that brief review. I stress it because it seems to me to be a corollary both of the failure of the League for the moment to provide us with collective security, and also of the conditions which would alone make any form of collective security effective as a deterrent. The conclusion I draw is this : That if Great Britain is to make a substantial contribution towards the establishment of what I have described once again as our greatest interest, she must be strongly armed for defence and for counter-offence. Sometimes it has seemed to me that hon. Members opposite were endeavouring to make some distinction between the purposes for which our armaments can be used. I could understand that if it were contemplated that in any circumstances these armaments could be used for purposes of aggression, or, indeed, for any purposes which were inconsistent with the spirit of the Covenant. But we all know that there is no question with us of anything of the kind. If that be so, I cannot myself see any object in trying to make a difference between armaments required for self-defence and armaments required for the purpose of fulfilling international obligations.

" If ever the time comes when the world establishes an international police force which will inspire us all with full confidence in its capacity to keep the peace, then there will be no need for us to trouble our heads about our own defence ; it will be done for us. But until that day comes—I am afraid it is a great way off yet—we must think first of the safety of this country and the safety of the peoples for whom we are responsible. When we have made what seems to us to be adequate provision for all that, then the size and the strength of the forces which we have built up will be a measure of the contribution which we can make to collective action for peace, whatever form that action may take. I would add only this last word. The value of any guarantee which we may give or of any treaty obligation into which we may enter must in the last resort depend upon our ability to implement the obligations or the guarantees upon which we have entered.

" I now turn to the situation with which we are more particularly concerned this afternoon. His Majesty's Government have expressed the view that recent events in Austria have created a new situation, and we think it right to state the conclusions to which consideration of these events has led us. We have already placed on record our judgment upon the action taken by the German Government. I have nothing to add to that. But the consequences still remain. There has been a profound disturbance of international confidence. In these circumstances the problem before Europe, to which in the opinion of His Majesty's Government it is their most urgent duty to direct their attention, is how best to restore this shaken confidence, how to maintain the rule of law in international affairs, how to seek peaceful solutions to questions that continue to cause anxiety. Of these the one which is necessarily most present to many minds is that which concerns the relations between the Government of Czechoslovakia and the German minority in that country ; and it is probable that a solution of this question, if it could be achieved, would go far to re-establish a sense of stability over an area much wider than that immediately concerned.

" Accordingly, the Government have given special attention to this matter, and in particular they have fully considered the question whether the United Kingdom, in addition to those obligations by which she is already bound by the Covenant of the League and the Treaty of Locarno, should, as a further contribution towards preserving peace in Europe, now undertake new and specific commitments in Europe, and in particular such a commitment in relation to Czechoslovakia. I think it is right that I should here remind the House what are our existing commitments, which might lead to the use of our arms for purposes other than our own defence and the defence of territories of other parts of the British Commonwealth of Nations. They are, first of all, the defence of France and Belgium against unprovoked aggression in accordance with our existing obligations under the Treaty of Locarno, as reaffirmed in the arrangement which was drawn up in London on 19th March, 1936. We have also obligations by treaty to Portugal, Iraq and Egypt. Those are our definite obligations to particular countries.

"There remains another case in which we may have to use our arms, a case which is of a more general character but which may have no less significance. It is the case arising under the Covenant of the League of Nations which was accurately defined by the former Foreign Secretary when he said :

"'In addition, our armaments may be used in bringing help to a victim of aggression in any case where in our judgment it would be proper under the provision of the Covenant to do so.'

The case might, for example, include Czechoslovakia. The ex-Foreign Secretary went on to say :

"'I use the word "may" deliberately, since in such an instance there is no automatic obligation to take military action. It is moreover right that this should be so, for nations cannot be expected to incur automatic military obligations save for areas where their vital interests are concerned.'

His Majesty's Government stand by these declarations. They have acknowledged that in present circumstances the ability of the League to fulfil all the functions originally contemplated for it is reduced ; but this is not to be interpreted as meaning that His Majesty's Government would in no circumstances intervene as a member of the League for the restoration of peace or the maintenance of international order if circumstances were such as to make it appropriate for them to do so. And I cannot but feel that the course and development of any dispute, should such unhappily arise, would be greatly influenced by the knowledge that such action as it may be in the power of Great Britain to take will be determined by His Majesty's Government of the day in accordance with the principles laid down in the Covenant.

" The question now arises, whether we should go further. Should we forthwith give an assurance to France that, in the event of her being called upon by reason of German aggression on Czechoslovakia to implement her obligations under the Franco-Czechoslovak Treaty, we would immediately employ our full military force on her behalf? Or, alternatively, should we at once declare our readiness to take military action in resistance to any forcible interference with the independence and integrity of Czechoslovakia, and invite any other nations, which might so desire, to associate themselves with us in such a declaration?

" From a consideration of these two alternatives it clearly emerges that under either of them the decision as to whether or not this country would find itself involved in war would be automatically removed from the discretion of His Majesty's Government, and the suggested guarantee would apply irrespective of the circumstances by which it was brought into operation, and over which His Majesty's Government might not have been able to exercise any control. This position is not one that His Majesty's Government could see their way to accept, in relation to an area where their vital interests are not concerned in the same degree as they are in the case of France and Belgium ; it is certainly not the position that results from the Covenant. For these reasons His Majesty's Government feel themselves unable to give the prior guarantee suggested.

" But while plainly stating this decision I would add this. Where peace and war are concerned, legal obligations are not alone involved, and, if war broke out, it would be unlikely to be confined to those who have assumed such obligations. It would be quite impossible to say where it would end and what Governments might become involved. The inexorable pressure of facts might well prove more powerful than formal pronouncements, and in that event it would be well within the bounds of probability that other countries, besides those which were parties to the original dispute, would almost immediately become involved. This is especially true in the case of two countries like Great Britain and France, with long associations of friendship, with interests closely interwoven, devoted to the same ideals of democratic liberty, and determined to uphold them.

" It remains for His Majesty's Government to state their attitude in regard to the proposal made by the Government of the U.S.S.R. that an early conference should be held for the purpose of discussion with certain other Powers of the practical measures which in their opinion the circumstances demand. His Majesty's Government would warmly welcome the assembly of any conference at which it might be expected that all European nations would consent to be represented, and at which it might therefore be found possible to discuss matters in regard to which anxiety is at present felt. In present circumstances, however, they are obliged to recognise that no such expectation can be entertained, and the Soviet Government do not, in fact, appear to entertain it. Their proposal would appear to involve less a consultation with a view to settlement than a concerting of action against an eventuality that has not yet arisen. Its object would appear to be to negotiate such mutual undertakings in advance to resist aggression as I have referred to, which, for the reasons I have already given, His Majesty's Government for their part are unwilling to accept. Apart from this, His Majesty's Government are of opinion that the indirect, but none the less inevitable, consequence of such action as is proposed by the Soviet Government would be to aggravate the tendency towards the establishment of exclusive groups of nations, which must, in the view of His Majesty's Government, be inimical to the prospects of European peace.

" Great Britain has repeatedly borne witness to the principles on which she considers the peace of the world depends. We do not believe that any stable order can be established unless by one means or other recognition can be secured for certain general principles. The first is that differences between nations should be resolved by peaceful settlement and not by methods of force. The second, admittedly of no less importance, is that a peaceful settlement, to be enduring, must be based on justice.[1] Holding these views successive British Governments have accepted the full obligations of the Covenant of the League of Nations, and done their best to discharge them; they have acceded to special instruments designed to pledge the nations afresh to refrain from resort to aggressive war; and they have reinforced the general obligations thus undertaken by specific undertakings within the framework of the League towards countries with whom they enjoy special relations or in which they have special interest. On the other side they have constantly lent, and are prepared to continue to lend, their influence to the revision of relations between nations, established by treaty or otherwise, which appeared to demand review. They will continue, whether by way of action through the League or by direct diplomatic effort, to exert all their influence on the side of bringing to peaceful and orderly solutions any issues liable to interrupt friendly relations between nations.

"So far as Czechoslovakia is concerned, it seems to His Majesty's Government that now is the time when all the resources of diplomacy should be enlisted in the cause of peace. They have been glad to take note of and in no way under-rate the definite assurances given by the German Government as to their attitude. On the other side they have observed with satisfaction that the Government of Czechoslovakia are addressing themselves to the practical steps that can be taken within the framework of the Czechoslovak constitution to meet the reasonable wishes of the German minority. For their part, His Majesty's Government will at all times be ready to render any help in their power, by whatever means might seem most appropriate, towards the solution of questions likely to cause difficulty between the German and Czechoslovak Governments. In the meantime, there is

---

[1] The first was the principle later contended for at Munich, after the second had been acceded at Berchtesgaden. It was Herr Hitler's proposal to seize by force what he had already been promised, instead of waiting for a transfer by agreement, that was so nearly to cause an eleventh hour war when the real causes for it had at long last been removed.

no need to assume the use of force, or, indeed, to talk about it. Such talk is to be strongly deprecated. Not only can it do no good; it is bound to do harm. It must interfere with the progress of diplomacy, and it must increase feelings of insecurity and uncertainty.

" There is another subject which is of such great importance that the House will rightly expect me to make reference to it. With regard to the unhappy situation in Spain the policy of His Majesty's Government has been plainly declared. That policy has consistently, from the outbreak of the conflict, been one of non-intervention in Spanish affairs and loyal observance of our obligations under the Non-Intervention Agreement. This policy was adopted in view of the dangerous international situation which threatened to develop with the first signs of civil strife in Spain. From the early stages of the conflict the prospect of open and active assistance to both Spanish parties from outside constituted a real menace to the peace of Europe. If nothing had been done to check this process, it might well have culminated in a general European war. His Majesty's Government, acting in concert with the French Government, came to the conclusion that the only way to avert this very serious threat was by doing their utmost to induce other European Powers to fall in with their own determination to adopt a completely impartial attitude to both parties in Spain and to refrain from giving material assistance to either side.

" His Majesty's Government are fully alive to the fact that repeated infringements of the practice of non-intervention from more than one quarter have taken place, and they deeply regret it. But serious as are these infringements, they do not alter the judgment of His Majesty's Government that the policy of non-intervention, even though infractions of this policy may take place, affords the best means of avoiding a major conflagration. In the meanwhile, His Majesty's Government, in a spirit of complete impartiality, have devoted their efforts to such humanitarian work as has been possible for the benefit of the Spanish people as a whole. They have greatly deplored the excesses committed during this strife as affecting the civilian population, and they have taken every opportunity which presented itself to convey to both sides their strong disapproval of the employment of such methods, which have earned public condemnation and are contrary to the rules of international law. It will be within the recollection of the House that so recently as on the 18th March last I expressed in this House my horror and disgust at the indiscriminate bombing which was being carried out at Barcelona at that time, and strong representations have since been made to the Salamanca authorities on this matter in conjunction with the French Government.

" I do not propose on the present occasion to enter upon a discussion of our conversations with the Italian Government. They have been carried a considerable distance and the results are full of encouragement to those who, like His Majesty's Government, regard appeasement in Europe as an objective to which the efforts of all men of good will should be directed. The House will remember that just before these conversations were opened, the Italian Government informed us of their acceptance of the British formula for the withdrawal of volunteers and the granting of belligerent rights. While gladly welcoming this assurance, I impressed upon the Italian Government, through their Ambassador, the necessity, if the conversations were to succeed, not only that they should lend whatever help they could along with others, in the bringing into operation of the withdrawal plan, but that in the meantime the situation in Spain should not be materially altered by Italy sending fresh reinforcements. It was never demanded or expected of the Italian Government that they should effect a unilateral withdrawal, and I think it right to say that, during these last weeks while the conversations have been proceeding, His Majesty's Government are satisfied of the fulfilment by the Italian Government of the conditions which had been indicated to them.

" The Italian Government have now again asserted their willingness loyally to assist in the execution of the British plan, and, what is perhaps most important, they have repeated a declaration which they made some time ago and which was made public here at the time, to the effect that Italy has no territorial, political, or economic aims in Spain or in the Balearic Islands. His Majesty's Government place full reliance upon the intention of the Italian Government to make good their assurances. They believe that, with the spirit of mutual confidence in which both Governments are addressing themselves to the task, it will be possible through these conversations to reach complete agreement.

"In an earlier passage of my speech I referred to the obligations, legal or moral, which lie upon us. We recognise that these obligations imply also that we should be in a position to fulfil them, and we have made and are making strenuous efforts to that end. Nevertheless, in accordance with our expressed intention of reviewing our programme from time to time in the light of changing circumstances, we have considered the position afresh, and we have decided that still further efforts are now called for. These efforts must be devoted to increasing production and accelerating the completion of the rearmament programme. The details of that programme have been from time to time laid before Parliament. Recently, in connection with the Estimates for the Defence Departments, statements have been submitted to the House of Commons as to the steps to be taken in the next financial year. The existing programme, however, has been carried out with the intention of interfering as little as possible with normal trade. In practice, notwithstanding this limitation, an increasing degree of priority over civil work has been gradually accorded to rearmament orders, with the result that in some cases the execution of orders for home and export trade has been delayed. The additional skilled and semi-skilled labour required by the programme has occasionally had to be provided by withdrawing labour from other activities. Only by such means has it been possible to undertake the large-scale programme of production which, in spite of some delays, is now continuously and rapidly increasing in volume.

"We had hoped that further acceleration, with its consequent interference with normal commercial work, might have been avoided, but, as I have already said, we have always made it clear that the Defence programme was flexible and was subject to review from time to time in the light of changes in the international situation. We have now come to the conclusion that in the present circumstances acceleration of existing plans has become essential and, moreover, that there must be an increase in some parts of the programme, especially in that of the Royal Air Force and the anti-aircraft defences. In order to bring about the progress which we feel to be necessary, men and materials will be required, and rearmament work must have first priority in the nation's effort. The full and rapid equipment of the nation for self-defence must be its primary aim.

" I gratefully acknowledge the way in which workers and employers have co-operated in carrying out the programme hitherto. Such co-operation will be even more necessary for bringing to practical and early fruition the plans to which I have referred, and the Government are confident that they can rely on the continued help and good-will of all concerned. In the view of the Government, it is not for them to try to dictate to the great industries the detailed action which will be necessary for overcoming difficulties. It is in accordance with our traditions that these industries themselves, through their joint machinery, should work out the details in the manner which is likely to be most effective. Steps are already being taken to inform organised workers and organised employers of the nature of the demands which the accelerated plans will make upon their industries, and thus to place them in a position to devise practical methods for meeting those demands by mutual arrangements and with a minimum of Government interference. By such means it is expected that the volume of production, which in the new circumstances is not sufficient for our needs, will be substantially increased.

" The building operations necessary for the expansion of the three Services will be expedited. This will facilitate the process of recruitment of Naval, Military, and Air Force personnel. The action already indicated will serve to accelerate the production of Naval equipment. Similar measures will be taken for completing at the earliest date possible the erection of new factories. Further capacity with a view to advancing the output of anti-aircraft and other guns will be put in hand. This priority will also enable us to expedite the programme of air-raid precautions. The satisfactory response to the appeal for recruits in connection with air-raid precautions is evidence of the widespread interest that is being taken throughout the country in this urgent question. By these and other measures within the Defence Departments themselves for the purpose of ensuring full and adequate co-operation with industry, we are satisfied that we shall be able to facilitate production and secure the necessary acceleration of the Defence programme.

" His Majesty's Government do not differ from those who feel that the increase of armaments alone is no sure guarantee for peace. They earnestly hope that it may yet be possible to arrive at a reasonable balance of armaments by agreement rather than by free and unlimited competition. They have, on the other hand, felt it right to make their view known that in the present state of the world, reliance upon the assertion of loyalty to the principles of the Covenant was not enough, in the absence of practical strength by which those professions might be supported. Accordingly, the policy of His Majesty's Government recognises, and is based upon, the necessity both of working untiringly to strengthen the cause of peace, and also of taking all steps requisite to make this country strong enough to meet whatever call may be made upon it. In their view the knowledge in all parts of the world that such steps are being taken with determination and despatch will be a valuable contribution towards international reassurance.

" I have endeavoured in what I have said to give to this House and to the world as full an indication as possible of the attitude of the Government upon the subjects which are at present occupying the thoughts of all nations. If I have not said all that hon. Members would like to hear from me, I would ask them to remember that, whether I would or no, I am inevitably speaking to a larger audience than is gathered here in this Chamber, and that whereas our thinking here is done openly, the thinking of other nations goes on behind closed doors. I do not expect that the decisions at which His Majesty's Government have arrived will be acceptable in all quarters of the House. Yet I have tried to put them in an unprovocative form, because I cannot think that there can be any difference of opinion among us as to what I have described as the fundamental basis of British policy, the preservation of peace and the association of peace with justice. We believe that in pursuance of that policy force should be our last resort and not our first. In spite of the shocks to which we have been subjected, we still hold to the truth of that maxim. We still intend to employ ourselves, and to urge others to employ, the methods of reason and diplomacy rather than those of menace and of force.

" Speaking here with all the knowledge that only the Government of the day can possess, and with a full sense of the responsibility which in such times as these must rest on the shoulders of those who administer the affairs of this great country, I affirm my conviction that the course we have decided to pursue is the best, and, indeed, the only one which is likely to lead us to our goal."

THE DANGER OF ARMED CAMPS

Despite the manifest importance of national unity on matters of foreign policy, the Opposition persisted in their attacks on the Government. On the 4th April, Mr. Arthur Greenwood moved on behalf of the Socialist Party :

> " That, as the foreign policy of His Majesty's Government cannot arrest the dangerous drift towards war and is inconsistent with their election pledges, this House is of opinion that the issue should be submitted to the country without delay."

This issue, however, was one which the Opposition leaders seemed more anxious to use as an argument than to fight over. It was indeed growing increasingly clear in the country that their programme of military alliances and provocatively self-righteous declarations would almost certainly result in war, and a War Party was likely to be extremely unpopular with the average voter. Mr. Greenwood's speech seemed designed to avoid any reference to the terms of the Motion he had proposed. He contented himself with taunting the Government with cowardice, declaring with a fine disregard of historical accuracy " that Great Britain had never been so humiliated since the seventeenth century when Van Tromp sailed up the Thames." Not only did the Opposition make no attempt to avoid the appearance of national disunity, but its members felt no obligation to ease the strained international atmosphere by any moderation in their utterances about foreign statesmen. The spokesman of the Socialist Party referred to a recent speech by the head o the Italian State as one of " bragg, bluff, braggadocio and cowardice." At the end of his speech, Mr. Greenwood made two references which read curiously in the light of after events. " We would rather have a peace conference before a war than one after the next war." " The people of this land, in the words of Disraeli, want peace with honour, and it is the responsibility of the Government to give our people that which they seek." At 4.50 p.m. the Prime Minister rose to reply.

"THIS is the thirteenth Debate on foreign affairs we have had in nine weeks. I should think that such concentrated attention upon one subject must be quite unprecedented in our Parliamentary history. I think this Debate can also stand out as memorable in one respect: I never remember before having listened to the opening speaker moving a Motion of Censure on the Government and speaking for sixty minutes without ever mentioning the Motion. The right hon. Gentleman the Member for Wakefield (Mr. Greenwood) made lengthy attacks upon the heads of other States; he sketched out imaginary and altogether inaccurate accounts of the policy of His Majesty's Government; but he kept studiously clear of the terms of the Motion, and, above all, the words 'General Election' never passed his lips.

"On the last occasion, less than a fortnight ago, when we were debating foreign affairs, I made a very lengthy and carefully considered statement upon the policy of His Majesty's Government, and it does not seem to me that I should serve any useful purpose if I were to repeat that statement this afternoon, even though I made it in somewhat different words. On that occasion, being very conscious that we were discussing issues of unusual gravity and magnitude, I tried to make my statement as unprovocative as possible, and my example was followed by my right hon. Friend the Chancellor of the Exchequer (Sir John Simon), who wound up the Debate; but we got no response from the other side, and to-day they are making this a party question, and hoping to exploit for party purposes the difficulties of the international situation. In that, I am convinced that they are profoundly mistaken, for from all the sources of information from which I have been able to draw, the policy of His Majesty's Government, as stated, has won the general approval of the whole country; and not only this country, but I may say practically the whole world, with the possible exception of Russia. Therefore, I am not disposed to think that an appeal to the country upon this issue is one which is likely to justify the Opposition's contention that it should be made. [HON. MEMBERS : ' Try it.'] Before I sit down I shall, of course, acquaint the House with my intentions as to a General Election, but for the moment I think I must examine a little more carefully the Motion which the right hon. Gentleman rose to move but failed to develop. The Motion begins by the assertion that :

" ' The Foreign Policy of His Majesty's Government cannot arrest the dangerous drift towards war.'

Perhaps I may let that pass, because, as has often been said before, it takes at least two to make a peace, but one Government can make war if it wants to do so. In that sense, therefore, it is true that neither this nor any other Government can frame any policy which will prevent some other Government going to war if it has made up its mind to act in that direction. But I would say that the general impression produced by the statement of the policy of His Majesty's Government has not led to the conclusion that it is drifting to war. Perhaps I may remind the House, in support of that observation, of some words which were used by the Prime Minister of Czechoslovakia after the speech which I made. He said :

" ' The declaration of Mr. Chamberlain has certainly been a great deed for the consolidation of Europe. History perhaps will recognise in the future that he in this hour has served peace well.'

The Motion then goes on to charge the Government with a policy which

' is inconsistent with their election pledges.'

" I think that on that theme, at least, we should have had some evidence from the right hon. Gentleman to show us in what respects he considers that the policy of His Majesty's Government is inconsistent with their election pledges. The right hon. Gentleman the Member for Hillsborough (Mr. Alexander) looks at me in an expectant sort of way ; perhaps he can supply the deficiency of his right hon. colleague sitting next to him, and tell us what it is the Opposition mean when they put down this on the Paper and cannot substantiate the charge by any evidence. I will give the right hon. Gentleman an opportunity of doing so now.

MR. GREENWOOD: "While thanking the right hon. Gentleman, I would point out that I have already read to the House the election pledges of the Government. Their policy now does not conform to them."

THE PRIME MINISTER: "Which election pledges?"

HON. MEMBERS: "1935."

MR. GREENWOOD: "If the right hon. Gentleman had taken the trouble to read the speech I made on a previous occasion, he would know that I quoted the charges then; I could have quoted them to-day; and I am prepared to do so now, if he likes."

THE PRIME MINISTER: "Very well, the right hon. Gentleman did not think it worth while, on a Motion of Censure, to repeat those charges, but he refers me to a speech which he made on a previous occasion when there was no Motion of Censure."

MR. GREENWOOD: "We might as well get the facts right. It was when I moved the previous Motion of Censure."

THE PRIME MINISTER: "That was on the Motion on which the right hon. Gentleman was not going to divide. But we will not waste time on that. We will examine the charge which the right hon. Gentleman has made. He said that we had stated in our election manifesto that the League of Nations would remain as heretofore the keystone of British foreign policy. I would like to go on and read a few more words. As a rule, you want to get the whole paragraph before you can properly weigh up the meaning of a particular sentence. It went on to say:

" ' The prevention of war and the establishment of settled peace in the world must always be the most vital interest of the British people, and the League is the instrument which has been framed and to which we look for the attainment of these objects. We shall, therefore, continue to do all in our power to uphold the Covenant and to maintain and increase the efficiency of the League.'

It is still the fact that we look forward to the time when the League will be so strengthened and so revitalised——"

F

Miss Rathbone: " What are you doing to strengthen it ? "

The Prime Minister: " —that it can fulfil its purpose, that it can be an effective instrument for the prevention of war and the establishment of settled peace in the world, and we shall do our best, as we said at the time, to increase the efficiency of the League until it is capable of performing its functions. It cannot perform those functions to-day. [Hon. Members: ' Why ? '] If hon. Members want to know why that situation has changed, I can give them the answer in the words of my predecessor, Lord Baldwin. Speaking on this subject as long ago as 23rd June, 1936, the same year as the speech was made to which the right hon. Gentleman referred, Lord Baldwin was talking about sanctions, and he said :

" ' The ultimate sanction is always war, and unless the sanction you apply is such as to bring the aggressor to his knees, war is inevitable.'

He went on to say :

" ' Where there is an aggressor it would be quite impossible for the nations that wished to exercise the power of military sanctions against the aggressor or a group of aggressors to do it unless they are in a position to do it at once and together. . . . If collective action is to be a reality and not merely a thing to be talked about, it means not only that every country is to be ready for war, but must be ready to go to war at once. That is a terrible thing, but it is an essential part of collective security.'

That was the explanation which Lord Baldwin gave of why it was not possible for the League to exercise the functions which had originally been designed for it and to secure collective security. If it be true that the League cannot properly be described to-day as the keystone of British policy, but only in the future, it is not because we have changed our policy. We are still intending to make the fullest use we can of the League within the limits which must be recognised, but we say that it is to-day in no state to fulfil the conditions which Lord Baldwin laid down as being essential to collective security. To deny that, as I understood the right hon. Gentleman to be trying to deny it to-day—a fact which has been admitted, as I quoted the other day, and stated in positive terms by the *Daily Herald*—to deny it to-day is merely a piece of wilful and transparent hypocrisy. I will deal with another alleged inconsistency between the policy of His Majesty's Government and the manifesto to which the right hon. Gentleman made no allusion to-day, but of which he has sometimes spoken before. He alluded to the passage in which it refers to Abyssinia. The passage ran as follows :

" ' In the present unhappy dispute between Italy and Abyssinia there will be no wavering in the policy we have hitherto pursued.'

The right hon. Gentleman has quoted that before, and it has always been received with loud cheers of derision, which I do not hear now, presumably because hon. Gentlemen are waiting for what is to follow. If you isolate this sentence from its context, it may give an entirely wrong impression. When you speak of a policy from which there will be no wavering, it is just as well to have in your mind what policy you are referring to, and the policy was defined on this occasion in the words which follow :

" ' We shall take no action in isolation, but we shall be prepared faithfully to take our part in any collective action decided upon by the League and shared in by its Members.' "

Mr. A. V. Alexander : " Or arranged separately with Laval ? "

The Prime Minister : " The right hon. Gentleman is now accusing us of following a policy which was inconsistent with the words which I have quoted."

Mr. Alexander : " Hear, hear. All the way through."

The Prime Minister : " I am pointing out that it was not inconsistent at all, and that what we said was that we would not act alone, but that we would be prepared to act with others as far as they would go. If I may once more quote my right hon. Friend Lord Baldwin, he said that collective security had failed

' because of the reluctance of nearly all the nations of Europe to proceed to . . . military sanctions. . . . The main reason of that was that there was no country, except the aggressor country, which was ready for war.' "

MR. ALEXANDER : " The real reason was given on 12th November, 1936—that he was afraid to tell the country the truth lest he should lose the Election."

THE PRIME MINISTER : " I am not going into an argument as to what my right hon. Friend meant by the statement which he made. It has nothing to do with this argument, which is as to the reason why collective security failed. The present policy of His Majesty's Government is perfectly consistent with the statement of our intentions regarding Abyssinia made at the time of the General Election of 1935. The criticisms that are made by hon. Members opposite can mean only one thing. They can only mean that hon. Members opposite think that what we ought to have done was the thing that we said we would not do, namely, to act in isolation. That is a policy which is all the more remarkable in a party which has consistently voted against the Estimates for the Defence Services. So much for that part of this precious Motion calling for a General Election.

" The right hon. Gentleman said that it was not for him to produce a policy and I agree that, in normal circumstances, it is not part of the Opposition's function to produce alternative policies. But when an appeal is made to the public the Opposition cannot rest upon mere criticism of the Government. They have to produce a policy of their own, and if the right hon. Gentleman is going to ask for a General Election now, he has to tell us what policy he is going to propose as an alternative to the one which has been stated on behalf of His Majesty's Government, and which has received the approval of almost the entire world. I hoped the right hon. Gentleman was going to tell us, but he said very little about it. I can only assume that the few words which concluded the last fraction of his speech were intended to give an outline of the policy which is set forth at considerably greater length and with equal obscurity of verbiage in the manifesto issued by the National Council of Labour—in the drawing up of which, I think I detect the right hon. Gentleman's master hand.

" I have carefully studied this document in view of the

coming General Election. I have tried to analyse in what the policy consists, and if I should make any mistake in consequence of the lack of explanation by the right hon. Gentleman, I hope he will tell me where I am going astray. In this document I find four different steps recommended, and they conclude with the statement that together, they constitute a decisive contribution—not merely a contribution be it noted, but a decisive contribution—to peace, and that they will make collective security a reality. They are, first, summoning the Assembly of the League; second, uniting the peace-loving countries, particularly France, the United Kingdom and Russia to make a common stand against the aggressor; third, the promotion of general negotiations among the Powers for the political and economic appeasement of Europe, and, fourth, intervention in Spain by permitting the free supply of arms to the Spanish Government."

MR. GREENWOOD : " It is not intervention."

THE PRIME MINISTER : " Does the right hon. Gentleman not agree with that analysis ? "

MR. GREENWOOD : " I agree with all but the last statement."

THE PRIME MINISTER : " At any rate, the fourth was to permit the free supply of arms to the Spanish Government. Let us see how far those proposals justify the claim that they constitute a decisive contribution to peace. I do not think anybody could say that summoning the League would have that effect. What could the League do to-day with its very limited membership ? It cannot really put into operation collective action. It can pass resolutions and make recommendations, but resolutions do not make peace and if, by any chance, it were to pass resolutions and nobody were to pay any attention to them, that would only make the League look foolish, and add further humiliations to those which have been suffered in the past.

" The second proposal is, certainly, of an entirely different character. It constitutes nothing less than a proposal for an offensive and defensive alliance between France, Russia and ourselves against some other Power or group of Powers. Is that what is called collective security ? Apparently the right hon. Gentleman thinks it is. The party opposite never bother to look at the mixture inside the bottle, as long as the label outside is right. When I think of all their past fulminations against pre-war alliances, which they used to accuse us of wanting, I am amazed at their being able to bamboozle themselves into thinking that if they take a pre-war alliance, and mumble these words, ' Collective Security,' over it, they can change its character and the consequences which are bound to flow from it."

MR. GREENWOOD : " Would the right hon. Gentleman mind correcting a misapprehension ? He really has misled the House. I have this document, the authorship of which he attributed to me for no reason which I can understand, and it reads :

" ' The British Labour Movement calls for an immediate meeting of the Assembly of the League of Nations and for special consideration by the European members of the League, particularly France, Great Britain and Russia, of the steps to be taken to bring appeasement in Central Europe and in Spain.'

I submit that, by leaving out the words ' for special consideration by the European Members of the League,' the right hon. Gentleman is deliberately misleading the House."

THE PRIME MINISTER : " I do not think so. These three Powers are to be the nucleus. It is true there is a general invitation to any other Powers, to all the other foxes to get their tails cut off, but I cannot think that it is very likely that that invitation will be enthusiastically received, and to all intents and purposes the real effect of this proposal would be to do what we, at any rate, have always set our faces against, namely, to divide Europe into two opposing blocs or camps. So far from making a contribution to peace, I say that it would inevitably plunge us into war.

" As to the third proposal, for general negotiations among all Powers for political and economic appeasement in Europe, I say that that proposal is inconsistent with the second one, the one that I have just been discussing. What a pretty beginning this alliance would make for general negotiations for economic and political appeasement in Europe. It may be a good plan to call a conference of all the world Powers together to discuss political and economic appeasement, although I myself think that the method of discussions between individual Powers is much more likely to be successful in removing such causes of friction and difficulty as may exist, but one thing is absolutely certain, and that is that a world conference which was preceded by an offensive and defensive alliance of this character would not have the remotest chance of success.

" The last point, which I call intervention, but which I think hon. and right hon. Gentlemen opposite prefer to call the abandonment of non-intervention, is the one to which they themselves attach the greatest importance of all. But what I marvel at most is the childlike simplicity of the party opposite in imagining that the removal of the embargo upon the supply of arms to the Spanish Government would at once result in the victory of the side that they favour. Is anybody so devoid of common sense as to suppose that you could confine the supply of arms to one side? If you remove the embargo on the supply of arms, it is bound at once to be followed by a whole flood of arms and ammunition and men pouring into Spain from the sympathisers of each side. It would not stop there. It would very soon extend to the sea, and you would have sinkings of ships, you would have drownings of troops, you would have perhaps naval battles ; and the European War would have begun. That, in my opinion, and in the opinion of my colleagues, would be the result of abandonment of non-intervention in Spain, and we have no intention of changing our policy in that respect.

" In this very brief analysis of the policy of the party opposite, I claim that I have shown that their alternative policy is both futile and dangerous. It is futile because it does not make a single constructive contribution to peace, dangerous because it would lead inevitably to war. I cannot imagine any better issue for an appeal to the country than the contrast between the policy of His Majesty's Government and the policy of the party opposite. I cannot imagine anything which would carry greater consternation into their ranks than if I were to say that I would take them at their word, but I am not going to torture them any longer with suspense. The right hon. Gentleman the Member for South Hackney (Mr.

H. Morrison) was right when he said the other day, just before he left for America, that after the last Debate he felt it was safe for him to go away. He knew, and so do hon. and right hon. Members opposite, that no Government with an ample majority ever went to the country at the demand of such a feeble Opposition. This is no time to disturb a country which is in the throes of its rearmament programme. The Opposition can be thankful that they are going to get off with a sound beating to-night, and that they will not just yet have to suffer an even more resounding defeat in the country."

TO MAKE GENTLE THE LIFE OF THE WORLD

Five days later, after the Houses had risen for the Easter recess, Mr. Chamberlain, speaking at Birmingham at a crowded Unionist meeting in the Town Hall, again outlined the nature of the policy he was pursuing.

" **Y**OU have given me to-night one of those occasions of supreme pride and pleasure that every now and then come to politicians to make up for the checks and disappointments to which inevitably they must be subject. These addresses which have just been presented to me have expressed to me in varying words the same message—a message of your affectionate confidence, of your support, of your approval of what I am trying to do. They tell me that you are standing beside me in the fight that I am carrying on, and have given me an encouragement and a stimulus for which I cannot sufficiently express my gratitude. They have pleased me all the more because they come from my own friends and fellow-citizens who have known me since I was a child, and who, when I come amongst them to-day, still receive me as one of themselves. If there is one other thing which has greatly enhanced their value to me, it is that they have been handed to me and shared by my wife, to whom I owe everything that a man can owe, a helpmate as perfect in the political as she is in the domestic sphere. I thank you from the bottom of my heart for your kindness and your trust, and I can assure you that as long as I am permitted to carry on my task it will be my constant endeavour to prove worthy of your good will. . . .

"This is the time when young men's fancy lightly turns to thoughts of Budget Day, when the Chancellor of the Exchequer is accustomed to retire into his cell, there to fast and pray and wrestle with the problems of taxation. He does not emerge until that day when, amid the hopes and fears of his fellow-countrymen, he opens his red box and discloses secrets which he has so zealously guarded. But now, after six years at the Treasury, I have handed over the responsibility of that great office to the extremely competent hands of my friend and colleague Sir John Simon. I only regret that when I called on him this morning he happened to be out, and I am

not able to say what he is going to say on the 26th of this
month.

" No one who has watched the growing expenditure on
armaments can doubt that the Chancellor of the Exchequer
has before him a difficult and unenviable task, and no one
questions, I think, the determination of this people to see this
business of rearmament through, recognising as we must
that it is our best security against war, that of all sacrifices
none is so terrible as those of war. You may have read that
at the beginning of this week we had in the House of Commons
a debate, a rather lively debate, on foreign affairs. That
was only the last of a whole series of debates on that subject,
and, although we are told nowadays that people do not read
of what goes on in the House of Commons, I cannot help
thinking that the general outlines of the Government's foreign
policy are fairly freely read.

" We are bound by certain treaties, entered into with general
approval, to go to the assistance of France and of Belgium in
the event of unprovoked aggression against either of those
two countries. But we have declined to commit ourselves
to a similar undertaking in respect of other countries farther
away, in which our vital interests are not concerned to the
same extent, and which might be involved in war under
conditions over which we would have no control. Now it is
quite true that in these days no one can say where or when a
war will end once it has begun, or what Governments may
ultimately be entangled in a dispute which originally might
have been confined to some remote corner of Europe. But
at least we ought to reserve to ourselves the right to say
whether we consider it necessary to enter into such a war or
not, and we ought not to hand over to others the determination
of our action when it might involve such tremendous consequences to ourselves.

" Sometimes we are told that if only we took a bolder
course, if we were to lay down here and now precisely the
circumstances in which we would or would not go to war, we
should give such a warning to the world that there would
in fact be no war. That would be a gamble, and it would
be a gamble not with money, but with the lives of men,
women and children of our own race and blood. I am not

prepared to enter into a gamble of that kind, and though the
stern necessity for war may arise in the future, as it has arisen
in the past, I would not give the word for it unless I were
absolutely convinced that in no other way could we preserve
our liberty.

" Then there are other critics who say they cannot understand what the policy of His Majesty's Government is, and
they conclude therefore that there can be no policy. You
may remember what Johnson said to a man who said he could
not understand his reasoning : ' Sir, I can give you a reason,
but I cannot give you understanding.' Our policy has been
stated often enough and clearly enough, but nevertheless, I
will state it again to-night. But before I come to that, I would
like to say to you what our policy is not.

" Our policy is not one of dividing Europe into two
opposing *blocs* of countries, each arming against the other
amidst a growing flood of ill-will on both sides, which can
only end in war. That seems to us to be a policy which is
dangerous and stupid. You may say we may not approve of
dictatorships. I think, perhaps, most of us in this room
do not approve of them, but there they are. You cannot
remove them. We have to live with them, and to us in the
Government it seems that, while we must continue to arm
until we can get a general agreement to disarm, it is only
common sense that in the meantime we should try to establish
friendly relations with any country that is willing to be friends
with us. We should take any and every opportunity to try
to remove any genuine and legitimate grievances that may
exist.

" During the recent weeks we have been engaging in
conversations for this purpose with the Italian Government,
with the result that a whole cloud of suspicions and misunderstandings has been blown away. There is to-day a good
prospect of restoring those old friendly relations which, until
they were recently broken, had lasted so long that they had
become almost traditional between our two countries.

" Anyone would think that such a happy change as that,
such a lightening of the tension, such a prospect of getting
rid of a state of feeling which was becoming a menace both to
Italy and ourselves, would have been welcomed everywhere,

and yet the whole of the Opposition, the Socialists and Liberals, with the notable exception of the veteran George Lansbury and George's friends who have the courage to express their approval, have denounced these conversations with the utmost bitterness. They have painted the most fantastic pictures of the subjects which we are supposed to be discussing. They have talked about vast loans, about surrenders to dictators, about the gullibility of the Prime Minister in believing a single word that was said to him, and even declare that they believe we were going to sacrifice the British Empire itself in a panic.

"I only ask you to have a little patience, to wait a little longer—and I do not think it will be very much longer—before our agreement with Italy is concluded and published, and then, if you are not of my opinion, if you do not believe that it is not the Prime Minister who has been fooled, but the Socialists and Liberals who have fooled themselves, I will be prepared to eat my hat.

"No, believe me, the Government have a very clear and definite foreign policy, which they keep always before them, and which they continue to pursue by various methods according to the circumstances of the time. The object of that policy is to maintain peace and to give confidence to the people, if that be possible, that peace will be maintained, so that they may all go about their occupations free from a sense of menace lurking always in the background.

"Our policy is based upon two conceptions. The first is this : That, if you want to secure a peace which can be relied upon to last, you have got to find out what are the causes of war and remove them. You cannot do that by sitting still and waiting for something to turn up. You have got to set about it. You have got to inform yourself what are the difficulties, where are the danger spots, what are the reasons for any likely or possible disturbance of the peace ; and, when you have found that out, you must exert yourself to find the remedy.

"The second conception is this : In any armed world you must be armed yourself. You must see to it that your preparations, or defensive and offensive forces, are so organised and built up that nobody will be tempted to attack you, but that, on the contrary, when your voice is raised for peace, it will be listened to with respect. These, then, are the two pillars of our foreign policy—to seek peace by friendly discussion and negotiation, and to build up our armed forces to a level which is proportionate to our responsibilities and to the part we desire to play in preserving peace.

" I may be asked : ' Where in all this does the League of Nations come in ? ' ' Why don't you call in collective security to your aid ? ' ' Must we take it that those splendid ideals which animated us when the League was started have got to be abandoned ? ' We have never mocked at the League. We do not yield to anyone in our devotion to those great and splendid ideals. We still intend to seize every opportunity that we can find to build up and strengthen the League and to restore it to a condition in which it may once again become an effective instrument for the preservation of peace.

" But to-day we have got to face the facts as they are. To-day we must, before we attempt to impose upon the League from which some of the most powerful countries in the world have become alienated, the formidable task of preserving peace, we must do a little clear thinking. Collective security can only be attained by the willingness and the capacity of the members of the League to take collective action of a kind which is effective enough to stop aggression. Is the League in such a state as to be able to do that to-day ?

" A little while ago I asked the Opposition in the House a question—and mind you this was before the recent events in Austria. I asked them whether they could name one single small State in Europe to-day, which, if it were menaced by a powerful neighbour, could rely upon the League alone to give it collective security. They did not—they could not—answer that question, because they knew the only honest answer would be that there was no such State, because there was no such collective security available. That is not to be disloyal. The true disloyalty to the League lies in pretending that the League to-day is capable of functions which are clearly beyond its power. Do not let us be guilty of that kind of disloyalty.

" Do not let us either abandon the idea of a bigger and better League in the future. Let us rather seek to create a new atmosphere of good will in the world, because that is the essential preliminary of a League that will work. I mentioned just now those events which took place just a month ago, and which terminated in the inclusion of Austria in the German Reich. I do not think that the people of this country would want to interfere in a case where two States desired to join together, but there were features about the methods which were employed in this particular case of union which were extremely distasteful to His Majesty's Government, and which profoundly shocked public opinion.

" One result of that shock has been in the general desire which has been manifest throughout the country to do something to demonstrate our solidarity, and there have been discussions in the Press and elsewhere as to the ways in which individuals can do something to show their willingness to put their services at the disposal of the country. One suggestion has been made that the Government should institute a voluntary register, so that men and women could enrol themselves for some form of public service. I very warmly welcome the spirit which lies behind that suggestion, but, after thinking it over very carefully, I have come to the conclusion that it would not be likely to give satisfactory results in peace time. It is no use to register for work unless there is some work to do for which the person who registered is suited, and I am afraid if we started a voluntary register we would find a great many people either registering for work not immediately wanted, or registering for work for which they had not the necessary qualifications. If it was to be of any use, it would have to be constantly revised, or otherwise it would quickly get out of date, and I cannot help thinking that this continual re-registering without any visible result would soon weary and would cause disappointment and disillusionment.

At any rate, I dare say many of you know the employment exchanges to-day have got exact particulars of the qualifications and whereabouts of over 12,000,000 workers in industry and commerce, and I may tell you, too, that we have already prepared a carefully thought-out scheme of compulsory registration which in an emergency could be put very rapidly and very smoothly into operation.

" At the same time I want to say to you that there is just now an exceptional opportunity for anybody who wants to take part in the national effort for defence preparation. If a young man, for instance, thinks he would like to make the Defence Service his career, he can enter the Regular Army, or the Navy, or the Air Force. If he prefers to stick to a civilian occupation in peacetime, but wishes to make himself ready for his part in defence if this country is ever attacked, he can join the Territorial Army, which provides the anti-aircraft units for home defence. Or he can become a member of the Auxiliary Air Force.

" Then again, if none of those things appealed to him, there is the great civilian service of Air Raid Precautions. The Home Secretary called the other day for 1,000,000 volunteers, men and women, for this work, but he said : ' I want the volunteers to be trained,' because, as he pointed out, one trained volunteer, who knows exactly what he would have to do if he were called upon, is worth two or three who only come in at the last moment when there is no time to teach them their duties. There are many ways in which a man may enter this service and obtain the necessary training. He may train to join the expanded police force which would be required in the case of war to preserve order, to prevent panic, and try to help people in distress. Or, again, he can train to join the Auxiliary Fire Brigade, which is going to be wanted to man the new large fleets of auxiliary fire engines which the Home Office has designed, and which would be quite useless unless there was someone to man them. Then, again, he could obtain training in elementary first aid, he could get training as an ambulance driver or as a member of a chemical staff, and, should he so wish, he could join the large army of air-raid wardens.

" All this means that those who take part in it have got to give up an hour or two a week of their spare time, but I feel confident that there are many who will feel that that is not too great a sacrifice, and if they will join one of these voluntary services, and if they will be ready to assist the local authority in any way that they may desire, they will have the satisfaction of feeling that they will have made their contribution to the great national effort for defence.

" I want to utter one word of warning. People are apt to think that, with all this talk of recruiting and arming and air raid precautions, the Government must be expecting that a war is going to come upon us very soon. If such an idea has occurred to you, get it out of your mind. The exact contrary is the case. As I have tried to explain to you, our whole policy is directed towards maintaining peace. But we are convinced at the same time that one of the ways to ensure peace is to make ourselves ready for war. Remember that there are many interested people who are watching very closely what is going on in this country. You must look upon these preparations not merely as a precaution against war, but as one of the most effective deterrents.

" I should have liked to have dwelt for a time upon some other topics. I should have liked to have shown you, as I could by many illustrations, that, in spite of all our pre-occupations with foreign affairs, we have not forgotten our home needs, and we are still doing many things to improve our social services, particularly in connection with housing and our various insurance schemes. I would like to have shown you how we are all the time taking measures to maintain the conditions under which our industry and our agriculture can continue to expand and prosper. But I must leave a fuller discussion of these topics to another occasion, because to-night I have rather thought it was my duty to tell you first of all of our efforts to keep this country out of war, and secondly to urge you to do your part in playing up and completing our defensive organisation.

" I have confined myself to those topics sadly and reluctantly. There are many here to-night who can look back some twenty years, and who may remember me as a member of our city council here, when all my ambitions were to do something to help the people whom we were serving to lead healthier and happier lives. To-day, when my responsibilities cover so much wider a field, I should be happy if I could still concern myself only with those same objects. To me the very idea that the hard-won savings of our people, which ought to be devoted to the alleviation of suffering, to the opening out of fresh institutions and recreations, to the care of the old, to the development of the minds and bodies of the young—the thought that these savings should have to be dissipated upon the construction of weapons of war is hateful and damnable. Yet I cannot shut my eyes to the fact that under the present conditions of the world we have no alternative but to go on with it, because it is the very breath of our British being, our freedom itself, that is at stake.

" Do not let us forget that this freedom has come down to us from the past, bought for us at a price. If we wish to keep it we must pay the interest on that price in each succeeding generation, but there is no need to look forward to the future with apprehension, and still less with despair. We pass no judgment here upon the political systems of other countries, but neither Fascism nor Communism is in harmony with our temperament and creed. We will have nothing to do with either of them here. And yet, whatever differences there may be between us and other nations on that subject, do not forget that we are all members of the human race and subject to the like passions and affections and fears and desires. There must be something in common between us if only we can find it, and perhaps by our very aloofness from the rest of Europe we may have some special part to play as conciliator and mediator. An ancient historian once wrote of the Greeks that they had made gentle the life of the world. I do not know whether in these modern days it is possible for any nation to emulate the example of the Greeks, but I can imagine no nobler ambition for an English statesman than to win the same tribute for his own country."

THE ANGLO-ITALIAN AGREEMENT

On 16th April, 1938, the Anglo-Italian conversations, whose initiation two months earlier had resulted in the resignation of Mr. Eden, were concluded by an Agreement. After Parliament reassembled, the Prime Minister on the afternoon of 2nd May asked for its approval of this Agreement.

"I BEG to move,

" ' That this House approves the results of the recent Anglo-Italian conversations as contained in the Agreement signed at Rome on 16th April, 1938.'

" To this Motion the Opposition have put down what, I think, is generally known as a reasoned Amendment. Any really impartial person who reads the terms of the Amendment will see that there is mighty little reason in it. It appears that the very idea of making any agreement with Italy arouses such violent emotions in the breasts of hon. and right hon. Gentlemen opposite that they lose all sense of reality and are tempted to commit themselves to assertions about the contents of the Agreement which have no warrant whatever in the actual terms. In these circumstances I am disposed to treat this Amendment as merely an emphatic manner of saying ' No,' and I do not propose to say any more about it. It seems to me that the best answer is not so much to be found in dissecting these overstatements and misstatements as in giving to the House the reasons why the Government are proposing to ask the House to say ' Yes.'

" I do not think that it will be necessary for me this afternoon to delve very deeply into past history, but, at the same time, if we are to obtain a proper consideration of the Agreement, I think it is an essential preliminary that I should say something about the conditions which prevailed before it was signed. I suppose it was inevitable that the termination of the Abyssinian affair, ending as it did in the conquest of Abyssinia and in the failure of collective action to produce the results which had been intended, should leave behind it a great deal of bitterness and resentment on both sides. By the Autumn of 1936 the relations between this country and Italy had become so unsatisfactory and even so dangerous that it was felt to be necessary to make some effort to improve them. Since it was in the region of the Mediterranean Sea that the interests of the two countries came most closely into contact with one another, it was there that any lack of confidence between us became most apparent, and was most calculated to give rise to harmful results. For these reasons, it was to that region that the two Governments directed their attention, and on 2nd January, 1937, they signed a joint declaration which came to be known as a 'Gentlemen's Agreement.' The Gentlemen's Agreement was designed to dispel suspicions and misunderstandings, but, unfortunately, it proved that it did little in that direction, and these suspicions, which were intensified and reflected by comments in the Press of both countries, continued to grow.

" When, later in the year, I succeeded my noble Friend, Lord Baldwin, in my present office, the situation was as bad as ever it had been, and it seemed to me then, and it seems to me now, looking back, that unless some further effort could be made it was in danger of rapidly becoming acute. In July of that year, in response to a friendly message which I had received from Signor Mussolini, I wrote to him a letter, in the course of which I suggested that it might be a good thing if the two Governments were to enter upon conversations with a view to seeing whether they could not clear away any misunderstandings which existed, and do something to restore the old and more cordial relations. Signor Mussolini responded very readily to this suggestion, but in July we were near to the holiday season and for that, and various other reasons, which I need not enter into now, it did not prove possible to give an early effect to these good intentions.

" On 11th December the Italian Government announced their decision to withdraw from the League of Nations, and the conversations between us had to remain in abeyance until January of this year, when they were revived in circumstances with which the House is familiar. On 21st February last, I announced the intention of His Majesty's Government to begin negotiations with the Italian Government with a view to concluding an agreement with them at an early date. Those negotiations began, they have been carried on in a spirit of mutual accommodation and good will and have resulted in the Agreement which was signed on the 16th of last month.

" I should like to pay my tribute to the statesmanlike

qualities of Lord Perth and his staff, on the one hand, and of Count Ciano, the Italian Minister for Foreign Affairs, on the other, in the handling of these negotiations, and on the careful and thorough manner in which they examined every aspect of a somewhat complicated situation. In that connection I should not like to fail in recording my sense of the contribution made also by Count Grandi, the Italian Ambassador in London, who has won for himself a position of confidence and respect in this country, and who certainly did much to facilitate the conclusion of this Agreement by his unceasing and effective efforts to remove doubts and misunderstandings.

" Before I come to examine the details of the Agreement I should like to say one or two words about its place in the general scheme of the Government's foreign policy. As the House has been informed on numerous occasions, the purpose of that general foreign policy is not only to establish peace but, if possible, to restore the general confidence that peace can and will be maintained, because without that confidence no progress is possible in international affairs. We can only attain that confidence if we can succeed in removing grievances, differences and suspicions which may, if unchecked, lead to war. That is not a task which can be accomplished in a moment, or all at once, but if we can remove the danger spots one by one, we may in time find ourselves in a position to arrive at the goal at which we are aiming.

" No one can doubt, I think, that before the signing of this Agreement the relations between Italy and this country, and between Italy and France, constituted one of those danger spots. His Majesty's Government believed that that danger could be eliminated by the application of good will and common sense to problems which arose, as we believed, very largely out of want of trust and confidence between us. But to accomplish that, it was necessary to face facts, however unpalatable those facts may be. It is in our willingness to face realities which we cannot change, and to make the best of them, that the difference lies between this side and the other side of the House.

" This Agreement has been designed to cover comprehensively the whole ground of the relations between ourselves and Italy in certain areas of the world, and it paves the way for future co-operation and understanding in those areas in which our interests are found to be parallel. The areas in question are the Mediterranean, the north-east corner of Africa and the Middle East. It deals with the future. It lays down certain guiding principles which should be taken to inspire our policy not only to one another, but also the policy of both of us to other Powers, and it contains, as right hon. and hon. Members will have seen, four separate but correlated sections. First of all, there is the Protocol itself, signed by Lord Perth and Count Ciano, to which are attached eight Annexes. Then comes an exchange of notes between the two negotiators and, thirdly, there is a Bon Voisinage Agreement, to which Egypt is a party in so far as their interests are affected, and, finally, an exchange of notes between Lord Perth and Count Ciano, on the one hand, and the Egyptian Minister in Rome, on the other, the effect of which is to associate Egypt with two declarations in the main Agreement.

" Let us examine the proposals in this Agreement. Let us begin with the Protocol itself. In it it will be seen that the two Governments, the Government of Great Britain and the Italian Government,

' animated by the desire to place the relations between the two countries on a solid and lasting basis . . . have decided to undertake conversations in order to reach agreement on questions of mutual concern.'

It goes on to specify the number and character of the questions which are dealt with in the several Annexes to which I have already referred. It points out that the said instrument is not to come into force at once, but on such a date as the two Governments together shall determine, and, further, the two Governments agree that after the instrument has come into force, negotiations will be opened in which Egypt will be included in order to try and arrive at certain definite agreements about the boundaries between the Sudan, Kenya and British Somaliland, on the one side, and Italian East Africa, on the other, and certain other matters, including trade, affecting the relations between these several territories.

" I now come to the Annexes. The first reaffirms the

Declaration signed in Rome on 2nd January, 1937, regarding the Mediterranean and the Notes which were exchanged between the two Governments on 31st December regarding the *status quo* in the Western Mediterranean. The second one has reference to a very important point, the exchange of military information, and when hon. Members recall, what I have said before, that the signing of this Agreement has been preceded by a good deal of what, I believe, has been unfounded suspicion as to the intentions of both sides, it will be seen that this Annex is a precaution against further suspicion of that kind, because it is an undertaking that information as to any major prospective administrative movements or redistribution of their respective naval, military and air forces is to be periodically exchanged between the two Governments. The forces concerned are those which are stationed in the overseas territories in or bordering upon the Mediterranean, the Red Sea, or the Gulf of Aden, and also Egypt, the Sudan, Italian East Africa, British Somaliland, Kenya, Uganda and the Northern part of Tanganyika. These are the territories included within the boundaries which are mentioned in the latter part of this Annex.

" I come now to the third Annex, which is one which deals with certain areas in the Middle East, and Saudi Arabia and the Yemen. It will be seen that the two Governments bind themselves to respect the independence and integrity of Saudi Arabia and the Yemen. They further agree that it is their common interest that no other Power shall interfere with the independence and integrity of both these countries. Article 4 of the Annex deals with certain islands in the Red Sea, and goes on to clarify and regularise the position as between Great Britain and Italy as regards certain areas in Southern Arabia which for a long time have been under the protection of the British Government. This applies in particular to the Aden Protectorate, where certain rights have been guaranteed to Italy by this instrument. Finally, in Article 8, provision is made for a revision of the terms if the circumstances should change, and for a duration of 10 years, after which the Agreement will be subject to three months' notice. In the fourth Annex, which concerns propaganda, both Governments declare that neither of them will employ methods of publicity or propaganda at their disposal in order to injure the interests of the other.

" In the Fifth Annex, which concerns Lake Tsana, the Italian Government confirm the assurance which they have previously given to us, that they were fully conscious of their obligations towards the Government of the United Kingdom in the matter of Lake Tsana, and that they had no intention whatever of overlooking or repudiating them. In the Sixth Annex the Italian Government again reaffirm the assurance they have given before to the League of Nations, that Italy is willing to accept the principle that natives of Italian East Africa should not be compelled to undertake military duties other than those of local policing and territorial defence. The Seventh Annex deals with the free exercise of religion, and it gives an undertaking on the part of the Italian Government in regard to such free exercise by British nationals in Italian East Africa, and also deals with the treatment of religious bodies in that territory. The last Annex, No. 8, deals with the Suez Canal and provides for a reaffirmation on the part of both Governments of their intention always to abide by the provisions of the Convention of October, 1888, which guarantees at all times and for all Powers the free use of the Suez Canal.

" I think the House will agree that these Annexes deal in a very careful and comprehensive manner with these possible sources of difference between the Italian Government and ourselves, and the fact that we have been able to reach complete agreement upon them shows how desirable it was that we should get together and discuss these things peacefully round a table. In case anybody should think that Palestine is purposely left out, I should like to mention that the subject of Palestine was also discussed between Lord Perth and Count Ciano, and that as a result the Italian Minister for Foreign Affairs has given our Ambassador an oral assurance that the Italian Government will abstain from creating difficulties or embarrassment for His Majesty's Government in the administration of Palestine, and our Ambassador has given a similar oral assurance that His Majesty's Government for their part intend to preserve and protect legitimate Italian interests in that country."

Mr. Dalton: "Why was this left oral, and not included in the document? What was the reason?"

The Prime Minister: "I have some difficulty in saying what the reason was, but, at any rate, the matter was not considered to be quite of the same order as the other matters which are made the subject of written exchanges, but we ourselves are perfectly satisfied with the oral declarations which we have received[1] and, on the other hand, I think I can say that the Italian Government are perfectly satisfied with the oral declarations we have given in return.

"Now I come to the second section of the Agreement, which consists of three exchanges of Notes. It begins on page 26 of the White Paper. The first one deals with Libya, and in a letter, Count Ciano informs our Ambassador that the Italian Government have given orders for a diminution of the forces in Libya, that withdrawals have already begun at the rate of 1000 a week, that they will continue at not less than this rate until the Italian Libyan effectives reach peace strength, and we are informed that that will constitute an ultimate diminution of these effectives by not less than half the numbers which were in Libya when conversations began. The third Note deals with the accession of the Italian Government to the Naval Treaty, the Treaty of London, and it informs us that the Italian Government have decided upon that accession, and that it will take place as soon as the instruments annexed to the Protocol come into force; but, in the meantime, the Italian Government undertake to act in conformity with the provisions of the Treaty. That, although, so to speak, a side-line, is also a matter on which I think we may all congratulate ourselves.

"In the second Note, on page 28 of the White Paper, three important assurances are given to us in respect of Spain by the Italian Government, and I will say something more about them when I come to explain how and when this Agreement will come into force; but it will be observed that in taking note of these assurances, the British Ambassador stated in his letter:

'that His Majesty's Government regard a settlement of the

[1] These promises have been duly honoured.

Spanish question as a pre-requisite of the entry into force of the Agreement between our two Governments.'

He further stated :

' That His Majesty's Government, being desirous that such obstacles as may at present be held to impede the freedom of member States as regards recognition of Italian sovereignty over Ethiopia should be removed, intend to take steps at the forthcoming meeting of the Council of the League of Nations for the purpose of clarifying the situation of member States in this regard.'

On page 32 we get to the third section of the Agreement, namely, that part which deals with Bon Voisinage between the Government of the United Kingdom, the Egyptian Government, and the Italian Government. The Egyptian Government is associated with this Agreement in respect of the Sudan, and the Agreement is to cover the period between the date of signature of the main Agreement and the completion of the negotiations dealing with the specific East African matters which are referred to in the Protocol. This Agreement will provide, therefore, for co-operation between the two countries in preventing the evasion of anti-slavery laws. I am sorry the right hon. Gentleman opposite should treat a matter so important to this country and the peace of the world with flippancy. I hope that when he comes to speak he will take it in a rather more serious spirit. This Agreement provides also for co-operation in preventing the enrolment of nationals of one party in native military formations of the other."

MR. WEDGWOOD BENN : " Do the words ' Italian East Africa ' mean the existing East Africa, Eritrea and Somaliland, or what the Italians call the Empire, including Abyssinia ? "

THE PRIME MINISTER : " The whole of the Italian possessions in East Africa."

MR. BENN : " In Abyssinia ? "

THE PRIME MINISTER : " Yes. The right hon. Gentleman said that I denied that there was frontier rectification. I never denied any such thing, and I challenge him to find any place where I did. There is nothing sinister about it. A considerable part of the boundary has never been demarcated. It is obvious it must be necessary for a complete understanding between us, and if we are, as we desire, to remove possible sources of difference, it is absolutely necessary that we should determine where the boundary lies, and that we should also agree upon any rights which people living on either side of the border may have on the other side of the border for the purposes of watering cattle, and so on. Finally, on page 34, we have the Notes exchanged between the Egyptian Minister in Rome, the Italian Foreign Minister and Lord Perth, under which Egypt is associated with the Declaration about Lake Tsana in Annex 5, and, as the Territorial Power concerned, with the Declaration about the Suez Canal which is found in Annex 8. I think that completes this brief analysis of the terms of the Agreement, and it will be observed that, whereas the Notes exchanged and the Bon Voisinage Agreement have already come into operation, the Protocol itself, with its Annexes, is not to come into force until such date as the Governments are hereafter to determine. I think the reason for that is very clear.

" The signing of this Agreement has already effected a radical change in the relations between our two countries. The clouds of mistrust and suspicion have been cleared away. We are able now to regard one another with determination to promote mutual friendship instead of hostility. Full effect cannot be given to this Agreement until we can regard the Spanish question as settled, and find ourselves, consequently, in a position to recognise the Italian conquest of Ethiopia."

MR. GALLACHER : " Of Spain."

THE PRIME MINISTER : " With regard to Spain, there have been suspicions, which have been frequently expressed, that Italy not only when the time came would refuse to withdraw volunteers in accordance with the Non-Intervention Committee's Agreement, but that she also was aiming at acquiring for herself some permanent position, either in Spain itself or in some of Spain's overseas possessions. Therefore, I desire to call particular attention to Count Ciano's letter, which is to be found on page 28 of the White Paper, in which he gave three specific assurances to the British Government. First of all, he said the Italian Government :

" ' Confirm their full adherence to the United Kingdom formula for the proportional evacuation of the foreign volunteers from Spain, and pledge themselves to give practical and real application to such an evacuation at the moment and on the conditions which shall be determined by the Non-Intervention Committee on the basis of the above-mentioned formula.'

Secondly, he reaffirms that

' if this evacuation has not been completed at the moment of the termination of the Spanish civil war, all remaining Italian volunteers will forthwith leave Spanish territory and all Italian war material will simultaneously be withdrawn.'

Thirdly, he

' repeats his previous assurance that the Italian Government have no territorial or political aims, and seek no privileged economic position, in or with regard to either Metropolitan Spain, the Balearic Islands, any of the Spanish possessions overseas, or the Spanish zone in Morocco, and that they have no intention whatever of keeping any armed forces in any of the said territories.'

" That is an important declaration. They are what I suppose are alluded to by the Opposition in their Amendment as ' illusory promises.' I wish to state, on the other hand, that His Majesty's Government accept them as being given in good faith and believe that the Italian Government intend to keep them in the spirit as well as in the letter. If you are to come to an agreement with another party with whom you have had differences, it is essential that you should approach the negotiations in a spirit of trust. Just as mistrust breeds mistrust, so does trust breed trust. I have no doubt that time will show who is right on that matter, and at present we had better leave it at that.

" With regard to the question of recognition of the Italian conquest of Ethiopia, I would like to remind the House that a number of different States, members of the League whose loyalty to the League cannot be questioned, have taken a different view on this matter from that held by His Majesty's

Government. They have taken the view that collective obligations in this matter were discharged on 4th July, 1936, when
the Assembly of the League passed a resolution abolishing the
sanctions. It is their view, therefore, that States members
were consequently free to take whatever action seemed good
to them in the light of their own situation and what they
considered to be their own obligations. That is a perfectly
comprehensible view and a good number of powerful and convincing arguments can be brought forward in support of it.
His Majesty's Government do not desire to criticise any States
who have taken that view, but so far as they are concerned
they, in common with many others, have held that this is not a
question which concerns ourselves alone, but that it is one
which requires consideration by the appropriate organ, the
League. The result of this difference of opinion is that some of
those who took part in collective action have already recognised the Italian position in Ethiopia. Others, again, have
taken action which implies recognition, or seems to imply
recognition. Others, again, have taken no action at all.
The result of that is a confused and anomalous situation, a
situation which does require clearing up.

" His Majesty's Government have taken the first step
towards clarification by asking the Secretary-General to place
an item dealing with this question on the agenda of the forthcoming meeting of the Council, which they consider to be
the appropriate organ. Let me make one or two points
clear. First of all, our action does not mean that we condone
or that we approve the methods by which Italy obtained
control of Abyssinia. Secondly, it does not mean that we are
going to ask the League to modify any resolution or any
decision which it took during the period of the conquest.
The League has expressed its judgment on the whole affair in
the plainest possible terms and there will be no going back on
that. In the third place, we do not intend to ask any other
State to take any action which they might deem incompatible
with their obligations. There is something further. Neither
any action which we have taken nor any action which we may
ask the Council to take, in itself constitutes recognition. It
neither binds us nor anyone else to recognition. The act of
ecognition remains within the sovereign rights of each

G

individual State. In other words, in so far as this country is concerned, the time and circumstances of recognition remain within our own discretion. I myself have always maintained, and many I think agree with me, that the only circumstances in which recognition could be morally justified would be if it was shown to be an essential feature of a general appeasement. That is the position of the Government to-day."

MR. CHURCHILL : " Is there general appeasement ? "

THE PRIME MINISTER : " The Mediterranean Agreement is a step towards general appeasement."

MR. BELLENGER : " What is the exact legal position ? Is it *de facto* or *de jure* ? "

THE PRIME MINISTER : " It is not *de jure* anyway, if the hon. Member means at the present moment. On the coming into force it will certainly be *de jure*. What I was saying was that the justification for recognition *de jure* would be that it was an essential factor in getting back to general appeasement. I do not think we could feel that we had got back or that we were taking steps towards general appeasement unless at the same time we could see that a Spanish settlement was within reach. That is a reason why we have made this Spanish settlement a pre-requisite of the entry into force of this instrument, and a pre-requisite therefore of the recognition of the Italian conquest."

MR. ATTLEE : " What does the right hon. Gentleman mean by a settlement ? "

THE PRIME MINISTER : " I prefer not to give a definition of it. At this stage it would be wrong to try to define the circumstances in which one could say that a settlement had been arrived at. It may be that later on we shall get nearer the time when we can give a definition."

MR. ATTLEE : " The right hon. Gentleman is asking the House to approve a Treaty that is to come into force on the specific terms that there should be a settlement in Spain, and now he says that he cannot tell the House what a settlement is. It is ridiculous. The House is entitled to know."

THE PRIME MINISTER : " There I leave myself to the judgment of the House. I cannot tell the House even when this Protocol and Annexes will come into force. No doubt the situation will clear itself up as time goes on. The right hon. Gentleman does not agree with that policy I know, but I do not think the House in general will feel that this is not a policy or that I am being unduly obscure at the moment in declining to say what is to be the final definition of the words ' settlement of the Spanish situation.'

" I think that is all I need say on the question of recognition, but I would like to tell the House that all through these negotiations we have been in the closest touch with the Dominions, who have been advised of the progress of them from the very beginning. Egypt, of course, in virtue of her special relations, has also been kept closely informed, and not only that, but on all questions which actually affect Egyptian interests there has been collaboration with them, and no decisions affecting those interests have been taken without prior consultation and full concurrence on her part. Then, of course, our special relations with France have naturally led us to keep her informed of our general intentions, and I think the House knows that the French Government have expressed their warm approval of our action. Not only do they approve what we have done, but they have paid us the sincerest flattery by deciding themselves to enter into conversations with the Italian Government, in the hope of concluding an agreement which, I understand, they expect to be of a similar character, and if they can be successful in that end, one may say that a further step will have been taken towards the clearing of the European horizon.

" France is not alone in approving of this Agreement, for we have had from the Balkan Entente, through their chairman, a message of warm congratulation upon the result. I think I may say that the Press of Europe, with hardly an exception, has given a sincere welcome to this Agreement ; and it will not have escaped the attention of hon. Members that the President of the United States has signified his sympathetic interest and considers that this affords proof of the value of peaceful negotiations. In this almost universal chorus of praise, is it not strange to find only those two parties opposite regretting and opposing an agreement which has done so much to lighten the tension in Europe and to avert the danger of war ? For my part, I repudiate the idea that it is impossible for democracies to come to terms and to understandings with

States where authoritarian ideas prevail. This Agreement proves the contrary, and I am encouraged by what has happened to hope that we have taken only the first step towards a healthier and saner state of things in Europe.

"I believe that for Italy and ourselves this Agreement marks the beginning of a new Era. In former days we had a close friendship with the old Italy, the Italy which, with our warm approval and sympathy, won her independence and her unity under Cavour and Mazzini and Garibaldi. [HON. MEMBERS: 'And Mateotti.'] To-day there is a new Italy, an Italy which, under the stimulus of the personality of Signor Mussolini, is showing new vigour, in which there is apparent new vision and new efficiency in administration——"

MR. A. V. ALEXANDER: "And new horrors."

THE PRIME MINISTER: "—and in the measures which they are taking to improve the conditions of their people. With the laying aside of temporary differences which this Agreement has brought about, I believe that we may look forward to a friendship with the new Italy——"

MR. ALEXANDER: "Never."

THE PRIME MINISTER: "—as firmly based as that by which we were bound to the old."

PEACE WITH EIRE

On 5th May, Mr. Chamberlain in moving the second reading of the Eire (Confirmation of Agreements) Bill in the House of Commons, was able to announce a further achievement in his policy of international appeasement and the termination of another long-standing feud—that with the Irish Free State. Here, Britain had been able to plead throughout that it had right on its side, but by doing so had merely increased and prolonged international ill-will. The Prime Minister's policy was one more in keeping with the realities not of the irrevocable past, but of the ever-changing present.

" I BEG to move, ' That the Bill be now read a Second time.'
" I should imagine that it would be necessary to go a
very long way back in our Parliamentary history to find
another occasion on which it has been possible for a Minister
in the course of a single week to put forward for the approval
of the House two Agreements between this country and
another country, each of which constitutes the termination of
a long and painful difference. That is my lot this afternoon.
Although the two agreements differ from one another in
themselves and in the conditions in which they were concluded, in almost every other respect I think it may be said that
both of them illustrate the fact that disputes, even when they
have been carried on to an extreme limit of acrimonious
discussion, nevertheless can be settled by peaceful discussion,
provided only there is a spirit of accommodation and good
will on both sides.

" Before I come to any comments or explanations that I
may wish to make about the Agreements I would like to say
one or two words about the procedure. The Agreements, as
is stated in the general Preamble, are subject to Parliamentary
confirmation, and this Bill is designed to provide that confirmation and to do anything else that may be necessary to
carry them into effect. If the Bill is carried, we propose to ask
the House to go into Committee on the Financial Resolution
which is required for part of Clause 2. The Financial Resolution deals with two things : First of all with the disposal of a
sum of £10,000,000 which is to be paid by the Government
of Eire, and the method of disposal is dealt with in the Financial
Memorandum accompanying the Bill ; secondly, there is
the transfer to the Consolidated Fund of certain charges in
connection with the service of the land purchase scheme, which
is dealt with in the Second Schedule to the Bill. There is also
a Resolution which will be moved in Committee of Ways
and Means covering Clause 3, Sub-section (4), which provides

that Customs Duties may be levied in certain events which are specified therein.

" I would like to give the House some idea of the general considerations which were present in the minds of the Government in conducting their discussions with Mr. de Valera and his colleagues and I think that the vast majority of the people of this country have regretted very deeply the long differences and disputes which have separated us from the people of what was formerly the Irish Free State. Those of us who can carry back our memories to the discussions on Home Rule in 1886 and 1893 remember the bitterness of the feelings which were aroused at that time and the devastating and disruptive effects which they had on English politics. Later on were the unhappy episodes which preceded and followed the Great War. When the Treaty of 1921 was signed many of us who accepted that treaty with some misgiving and reluctance nevertheless hoped that at any rate it had settled the Irish question. But those hopes were doomed to disappointment, and the withholding of the Land Annuities which were due under that agreement, and the changes in the Irish Constitution seemed to leave the Irish question as unsolved and insoluble as ever.

" The conference which was held in 1932 between Mr. de Valera and some of his colleagues and British Ministers led to no result, and indeed it was not until the first Coal-Cattle Agreement was made that there seemed to be any approach towards more amicable relations. But in those circumstances my right hon. Friend the Secretary of State for the Dominions began very cautiously and carefully to prepare the way by establishing personal relations with the Irish High Commissioner, and later on with Mr. de Valera himself, and I have no hesitation in saying that we could never even have begun the conversations which have just terminated so successfully if it had not been for my right hon. Friend's inexhaustible patience and sympathy. At length the time arrived when it seemed possible to establish personal contacts with the Irish Ministers. We determined that we would make the scope of these discussions as wide as possible, because it was quite evident that if we could obtain anything in the nature of a general settlement, that would justify concessions far more generous than we should have been able to submit to this House for approval if a more limited agreement had had to stand entirely upon its own merits.

"In order to obtain a complete general settlement, four subjects came up for review. The first was the question of partition; the second, of defence; the third, finance; and the fourth, trade. With regard to the first, the question of the ending of partition, Mr. de Valera and his colleagues attached to that subject primary importance, and they repeatedly told us that if that question could be settled to their satisfaction, as far as they were concerned the Irish question would be at an end. But on our side we took the view that the question of partition was not one for us; it was one which must be discussed between the Governments of Southern and Northern Ireland. Any question of our putting pressure on Northern Ireland to come into an arrangement did not commend itself to us; we could not even think of such a thing. But when we had made that perfectly plain, the subject of partition was laid aside, and we proceeded to the discussion of the other three subjects that I have mentioned. Those subjects we were able to agree upon, and they form the substance of the three Agreements, which are indeed separate Agreements but are linked together by a general Preamble saying that they are to be treated as one interconnected whole.

"If I may take first the trade Agreement, I would say that it is an arrangement which can stand on its own bottom. It is one which may be considered to be equally beneficial to both parties. Broadly speaking, it provides that goods from Eire can be admitted to this country free of Customs Duty other than revenue duty and subject to certain quantitative regulations on agricultural produce. On the other hand the Government of Eire guarantees the continuance of free entry into Eire for United Kingdom goods which already enjoy entry free of duty. The Eire Government undertake to remove or reduce their duties upon certain other United Kingdom imports and to arrange for a review of the existing protective tariffs by the Prices Commission. The existing preferential margins are to be maintained, and a preference is assured for United Kingdom goods in any new duties or any adjustment of the duties which already exist. In case of any

G *

difficulty arising there is a provision for consultation between the two Governments.

"I would just say a few words upon Clause 3, Sub-section (4), which requires a Resolution in Committee of Ways and Means. It will be seen that that Sub-section has reference to Article 4, Sub-section (3), on page 9 of the Agreement. Under that Sub-section in certain circumstances it is contemplated that the Government of the United Kingdom may impose such duties as may be necessary upon eggs and poultry exported from Eire to this country. There is no present power to impose such duties, and that is the reason why we have to include Sub-section (4) of Clause 3. As I have said, this Agreement carries its own justification with it, and it is not necessary, I think, for me at this stage to enter into any description of the details of a somewhat long and complicated arrangement, but I may say that we believe that this Agreement will stimulate the natural tendency of trade between the two countries, and I think that the coal-mining industry in particular will welcome the advantages that they may expect to obtain from it.

"The Agreements on defence and finance are of a totally different character. It cannot be said that, on the face of them, either of them constitutes a good agreement for this country, because both of them make very large and impressive concessions to Eire without on the face of it any corresponding advantages. If you are to find those advantages, you must look outside the Agreements, and must seek them in those intangible, imponderable, but nevertheless invaluable fruits which have on various occasions in the past rewarded a liberal and unselfish act of generosity by a great and powerful country towards a State weaker and poorer than itself.

"If you exclude the annual sum of £250,000 payable by the Government of Eire in respect of damage to property, the British claims against that Government amount, if they are capitalised, to over £100,000,000. It is quite true that the Government of Eire does not admit those claims; its view is that they are wrong in essence, that they ought never to have been made, and that they are not sustainable in equity. But the fact remains that the special duties which were imposed by this country in order to recoup us for the sums which were being, in our view, wrongfully withheld, have amounted to over £4,000,000 a year, and that in the absence of this Agreement, there appeared to be no reason why we should not continue to exact those duties. Under this Agreement we have wiped out the special duties, and we have withdrawn all our financial claims in return for a lump sum of £10,000,000. Nobody, I think, can deny that that is generous treatment. Nevertheless, I hope the House will agree that the Government was right to end this dispute even at that price, because, if we were ever to end it at all, some compromise was inevitable. The continued exaction of these duties from Eire was gradually impoverishing that country; it was gradually reducing its potential value as a customer of our own. And, finally, we surely should recollect that in this case we are dealing with no foreign country; we are dealing with a country which is a partner with us in the Empire, and we should deal with it, therefore, on terms of partnership rather than on terms of competitorship.

" I pass to the Agreement on Defence. There was no part of our discussions with the Ministers from Eire which gave us occasion for more prolonged and more anxious thought than this subject of Defence. The request was made to us by those Ministers that we should hand back to the Government of Eire the full and unrestricted possession of certain ports, and that we should repeal certain Articles in the Treaty of 1921 which gave us rights in those ports. I think it will perhaps be for the convenience of the House if I read two Articles of the Treaty of 1921 which, if this Bill becomes law, will cease to have effect. They are Article 6 and Article 7. Article 6 reads as follows:

" ' Until an arrangement has been made between the British and Irish Governments whereby the Irish Free State undertakes her own coastal defence, the defence by sea of Great Britain and Ireland shall be undertaken by His Majesty's Imperial Forces; but this shall not prevent the construction or maintenance by the Government of the Irish Free State of such vessels as are necessary for the protection of the revenue or the fisheries. The foregoing provisions of this Article shall be reviewed at a conference of representatives of the British and Irish Governments to be held at the expiration

of five years from the date hereof, with a view to the undertaking by Ireland of a share in her own coastal defence.'

Article 7 says :

" ' The Government of the Irish Free State shall afford to
His Majesty's Imperial Forces (*a*) in time of peace, such
harbour and other facilities as are indicated in the Annex
hereto, or such other facilities as may from time to time be
agreed between the British Government and the Government
of the Irish Free State ; and (*b*) in time of war or of strained
relations with a foreign Power, such harbour and other
facilities as the British Government may require for the
purposes of such defence as aforesaid.'

In the Annex the ports in question are specified as Berehaven,
Queenstown and Lough Swilly, and in those ports the defences
are to remain in charge of British care and maintenance
parties. I think hon. Members will have appreciated that the
really important part of those passages which I have read out
refers to the right which is given to the British Government to
have the use of those ports in time of war or of strained
relations with a foreign Power. I believe that, at the time
when the Treaty was signed, great importance was attached
to that particular provision. I do not by any means under-
rate its importance now, but I must point out to the House
that when the Treaty was signed, that provision was based on
the assumption of a friendly Ireland, and that, if you had an
unfriendly Ireland, the situation would be completely changed,
because you would have to send troops to Ireland then to
protect your rights in the ports. We had to recognise in the
discussions that we had a far better chance of having a friendly
Ireland if we handed back those ports to them than if we were
to insist upon treaty rights the effect of which would be to
perpetuate a grievance in Ireland which constituted in their
eyes an affront to their independence and self-respect.
Nobody who knows anything of Ireland would under-
rate the genuineness and the seriousness of any feeling of that
kind in the minds of the Irish people. I observe that Mr. de
Valera, speaking in the Dáil in support of this Agreement on
27th April, said :

" ' The Articles of the 1921 Treaty that gave most offence, were these '—

that is to say, the two Articles I have just read—

' because they meant that part of our territory was still in British occupation.'

After most careful consideration of all the circumstances, and after due consultation with the Chiefs of Staff, we came to the conclusion that a friendly Ireland was worth far more to us both in peace and in war than these paper rights which could only be exercised at the risk of maintaining and perhaps increasing their sense of grievance ; and so we have agreed that, subject to Parliamentary confirmation, these Articles shall be repealed, and that the ports shall be handed over unconditionally to the Government of Eire. We do that as an act of faith, firmly believing that that act will be appreciated by the people of Eire, and that it will conduce to good relations. I would remind hon. Members that again in the course of the speech to which I have referred, Mr. de Valera repeated what he had said on more than one occasion before, namely, that the Eire Government would not permit Irish territory to be used as a base by any foreign Power for an attack upon this country. He further announced his intention to put those ports into a proper state of defence so that he could implement that assurance.

" I think I need say no more upon the Agreements, but I would like to say one or two words about the position of Northern Ireland. I have already told the House that we declined altogether to discuss the question of partition, and the Government of Northern Ireland were of opinion that the other matters which were the subject of agreement were not within their competence. At the same time, they did make representations to us that it was possible that some provisions in our Agreement with Eire might materially and injuriously affect their economic interests in Northern Ireland, and they pressed us repeatedly to do all that we possibly could to safeguard those interests for them. We listened to what they had to say on that subject with very great sympathy. We were extremely anxious that Northern Ireland should not suffer in any way by an agreement which was made primarily to restore good relations between this country and Southern Ireland. We were able to meet in a very considerable degree the suggestions which they made to us, and the various concessions to which we agreed were recapitulated by the Prime Minister of Northern Ireland in a speech which he made in their Parliament. I would just like to read to hon. Members a short passage from that speech which shows how the matter presents itself to Lord Craigavon at this juncture. He said:

"'I desire to avail myself of this, the earliest opportunity, to express my gratitude to the Government of the United Kingdom for their appreciation of the difficulties with which we were confronted and the readiness they evinced to meet our wishes in reaching a solution. I am happy in paying this tribute to their understanding and sympathy. Taking the long view, Ulster will greatly benefit, and her prospects in regard to rearmament work be very materially brightened.'

That, I think, will commend itself to hon. Members as being a very satisfactory statement from the point of view of Northern Ireland."

SIR WILLIAM DAVISON: "Will my right hon. Friend say what the concessions to Northern Ireland are?"

THE PRIME MINISTER: "I would refer my hon. Friend to the statement made by Lord Craigavon, in which he detailed them, but I need hardly take up time in going through them now. They are fairly numerous."

SIR W. DAVISON: "What will they cost the Exchequer of this country—the concessions which are made, and of which I entirely approve, to Northern Ireland?"

THE PRIME MINISTER: "I will ask my right hon. Friend to try and give to my hon. Friend the figures which he desires. Now I think I have concluded what I wished to say. I wish to commend this Bill to the House as opening a new chapter in the relations between Eire and ourselves. The members of my family have more than once in the past made an effort to improve those relations, and if I feel some confidence that the prospects of a settlement this time are more hopeful than they were before, it is because the conditions which accompanied our negotiations were themselves far more favourable than we have ever had the good fortune to meet on previous occasions. These discussions have been carried through in a spirit of accommodation and good will. I would like to pay my tribute to Mr. de Valera and his colleagues for the way in which they played their part in these discussions. We could not always agree with them, but we always felt that we had before us men of sincerity who were genuinely anxious to meet us and to come to terms with us if they could.

"In spite of all the controversies of the past and all the heat that has been generated, this country and Eire cannot do without one another. Our natural interests and our geographical position inevitably tend to bring us together, and what has kept us apart has been, not a divergence of interests, but something which ought to be far less important, and that is a difference of opinion. Somebody sent me the other day a passage from John Selden's *Table Talk*, written some 300 years ago, which perhaps the House will allow me to read, because although it is quaintly expressed, it seems to have a bearing upon this subject. He writes :

" ' That was a good fancy of an old Platonic ; that the gods, which are above men, had something whereof men did partake (an intellect knowledge), and the gods kept on their course quietly. The beasts, which are below men, had something whereof man did partake (sense and growth) and the beasts lived quietly in their way. But man had something in him whereof neither gods nor beasts did partake, which gave him all the trouble and made all the confusion we see in the world ; and that is opinion.'

I hope that that difference of opinion with Eire is now at an end. I trust the House will give us this afternoon their unanimous support, and I would ask hon. Members to bear in mind that what we have done has obtained the warm approval, not only of many people in this country, but of others outside our shores, in the Dominions, in the United States of America, and indeed everywhere where men desire to see the establishment of peace and good will."

THE FEAR OVER COUNTLESS HOMES

The provisional Agreement with Italy was stigmatised by the Opposition as " morally repugnant and degrading." " The Prime Minister," Mr. Attlee declared, " is widely and justly distrusted in the country, and he will not get away by the kind of practice he has put in operation to-day." Mr. Chamberlain, however, disregarding criticism and abuse alike, persisted in his policy, knowing well the strength of the forces—so long accumulating—that were threatening to plunge the world into the irretrievable disaster of another great war. On 12th May, at the annual Conference of Women's Conservative Associations at the Albert Hall, he again explained his policy.

"I N my dual capacity as Prime Minister and Leader of the Conservative Party there is no aspect of Government policy which lies outside my province.

" I should not feel that I was properly fulfilling my function if I did not attempt to give a lead, both in the direction and the pace of the various Government activities. At the same time, I am not a dictator.

" If the policy that I and my colleagues are pursuing were not to meet with the support of those who have put us in our present positions, we would not retain our offices for a week. Therefore, it is essential that the relations between us should be those of mutual confidence and trust.

" For that reason, although talking about myself is not one of my favourite occupations, I do think that on this occasion of my first official duty to you in my new capacity, it would not be inappropriate if I were to tell you my personal attitude to politics, the things for which I stand, my purposes and my aims, in order that you may judge whether they are such that you are prepared to support.

" I always think that a man's character and principles are influenced very largely by his upbringing. Children generally model themselves on the standards that they see adopted by their elders, especially if they know that those elders are generally respected. Now I was brought up in a household where we were taught the importance of telling the truth even though we got into trouble in doing so. Perhaps that is a reason why I have developed this habit of plainly saying what I believe to be true, which has caused so much stress and lamentation among my political opponents. Another rule of conduct which was also impressed on me when I was young was that you should never promise anything that you did not think that you were able to perform.

" I would like to illustrate this family tradition with an anecdote. My grandparents lived in London and my grandmother had a rock garden. My father as a boy was interested in chemical experiments, and one day thought it would be interesting to see what would happen if he buried a charge of gunpowder in the rockery. He did so, and the experiment was a great success—the rock garden went up into the air.

"Unfortunately, when my grandfather returned in the evening he took a rather serious view of the incident, and asked my father where he got the gunpowder. He said he had purchased it with threepence borrowed from a school friend —and corporal punishment was then administered. After the ordeal was over my grandfather said : ' Remember what I am about to say to you. I have punished you not because you blew up your mother's rockery, but because you have borrowed money which you have no means of repaying. Remember when you want money come to me, and then you will not have to repay it.'

"Although my grandfather was rather a stern parent, his principles were admirable. They have not been forgotten either by his son or his grandson, both of whom lived to be Chancellors of the Exchequer.

"But there was something else in the example of my father's life which impressed me very deeply when I was a young man, and which has greatly influenced me since I took up a public career. I suppose most people think of him as a great Colonial Secretary and tariff reformer, but before ever he went to the Colonial Office he was a great social reformer, and it was my observance of his deep sympathy with the working classes and his intense desire to better their lot which inspired me with an ambition to do something in my turn to afford better help to the working people and better opportunities for the enjoyment of life.

"At first I thought anything I could do in that direction would be done locally in serving on the council of my native city, but when afterwards I decided to enter upon national politics, the background was still the same, and I have not yet lost sight of it. Since I was a young man great improvements have taken place in our social services. In those days there was no free education, old-age and widows' pensions, no health and unemployment insurance, no maternity and child welfare centres, no working-men's compensation. The material conditions of the working people then were much harder than they are to-day, and their opportunities for recreation and amusement were much more restricted than they are in these days; and, indeed, most of them had little leisure from toil to amuse themselves at all.

"So, looking back, I see great improvements; but what strikes me is this—if you put all these things together, they constitute a veritable revolution in our social life, but it has been carried through without upsetting the Constitution, without violence or doing serious damage to any section of the community; and that is a striking testimony to the value of our democratic system.

"We in this country dislike violent changes, yet, although we may be slower in making these changes than if we were more highly organised, our progress is steady and continuous, and each step is firmly consolidated before the next step is taken. At the present time we are engaged in unprecedented expenditure on armaments, and yet even now we are still steadily improving and extending our social services.

"We are clearing away slums, controlling and reducing overcrowding, improving our health services, and particularly the maternity services, in which I have always taken a special interest, and quite recently we have been providing an improvement in extending facilities for the young to train and discipline their bodies to grow up and be strong and healthy.

"These increased facilities are more needed to-day than ever before because our young people have so much leisure at their disposal. It is a wonderful reflection to-day that something like eight million people are having holidays with pay. That is a practice I introduced into my own works twenty years ago, before I gave up business for politics, and to-day it is becoming the rule that if we are to get full enjoyment out of holidays we must be physically fit. I hope our efforts to provide physical fitness will mean that, when holidays come, holiday-makers will be able to get the best out of them.

"Home affairs to a large extent can be directed and controlled by ourselves. If that was all we had to think about, how much simpler would be the task of governing the country, but in these troublous times we cannot for long have out of our minds other affairs over which we have little control. They take place outside our shores but may profoundly affect our lives in the future. We are like people living at the foot of a volcano. It is so long since an eruption has taken place that we go about our business without thought of fear. Every now and then there comes a sudden blast of steam or subterranean rumbling from the mountain, which reminds us it is still alive, and then we remember it blew up once before and we begin to wonder whether it is to be our fate to be smothered in ashes or see our homes destroyed and devoured by burning lava.

" I know from many letters I receive that the fear of war has been hanging over countless homes for many months past and filling the hearts of mothers and wives with gnawing anxiety lest their menfolk may have to take part in it. If there are any of them here to-day, I should like to speak a few words of comfort to them. The main object of this Government's foreign policy is the establishment and maintenance of peace, so that, instead of building up armaments against one another, we may settle our differences and then devote ourselves to make the world a better place to live in.

" I only wish it was possible to establish peace by just declaring that we would not go to war, and inviting everyone else to do the same. If we were to do that, we would merely be inviting people who are not of the same mind as ourselves to take advantage of us.

" It is important to remember that although it takes two to make peace, only one can make war.

" If anyone was to attack us, we should have to defend ourselves. That is the purpose of our rearmaments. We have to make ourselves so strong that it will not be worth while for anyone to attempt to attack us. That is only half of our peace policy, because if we are to get a settled peace established, we have got to try and find out what are the likely causes of war and to remove them. We can only do that by entering into friendly conversations with those Powers who have grievances or think they have grievances against their neighbours. That is the other half of our peace policy.

" In our view, we ought not to refuse to take opportunities

which may present themselves for such conversations because other Powers do many things we don't like, if by taking advantage of those opportunities we could put an end to the old quarrels, settle our differences, and avert the danger of war. These are the two related members of our foreign policy —on the one hand, building up of defence forces and on the other hand entering into friendly conversations and relations with other Powers. That policy is already bearing fruit.

" When I remember all the long years of our differences with Ireland, all the bitterness and hatred engendered in the past in the course of that struggle, I am amazed at the universal approval which has welcomed the success of our efforts to reach agreement with Mr. de Valera's Government in Southern Ireland. It involves large concessions and sacrifices on our part, but in the view of His Majesty's Government all that we give away will be repaid if we can once and for all close an old, unhappy chapter and open a new one of trust and friendship between our two countries. We are confident that our expectation of that happy result will not be found to be disappointed, but that these new relations we have now opened with a country which we are to call Eire, will result in increased strength and prosperity for two nations which have been placed by Providence side by side, and which cannot afford to quarrel with one another.

" Still more important to the cause of world peace is the Agreement we have made with Italy. I have not changed in any respect the opinions I expressed about the Italian conquest of Abyssinia at the time. But, after all, the League of Nations was not able to stop that conquest or restore the situation to what it was before, and in the meantime relations between Italy and ourselves had been poisoned by the action which we, in common with others, took in pursuance of our obligations under the Covenant.

" Those relations were deteriorating so fast that we were rapidly approaching a situation full of danger which might easily have led to our being involved once again in war. When I became Prime Minister I made up my mind that it was necessary for us to make another and a determined effort to avert that dangerous situation. I believed that the quarrel between us rested largely upon unfounded suspicions and misunderstandings. And the ease with which, once we had broken the ice and begun conversations, we were able to reach agreement on every aspect of the situation which we discussed shows, I think, that I was right in that view and that there was no real and solid foundation for supposing that our interests were opposed to one another.

" You probably know that we cannot put the Agreement into full operation until we can regard the Spanish situation as settled, and consequently find ourselves in a position formally to recognise the Italian situation in Abyssinia. But already the mere fact that we have made this Agreement has resulted in a perceptible easing of the tension.

" The approval with which the Agreement has been received in France, in the countries of Central and Eastern Europe, in the Dominions, in America, and even in Russia, shows that it is generally recognised as a long step forward in the direction of general appeasement and peace.

" Now, is it not strange that, when the whole world seems to be rejoicing at this Agreement, there should be one quarter from which it is criticised and scoffed at ? And that quarter is, as perhaps you would expect, in the two branches of the Opposition in the House of Commons.

" The Opposition pay lip service to the cause of peace, but with them party interests come before country, and they don't scruple to misrepresent the motives and the actions of the Government if by so doing they think they can discredit it with the electors. Their latest device is to make personal attacks upon the Prime Minister and to declare that he has abandoned the League and become a Fascist.

" I do not think that personal attacks are very effective, nowadays, unless they put the victim off his sleep, and I can assure you that they have not done that, or unless the charges which are brought can be shown to be true. In this case they are the very reverse of the truth. I am, and always have been, against any form of dictatorship in this country, whether it be of the Right or of the Left. The introduction of Fascism here would certainly breed Communism and vice versa, and both Fascism and Communism alike are utterly inconsistent with our democratic notions of equality and liberty.

" But if in other countries it is found that Fascism or Communism suit their conditions, I do not see why we should try to impose our ideas upon them so long as they do not try to impose their ideas upon us. After all, we have to live with these countries, we have to trade with them, we have to work with them in all matters which require international co-operation. Surely in those circumstances it is only common sense to try to make our relations with them as amicable as possible instead of nagging at one another until we all lose our tempers.

" As for the League, anybody who has read the speeches that I have made about it during the last few years must know that I have repeatedly pointed out that in its present condition, when the League includes only a minority of the Great Powers, it is incapable of carrying out the intentions of its founders. To pretend that this maimed and mutilated League can really afford security to the smaller Powers of Europe is not loyal to the League ; it is disloyalty, because, if anybody believes it, it would mean that they would be putting upon the League a burden which it is clearly unable to carry.

" I have said, and I repeat here, that the ideals for which the League was founded are great and splendid ideals, and those who still retain their faith in them, as I do, can surely best show their loyalty by striving to bring the League back to health and strength so that it may become in truth what it was meant to be from the beginning—a world organisation embracing all political systems, uniting all in a common determination. And when we have done that, then, indeed, we may entrust to the League the peace of the world in the sure and certain conviction that it can preserve it.

" In the meantime, until we can be satisfied that every one else is as peacefully minded as we are, we have no alternative but to go on building up our defence forces.

" I deplore the necessity for that, but, in the present circumstances, I believe it to be essential. We have been carrying out our programme of rearmament as rapidly as possible under peace conditions and in accordance with our desire to interfere as little as possible with the course of ordinary trade. . . .

" If I may sum up my conclusions, I would say that what we have already achieved encourages us to believe that we are on the right road. In a complicated situation you can't expect to straighten it out all at once. What we have to do is to take the danger spots one after another, eliminating them one by one, and if we can go on doing that, we shall advance steadily and surely towards our goal until the time will come when we can finally put all our fears behind us and go about our business once more in tranquillity of mind."

REPAIRING THE BREACHES

The twin pillars of the Prime Minister's policy were the freeing of Europe from quarrels maintained by the dead hand of the past, and the simultaneous repair of those breaches in our defences caused by the policy of unilateral disarmament. For long the country had been deluded by the belief enthusiastically preached by the Socialist Party and the "intellectuals" of the Left that it was possible for a rich nation to maintain peace in a hungry and predatory world by disarming without waiting for her neighbours to do the same. With characteristic inconsistency, seeing that it had opposed every measure of national defence for years, the Opposition was now accusing the Government of having neglected the armed forces of the Crown, particularly the Air Force, whose parliamentary chief, Lord Swinton, feeling that the Air Ministry at such time should be represented by a Minister who could defend it in the Commons, had just resigned. On 25th May, in reply to what was virtually a Socialist Vote of Censure moved by Mr. Hugh Dalton, the Prime Minister made an important statement on the condition of the Air Force and the measures that the Government were pursuing to restore British power in the air.

"THIS Debate was originally fixed to take place last week. I should like to begin by expressing my regret to right hon. and hon. Gentlemen opposite that, owing to my personal physical weakness, I was not able to be present on that occasion, and also my appreciation of their courtesy in consenting to postpone the Debate until I was able to take my place here again. The hon. Gentleman the Member for Bishop Auckland (Mr. Dalton) began his speech by complaining that we have treated the Motion as a Vote of Censure, but I think he will see that it was inevitable that we should do so owing to the terms in which it is couched. Although it does not actually declare that this House has no confidence in the Government, there are in the terms of the Motion two implications which come as near as no matter to the same thing. The first implication is that the condition of the country's air defences and the administration of those defences by the Air Ministry are so bad that a searching inquiry is necessary; and the second implication is that the Government cannot be trusted to make that inquiry itself, but that the inquiry must be handed over to some outside, independent, or, as the hon. Gentleman said, impartial body. What is that but want of confidence? If the hon. Gentleman had confidence in the Government, he would not require to take the matter out of their hands and give it to somebody else. I think it is a little unreasonable of hon. Gentlemen opposite to put down a Motion in those terms and then complain that we treat it as a Vote of Censure.

"As to the first of the implications, let me say at once that I am not here to deny that there have been delays, disappointments and checks in the programme, which has been altered from time to time and expanded according to what we consider to be the needs of the moment. I do not deny that. But, on the other hand, I have no hesitation in saying that in the Air Force as it stands to-day the country has a defence of which any country might be proud, and if it were put to the test to-morrow, with whatever deficiencies there may be, I venture to say that it would prove to be one of the most formidable fighting machines in the world. If I am obliged, as I am, to reject the request for an inquiry, I do so for the same reasons as I rejected a similar request on 15th March last. But I am not going to treat this matter as a question of controversy between parties this afternoon, because I recognise that the very fact that the Opposition have put down this Motion means that they are proceeding on the assumption—an assumption indeed which was made by the hon. Member for Bishop Auckland—that it is not only desirable, but it is essential that we should have an Air Force complete and efficient in all respects as speedily as possible. We are all agreed about that.

" If that be so, then I say that my first and principal reason for rejecting an inquiry is that I do not believe that an inquiry would help in achieving that purpose. I believe that at this time when, above all, what we want is speed and rapidity in making up any deficiencies that exist, an inquiry, to which one could give only the most general terms of reference, an inquiry which would almost necessarily have to be a sort of fishing or roving inquiry to see what was wrong, would be a process which would distract the attention and dissipate the energies both of the Air Ministry and of the aircraft industry as a whole. I put it to the House——"

MR. GARRO JONES : " That is what you told us before."

THE PRIME MINISTER : " I heard a speech lasting more than an hour from the hon. Member for Bishop Auckland, and I think it is a little early to begin interruptions of my speech, especially as I am not now saying anything which is controversial or provocative. I put it to hon. Members that no Government can dispense with its own responsibility for the efficiency of the Defence Services of the Crown. I put it to them that what is wanted at this moment is not any digging up of the past or attempts to place the fault, if fault there be, here or there. What we want is a continuous review by the man who is principally responsible—that is my right hon. Friend the Secretary of State for Air—of all the circumstances of the case and the devotion of his whole mind to the removal of faults and the prosecution of the programme.

"Since this Motion was originally put down, there have been changes at the Air Ministry and I shall have something to say about my Noble Friend Lord Swinton and his administration of the office. My right hon. Friend the present Secretary of State for Air is a man of whom the House has had knowledge now for a great many years, and I think the reputation which he has established in the various offices he has already held will be some guarantee that his methods will be thorough, and that he will omit no pains in order to carry out the duties which are expected of him. I think it was made clear in the letters which passed between Lord Swinton and myself, when he offered his resignation and I accepted it, that I accepted it, not because I was dissatisfied with his administration, but because I recognised, as he recognised, the difficulty of carrying on a great spending Department at a time of rapid expansion, and at a time when it was the focus of attention both in this House and the country, when the head of that Department was not in this House to answer for himself.

"My Noble Friend has been criticised for faults which are alleged to have existed in the administration of his office. I do not think that any charges that have been brought against him have been brought with any malicious motive, but I do think they have been brought with insufficient appreciation of the magnitude and difficulty of the task which was laid upon him. When he took office, with no powers of compulsion but only those of persuasion, he was called upon, at short notice, to carry out an enormous expansion of the organisation of the Air Force. He was called upon to equip it with new types of machines which had not passed the stage of design, and at the same time to make all the necessary preparations for the recruitment and training of the increased personnel which was necessary to man the force.

"Not only that. He had to take account of what might happen if the last emergency arose and if we should be involved in war. He had to take account of the fact that the capacity of the country was quite insufficient to maintain our forces in the early period of a war, and he consequently had to devise

and put into operation a system under which the war potential
of the country could be increased to an extent which had
not hitherto been dreamt of. To do that he necessarily had
to enlist the services of firms who were entirely without
previous experience of the work they were called upon to do.
That is a very brief summary of the task laid upon my Noble
Friend. I cannot help feeling that it must be extremely difficult
for anyone who has not himself had experience of manufacturing on a large scale or of suddenly expanding some
organisation from very small proportions to very large ones
—it must be difficult, I say, for anyone who has not had
that experience to realise the tremendous stress and strain
which such a task involved upon those who are concerned
with it.

" I would like the House to recollect, too, that the situation
was enormously complicated by the fact that the conditions
in which it was carried out were entirely exceptional. It was
not like some period of expansion, let us say, in navies when
all that is required is to repeat many times, no doubt with
some developments, designs already accepted, tried out and
tested in actual service. Those three years of which I speak,
during which the expansion of the Air Force has had to
take place, coincided with one of those forward leaps which
periodically take place in applied science, and in this particular
case the features of this advance took three forms. The
development of the all-metal monoplane, the design of new
engines of unprecedented efficiency and the invention of
the variable pitch air-screw. The combination of those three
new features in aircraft construction not only completely
altered the design, but it necessarily altered the strategy which
had to be employed in the use of these newly developed
machines.

" During those three years the design of aeroplanes has
been changing all the time like a kaleidoscope. We have
heard again from the hon. Gentleman opposite of the delays
that have been caused by changes in design and the necessity
for a reduction in the types of machines to a comparatively
small number of standardised patterns. I agree that it is
desirable to reduce the number of types and to standardise
them as far as possible as a general principle, because the

nearer you can get to standardisation the easier it is to engage in economical quantity production. But I would suggest to hon. Members that in a transition period, and that is what we have been passing through, a transition period from old designs to new designs of an entirely different character, you can easily carry that principle too far. It would not be right to put too severe a brake upon the inventive genius of our people in manufacture and design, if we want to get the best results, and the modern type of aircraft fitted with engines such as I have described is not really ready for standardisation until you have had an opportunity of testing its performance by the ability of the human body to stand the tremendous stresses which are involved. Therefore, while it is undoubtedly the policy of the Air Ministry always to be reducing the number of types it has in use, and to standardise their construction as far as possible, yet I say that during this transition period it was inevitable that the number of types should be considerably in excess of the number to which you would hope to get down when you had had further opportunities of experience.

" Lord Swinton's work during those three years has been largely one of building foundations, and we are now beginning to see the fruits of his labours. I have not the slightest doubt that upon the foundations which he has laid, my right hon. Friend the Secretary of State for Air (Sir Kingsley Wood) will be able to build a firmly based structure of further additions and developments. But there are three indispensable pieces of preparatory work which have been done by Lord Swinton, and for which we owe him gratitude. First of all he has consistently stimulated experimentation so that we might get the best types of machines that could be devised, and I think it is satisfactory that the orders that we have been placing recently are orders for machines which have the highest records for performance and for maintenance when they are actually in operation. As regards speed, it is some time ago since a Hurricane machine flew from Edinburgh to Northolt in forty-eight minutes. That was a remarkable demonstration of the speed of these new machines, and what was perhaps quite as interesting was that that journey was made in bad visibility by night."

H

SIR HUGH SEELY: " With a sixty-mile-an-hour wind behind."

THE PRIME MINISTER: " What does the hon. Member mean to imply by that ? "

SIR H. SEELY: " If it is a question of speed, I am pointing out that there was a sixty-mile-an-hour wind behind the machine."

THE PRIME MINISTER: " Is the hon. Member trying to depreciate its performance ? "

SIR H. SEELY: " If that is considered to be the normal speed of a Hawker Hurricane, I am pointing out that it certainly is not so, because the wind behind on that flight is well known to have been between fifty and sixty miles an hour."

THE PRIME MINISTER: " I will not argue that, and I am not saying that that is the normal speed. I did not say so. I was going on to say that the pilot was able to find his way and steer a correct course by his instruments alone and that that showed that, while we have developed these great speeds, we have not neglected the question of safety or of adaptability. It is interesting to compare the speeds that are being achieved to-day with those which were achieved only a comparatively short time ago, and, of course, when the hon. Gentleman compares the output of aeroplanes to-day with the output of aeroplanes during the War he is comparing two things which are as different from one another as chalk from cheese. The Bulldog squadron which was formed long after the War in 1929 had a top speed of one hundred and sixty-three miles an hour ; the first squadron of Gauntlets which was formed in 1935 had a top speed of two hundred and thirty miles an hour ; but now we are well over speeds of three hundred miles an hour, and the Spitfire, to which I think the hon. Member alluded, is, I am informed, the fastest fighter in service squadrons anywhere in the world. It is shortly coming into service. In speaking of bombers, I cannot, of course, disclose the range of the bomb loads of the latest types, but those which are now in service are, I understand, the fastest bombers in the world, and the new types which are now on order show such a marked advance in all respects upon those which are now in service that I think it is very unlikely that their performance will be surpassed by the bombers of any other country.

"The second task of my Noble Friend was to devise a scheme for the expansion and for the training of personnel. The hon. Member said, quite truly, that there was no difficulty in the recruiting of the necessary numbers, and I think he rightly insisted that the important point was the training. In accordance with the plan of the Air Ministry, there are now thirteen civil schools devoted to preliminary training, there are eleven training schools for Service flying, the capacity for the trade training of men and boys in the Air Service has been increased sevenfold, and Lord Swinton also created the Royal Air Force Volunteer Reserve, for which there are now twenty-two centres in operation. I am not sure whether hon. Members have already been told, but there are now over one thousand volunteer pilots who have qualified to fly solo.

"Then may I say one word about the new war potential? That involved the building of new factories and very large extensions of those which were already engaged in aircraft construction. It also involved the creation of a shadow factory system, which for the time being is being fully employed, while we are building up the force, but which it is intended later on to keep in reserve for an emergency only, placing with the shadow factories such orders as are necessary to maintain the craftsmanship and the experience of those who will run them. This shadow factory system is giving us an enormous increase of productive capacity in war and it covers not only the manufacture of aircraft and engines, but there are shadow factories also for the production of carburettors, bombs, and air-screws. These factories are laid out on the very latest model of factory equipment, and they are, I am told, second to none in the world. I believe I am right in saying that there is no part of the development of the air defences of this country which has made a deeper impression upon foreign visitors than has this shadow factory system. I should like to say that in the whole of that scheme we have had invaluable assistance from Lord Weir, and although he has now retired from active participation in the work of the Ministry, we shall continue to have value for the work which he has done in the future development of the force.

"I would like to say a word or two about mass production. It was not mentioned by the hon. Member, but it often is mentioned, and, as far as I know, the words have never yet been accurately defined. I myself I think would understand the term 'mass production' as the production by labour-saving machinery of very large numbers of identical articles. The Ford Company have recently completed the four millionth V.8 engine under the sort of conditions under which mass production is carried on effectively, but I am told that in the ordinary motor car engine, such as the one that I have just mentioned, there are somewhere about 1700 parts. I do not think it is realised that in the case of a modern bomber there are 11,000 parts in the engine alone, and that, apart from that, in the planes there are upwards of 70,000 separate parts for which between 6000 and 8000 separate drawings are required. That is a very different proposition from the mass production of a motor car, and, moreover, in the design of an aeroplane there is so much variation of line, due to the various curves and tapers of the machine and so on, that there is necessarily extremely little uniformity among those parts, and the actual numbers of any one part are therefore comparatively small.

"It will be seen from what I have said, therefore, that although we have in fact placed very large orders with individual firms or shadow factories, running up to such numbers as 700, 800, or 900 machines, when you come to the actual number of parts which can be duplicated, they are not comparable with the numbers that we commonly associate with the term 'mass production.' It is, of course, possible to apply special methods to reduce time and labour when you have large orders for aeroplanes—and the larger the order the more nearly you approach mass production methods —but I think the House will appreciate that when you are dealing with a complex, delicate mechanism like that of these modern aircraft, the technique must necessarily be very different from that which is employed when you are turning out your grosses of screws or nuts or even of cardboard boxes.

"The hon. Member has also made criticism of the administration of the Air Ministry and he has given us a tremendous catalogue of charges, only a fraction, I understand, of those which he might have made, against the work of the Air Ministry. It is obviously quite impossible for me attempt to make an answer to those charges now. To my mind they suggested a foundation of truth and a great deal of elaboration, shall I say, of their truth afterwards, but again I put it to the House, assuming that there is a certain amount of truth, that there have been mistakes, that there have been delays, that there have been changes when there should not have been changes, and that there have been gaps when there should not have been gaps, how is an inquiry going to help us to put that right now? There are changes that have taken place quite recently, but before the appointment of my right hon. Friend, in the organisation of the Air Ministry. They were described by my Noble Friend the Chancellor of the Duchy of Lancaster (Lord Winterton) the other day. They have passed the test of experience like their predecessors, and I do believe myself that they are designed to carry out and are capable of carrying out effectively that acceleration and expansion of the programme which was recently decided upon by His Majesty's Government. My right hon. Friend will himself be speaking later in the Debate, and I do not want to trespass in any way upon what he is going to say hereafter. I think, therefore, I had better leave this question of the charges that are made about the past or the changes that have recently been made in organisation, with any fresh ideas which my right hon. Friend may desire to put before the House. I had better leave all that to him to give us when he comes to speak later in the evening.

"I would like now to turn to the remarks which the hon. Member made about a ministry of supply, a proposal which has had a good deal of publicity, though there appears to be a good deal of difference of opinion as to what exactly is wanted. There is the hon. Member for Oxford University (Sir A. Salter), for example. He has put forward a plan for a ministry of supply which would be limited to the requirements of the Air Ministry and which would not have, as I understand, any powers or duties which it is not possible for either the Air Ministry or the Committee of Imperial

Defence to exercise now. Then again there is Lord Mottistone, who has a desire to see the old Ministry of Munitions revived, with the same constitution, the same powers and duties, that the Ministry of Munitions had in the War; and that I understand to be favoured by the hon. Gentleman opposite. Then again my right hon. Friend the Member for Epping (Mr. Churchill) has revived a memorandum which he wrote some time ago, in which he evolved a scheme of his own, a scheme for a ministry with, as I understand, at the present time intermediate but unspecified powers, and a scheme which would combine supply and design for the Army and the Air Force with certain odds and ends for the Admiralty.

" The only point that all these schemes have in common is that they contemplate that a new minister should be appointed. That is, of course, a proposal which always carries with it a certain amount of interest. My first comment upon all or any of these schemes must be that, whatever their merits, they surely are inopportune at the present moment. Whichever form of ministry of supply we adopt, it must inevitably mean a certain dislocation of the present machine, and that must be followed, therefore, by a check and a setback in the programme which is being developed by the existing organisation. It seems to me that that difficulty is only to be overridden if there are some superior interests to be served. Either the new ministry of supply will be so superior to the present system that it will very quickly overtake the arrears, and thereafter give us greatly increased output, or else—and this would not apply to the proposal of my hon. Friend the Member for Oxford University—it follows that the present system is deficient in co-ordination, and that the new scheme would put an end to that deficiency and consequently promote efficiency and progress, which are now being hampered by overlapping.

" The hon. Member suggested that the fact that Canada had not been able to get delivery of orders placed for guns in this country years ago conclusively proved the necessity for a ministry of supply; but if Canada or other Dominions had not been able to get their orders fulfilled, that was not because there was no ministry of supply here, but because all available capacity for production of the things they wanted was being occupied in production for our own purposes. If we have to some extent broken in upon that state of things, if we have, for instance, exported a certain number of aeroplanes to the Dominions and other countries, we have had to do it at the expense of our own defences here in so far as they were military machines which we could use. The hon. Member is quite right in saying that other considerations have to be taken into account. Certainly it would be extremely unfortunate if we were to announce to all the world that we were not going to supply a single aeroplane or item of munitions to anybody until we had completed our own programme, for in that case we might indeed alienate our friends and destroy a good will for which we shall be very thankful hereafter.

" Let me say at once that I think hon. Members may dismiss any idea that you require a ministry of supply to stop overlapping or to prevent one Department from taking away supplies which ought really to go to another. There is ample machinery existing to-day and working daily for preventing overlapping and for allocating priority in all the things that matter. I wonder sometimes whether hon. Members realise how far the system of co-ordination has been carried to-day in commodities which we require for war-like purposes. The House has been told on other occasions of a body which is known as the Principal Supply Officers' Committee—a sub-committee of the Committee of Imperial Defence. That is the body which is responsible for this work. It contains representatives of all the Departments that are concerned in war supplies—the three Service Departments, the Treasury, the Board of Trade, the Ministry of Labour, the Home Office, and also the Dominions and India. It deals with all the commodities that are required in war— ships, guns, aeroplanes, tanks, explosives and propellants, motor vehicles, clothing, raw materials, machine tools and so forth. I could enlarge the list almost indefinitely."

MR. CHURCHILL : " Will my right hon. Friend say how often it meets ? "

THE PRIME MINISTER : " Continuously; it is in continuous session. Let me explain to the House how this committee works. In the case of every one of these commodities—and I have given only some—it assesses what would be the probable demand for that commodity in war-time, based, of course, on certain hypotheses as to the conditions of the war. It has inspected hundreds of factories all through the country. It has now allocated the capacity for each of these commodities, and where the capacity does not fully exist, it has taken, or is taking, steps to supply the deficiency. It handles all questions of priority as between one Department and another, and that covers not only materials, but labour. It has the closest relation with industry because it has on it representatives of industry, leading men who are in close touch with it and who act, in fact, as chairmen of some of its sub-committees. This is an organisation which was founded as long ago as 1924. It has been gradually building up this system. There was nothing like it before 1914, before the Great War, and I am bound to say that I find great difficulty in seeing how it will be possible to improve upon it to-day for the particular purposes for which it has been constituted.

" Do not let us be led into accepting the idea of a ministry of supply as being something innately superior to our present system. Let us be clear what it is that our present system is doing and what more we might expect to get from a ministry of supply if we set one up. My own view—and I, at any rate, have not looked at this matter from any departmental point of view; I am not concerned with the prestige of one Department against another—is that, although in actual war a ministry of supply would be essential—and, indeed, we have all the plans ready for such a ministry which could be put into operation at once in such circumstances—I do not believe that a ministry of supply in peace-time will be effective, as the Ministry of Munitions was effective in the Great War, unless you give that ministry of supply the same powers as the Ministry of Munitions had. The hon. Gentleman agrees with me. He specified some of the powers—he did not specify them all."

MR. DALTON: " What I said was that, in my submission, the ministry of supply should have the same powers over all stages and processes of manufacture from design at one end to inspection, testing and delivery at the other."

THE PRIME MINISTER: "It has to be a great deal more than that if it is to be an improvement on the present system. I submit to hon. Members that you can do a great deal to-day by persuasion, by voluntary effort, and by co-operation with labour and with employers; but if you want to produce the sort of effect you had in the Great War, when the Government had absolute control over the whole of industry throughout the country, you must give this ministry the same sort of powers. I would remind hon. Members that among those powers were not only the power of controlling factories, but the power of relaxing trade union practices and regulations, the power over strikes, the power over dilution——"

MR. KIRKWOOD: "You are not going to get that."

THE PRIME MINISTER: "That is what I am pointing out. I think we can do what we want without. What I am saying is that I do not think it is any use setting up a ministry of supply with the same limited powers that we have already. If you want to go further than that, you must have these further powers over industry and over labour, and I doubt very much whether we should be justified in asking for such powers, or whether, if we did ask for them, Parliament would give us them in time of peace. The analogy of war-time is really misleading. We are not at war.

"I need only remind hon. Members of one feature of the Ministry of Munitions Act to bring to their minds how very different are the conditions to-day. Under that Act one of the Sections provided that men could volunteer for service in controlled factories. If they volunteered for that service they had to enter into an undertaking to move from factory to factory according as they were instructed by the Ministry of Munitions. What did they get in return? They got a badge which exempted them from being called up for military service in France. We have no such persuasive powers at our disposal to-day, and I think hon. Members should always bear in mind, in considering this question of a ministry of supply, what an immense difference there is between times of peace such as we, at any rate, are enjoying, and times of war, or times when war seems imminent. Without those powers the only effect of setting up a ministry of supply

H *

would be that you would have to take the actual individuals who are now carrying on certain work in the Air Ministry or the other Service Departments, put them together in some new building, and label them ' Ministry of Supply.' That would be all the difference you would get. You would set back the work that is being done now and, as far as I am able to see, you would add nothing whatever to it. For the reasons I have given, the Government are not prepared to set up a ministry of supply any more than they are prepared to grant the inquiry which is being asked for by the party opposite. Nobody must imagine from that that we are not straining every nerve to complete our programme at the earliest possible moment.

" The hon. Member has again brought up the question of air parity. I do not accept his statement that we have abandoned the idea of air parity, but I repeat what I have said before, that in estimating air parity the number of machines which constitute first-line strength is only one of many factors which have to be taken into account. I very much deprecate the picking out of any particular country for continual comparison in considering our air affairs. I think it is unnecessary, because we have to work on general principles, and I very much prefer a general statement, which cannot then be taken as being in any way a challenge to anybody else. We are all sinners, no doubt, and I do not pretend to be more virtuous than other people. I only say what occurs to me now, that I do not think it is helpful to make comparison with particular countries, and that it is better, so far as we can, to keep our discussions upon this point upon general lines.

" I have said repeatedly in many Debates on this subject that our programme is flexible ; it is a programme which is capable of expansion, or even of reduction ; and it is a programme, therefore, which must vary from time to time in accordance with the international situation. I do not mind saying—and I pick out here something which I think I heard just now—that to me the important thing is not the programme, but its execution. What the Government have set themselves to do is to get the maximum execution possible, at least in the next two years. In these days, when foreign conditions are continually changing, it is difficult to look forward with any confidence to what the conditions may be over a longer period than two years, but our view is that it is our duty to obtain the maximum production of aircraft, and all the necessary accessories and equipment, that this country can give us in the course of the next two years. That is really the programme we have set before ourselves for the present. All I would say to hon. Members in conclusion is : I beg you most earnestly not to take away the attention of my right hon. Friend from the task which we have set him in order to carry out some inquiry, which, I veritably believe, however effective it was, would not help in the task to which, I feel, we all desire to address ourselves."

THE MEANING OF WAR

Disregarding the attacks being made upon him by the Opposition in the House of Commons, the Prime Minister on Saturday, 2nd July, made a further declaration of British Policy at a National Government rally at Kettering. In the course of it he uttered a grave warning to the world that " there are no winners in war."

"I AM glad to give you the opportunity of seeing for yourselves that although I am daily subjected to a barrage of missiles by our bloodthirsty pacifists in the House of Commons, I am none the worse for it. Indeed, I can tell you that at no time in my life have I enjoyed better health and better spirits than I do to-day.

"In the National Government naturally the Conservative Party is the predominant partner, but I do not forget that I have no more loyal colleagues in the Cabinet than the representatives of the Liberal and Labour sections. It is a curious thing that although the crisis which brought us together is every day receding further and further into the background, yet our association gets all the time closer because we can see how greatly this country has benefited by our association, both in the measures which we have carried and which, perhaps, no strictly party Government could have carried, and also in the enhanced influence which we can exert in foreign affairs owing to the fact that we represent such a wide front of national unity.

"I feel inclined to ask some of those old-time Liberals who have not up to now seen their way to throw in their lot with us whether the time has not come to reconsider their attitude. That old fiscal controversy which used to be so acute between us is not a live issue in politics to-day, and when I think of the social reforms that we have carried through and our attitude towards the agricultural and industrial problems of the day and, above all, of our conduct of foreign affairs, in which the largest measure of national support is so pre-eminently desirable, I cannot see anything inappropriate or difficult about their co-operation with us.

"It is a striking fact and a tragic one that at the present time foreign affairs are dominating the minds of the people of this country almost to the exclusion of subjects which in ordinary times would have occupied their whole attention. Indeed, we are not alone in that respect; for I think all the

peoples of the world are asking themselves this same question :
' Are we to be allowed to live our lives in peace or are we to be
plunged against our will into war ? '

" When I look round the world I must say I am appalled
at the prospects. War, accompanied by horrible barbarities,
inflicted either wittingly or unwittingly upon civilian populations, is going on to-day in China and much nearer to us in
Spain. Almost every week we hear rumours of war on this
question or on that in other parts of the world, and all the
principal nations are spending their precious savings on
devising and manufacturing the most efficient instruments
for the destruction of one another. I wonder whether, since
the world began, has it ever seen such a spectacle of human
madness and folly ?

" During the last twenty years we and our allies and associates have been telling ourselves that we won the Great War.
There have been disputes about the man who won the war
and even about the country that won the war, but nobody
has ever doubted that we were the winners.

" Well, we fought to preserve this free democracy from
foreign domination and dictation, and to maintain the rule of
order and law rather than the rule of force. Certainly we
succeeded in preserving our freedom, and if our liberties
were in danger again, and if we were sure that there was no
other way of preserving them except by war, we would fight
again. But think for a moment what the use of force involves
us in.

" When I think of those four terrible years and I think
of the 7,000,000 of young men who were cut off in their
prime, the 13,000,000 who were maimed and mutilated, the
misery and the suffering of the mothers and the fathers, the
sons and the daughters, and the relatives and the friends of
those who were killed, and the wounded, then I am bound to
say again what I have said before, and what I say now, not
only to you, but to all the world—in war, whichever side may
call itself the victor, there are no winners, but all are losers.

" It is those thoughts which have made me feel that it
was my prime duty to strain every nerve to avoid a repetition of the Great War in Europe. And I cannot believe
that anyone who is not blinded by party prejudice, anyone

who thinks what another war would mean, can fail to agree
with me and to desire that I should continue my
efforts.

" Ever since the beginning of the war in Spain my colleagues
and I realized the inherent danger in the situation, that it
might lead to war in Europe; and it was because of that
consideration that, in conjunction with the Government of
France, we decided very early upon a policy of non-intervention with the express purpose of confining the civil war
to Spain and preventing it from becoming a general conflagration. We have had endless difficulties in that policy,
but in spite of them all, in spite of the sneers and the jeers of
the Oppositions, we have succeeded in our main objects.
We have kept other countries out of the war, and to-day, at
long last, the British plan for the withdrawal of foreign
volunteers from Spain has been accepted, and we are hopeful that it will not now be long before they leave that country
to Spaniards.

" The situation has been complicated by the bombing by General Franco's aeroplanes of British ships
entering the zone of hostilities in Spanish ports, and the
Government have been fiercely denounced by those great
patriots who sit opposite to us in the House of Commons
for allowing the British flag to be insulted, and particularly
for allowing British property to be destroyed. There is
nothing like your Socialists for standing up for British
property. Well now, a long time ago we gave a warning
to British shipowners that, while we were intending to
give them full protection so long as their ships were on the
high seas, we could not undertake to protect them after
they had entered territorial waters in the zone of fighting, and
we said that, because, after very carefully examining all the
possible means of giving them protection, we were satisfied
that we could not do so without at any rate a very considerable
risk of being ourselves involved in the war.

" Well, now, the risks which are run by these ships literally
mean that the rate of freight which has to be paid is very high,
and shipowners are getting as much as four and five times the
ordinary rates of freight for voyages to these ports. We have
given this warning. If, in spite of it and for the sake of making

these profits, these shipowners still send their ships to these waters and then get bombed, is it reasonable that we should be asked to take action which might presently involve not only them but you in the horrors of war which I have been trying to describe, and you are not getting any profits at all ?

" I should consider that if we were to listen to demands of that kind we should be betraying our trust to the people of this country. That does not mean that we condone bombing of ships from the air, or that we recognise an aerial blockade of ports. We have on numerous occasions made protests to General Franco about particular incidents, and he has in reply given us the most emphatic assurances that it is not, and never has been, the intention of his Government to single out British ships for deliberate attacks, and if some of them have been struck—so he tells us—that is just because it is extremely difficult to ensure that a bomb dropped from a high-flying aeroplane will only hit the objective at which it is aimed and not sometimes hit other things, like ships which may be in the immediate neighbourhood.

" I find it a little difficult to reconcile that explanation with some of the facts which are known to us, but perhaps, after all, Franco's airmen do not always rigidly adhere to their instructions. However that may be, it remains true that as long as this war goes on and British ships are carrying cargoes into the ports of the Spanish Government, so long the danger of incidents of this kind will remain. Much the best solution would be the cessation of hostilities altogether, and if at any time we can see any prospect of offering our services to bring that about with a reasonable chance of success, you may be sure we shall not let that opportunity pass by us.

" Before I leave the question of foreign affairs I should like to call your attention to the attitude of the two Oppositions in Parliament. I do not believe any living person can recollect a time when foreign affairs were the subject of such constant challenge, such repeated debates and such heated and violent denunciations.

" At the present time, as the Foreign Secretary is a member of the House of Lords, most of that sound and fury descends on my head. I do not grumble at that. I try to give as good as I get.

" When Mr. Lloyd George complains, as he did the other day, that I am a very obstinate man, my reply is that I am not going to be diverted from the policy which I believe to be right for this country by criticism which seems to me to be as ill-informed as it is ill-natured.

" What I do regret about the attitude of the Opposition is the impression it creates abroad of national disunity. I believe that to be a completely false impression.

" I do not believe that the country desires us to abandon our efforts to establish and maintain peace—efforts which, as I am continually hearing, have already changed the atmosphere on the Continent for the better. I do not believe that the people want us to substitute for that attitude one of challenge and aggression, which may sound very heroic, but which is apt to involve us in frightful consequences.

" We are day by day building up the strength of this country. The stronger a country is, the more it can afford to be patient, and even generous. In our view our strength should be kept in reserve until we are satisfied that only by its use can we preserve our own or our vital interests. . . .

*   *   *   *

" . . . I am not sure that the public fully realises the gigantic effort we are making in this defence programme. Our shipbuilding yards have a tremendous number of warships to build. Orders for new warships that we have placed since April, 1935, amount to something like half the tonnage of the entire fleet as it existed at that time.

" We are beginning to see the results to-day in these powerful new cruisers and destroyers, along with a lot of smaller craft, which are joining the fleet in a continuous stream. Our enormous programme of battleship construction and reconstruction will ensure our continued supremacy in capital ships.

" It is not possible for me to give details of the additions which have been made to the Air Force, but the number and quality of our fighter and bombing machines are becoming more formidable every day.

" New factories are to be built at Crewe for an increased output of aero engines by the Rolls-Royce company. All these factories will be fully employed for a long time by the orders that have been placed with them, and side by side with these factories comes the personnel. Recruiting has been very satisfactory.

" A striking example is the Territorial Army, which is called upon to play a vital part in our defence. Territorials are asked to man the anti-aircraft guns and searchlights. These formations were doubled during the year, and they are going to be redoubled so that the numbers will be about 100,000. The Territorial Army as a whole has increased during the last three months by something like 20,000 men.

" May I say one word about Air Raid Precautions. Our plans are steadily developing with the co-operation of local authorities and a large number of individuals.

" Do not make any mistake about the nature of these preparations. I have been told that when some people see strange creatures going about in gas masks and protective clothing they begin to think that the Government must be anticipating that an attack is going to be made upon us in the immediate future.

" These preparations do not mean that war is imminent. They do not mean that war is ever coming. It will not come if we can help it, but we have to recognise that aerial warfare has introduced new conditions and involved the general population in war in a way different from the time when wars were carried on only by armies and navies.

" We cannot any longer make our preparations by building warships or training troops in some remote and isolated spot. We have to take the public into our confidence. We have to ask them to give a hand.

" These are not symptoms of war—they are merely manifestations of prudence and of common sense. I would beg you to remember this too—what is being done here about Air Raid Precautions is being done in a great many other countries as well. As surely the effect upon all the peoples must be the same ; it must make them all realise what war would mean to-day to their kith and kin if it came.

" This surely must strengthen their determination to avoid a conflict if that be possible, and it would be quite a mistake to suppose that public opinion has no effect even in countries which are governed by dictators. To me, that is a consideration which seems to give good grounds for hoping that we have in store for us a wiser and a happier future if people will be led to settle their differences by discussion instead of risking the frightful consequences which would ensue from war. That is the goal to which the Government are advancing, and, though progress is slow, and though we have from time to time our setbacks, yet we can say that we have made progress.

" If we can keep the end steadily in view, if we can refuse to be turned aside by opponents and critics, I for one am confident that we shall achieve it. In the meantime we must pay whatever price is necessary to ensure our own safety. There is one thing that does help us to keep up our courage and our strength, and that is the consciousness that we have behind us the support, trust and confidence of the nation.

" Expenditure on armaments is mounting, and there can be little doubt that it is imposing a severe strain on our financial resources. Fortunately, under the National Government, those resources have been steadily built up and have accumulated for seven years, and I have no doubt they will be equal to the strain.

" Just as a prudent householder, faced with expenditure which has become necessary for the preservation of his property, abstains for a time from buying a new motor-car for himself or new jewellery for his wife and daughters, so we must watch that expenditure which we control very carefully until the time comes when we can relax our efforts to build up our armaments and turn to more congenial pursuits.

" It is true that there is a great deal in the prospect which still calls for watchfulness, but the Government is not asleep, and every month that passes adds to the probability that we will come safely through our troubles."

AN INVESTIGATOR AND MEDIATOR

At the City of Birmingham Centenary Banquet on 14th July, Mr. Chamberlain spoke of the difficulty of applying in practice those principles of international law and order, reason and good faith in which all Britons believed. " It is much easier to formulate maxims of this kind than it is to apply them in practice ; and those who endeavour to steer by these general but deep-seated principles must expect to suffer many disappointments and set-backs, to have their motives misrepresented and their sincerity doubted." Throughout the whole of the troubled summer of 1938 that was the Prime Minister's lot. He was confronted with three major crises—the Japanese invasion of China, the long drawn-out Civil War in Spain and the ideological passions to which it gave rise in this and other countries, and the problem of the Sudeten-German minority in Czechoslovakia. The last was threatening to become the most serious of all, for the Germans with their new-found strength and their ideal of racial nationalism were showing signs that they were prepared to wait no longer for the ending of a wrong which had continued unrighted for twenty years, while the French were committed by their policy of military alliances to go to the assistance of Czechoslovakia if that country were attacked by Germany. Moreover, though the British Government had persistently refused to commit itself in advance to unconditional intervention in support of Czechoslovakia, Britain's obligation to assist France if attacked was very likely to involve her in such hostilities. The Prime Minister and his colleagues were, therefore, making every effort to find a peaceful solution of the impasse between the Czech Government and the Sudeten-Germans, which should secure the just rights of the three and a half million Germans included by the Treaty of Versailles in the composite Czechoslovak State, without the use of force by any of the parties concerned. In this search for a settlement by negotiation, Mr. Chamberlain was persistently vilified by the leaders of the Opposition, who, regardless of the fact that the nation was anything but united on this issue, declared that every effort to ensure the long-overdue consideration of the demands of the German minority was an abject concession to the threats of Dictators, against whom an uncompromising armed front should now be formed regardless of consequences. On 26th July the Opposition initiated the twenty-fourth debate of the Session on foreign affairs, and Sir Archibald Sinclair moved a reduction of the Foreign Office Vote in a speech that accused the Prime Minister of " trying to hustle the Czech Government in their negotiations " in a craven desire to placate the Dictators. At twenty minutes to five in the afternoon, Mr. Chamberlain rose to reply.

"THE right hon. Gentleman (Sir Archibald Sinclair) who has just addressed the House has moved a reduction of the Vote, and, of course, his business is to put a different point of view from that which the House would expect of me; nevertheless, the right hon. Gentleman did not on this occasion unduly stress disagreement and, in the concluding part of his speech, he said that everybody would agree with what he understood to be the main aim of the Government. I think that must be so. I cannot imagine anyone in any part of the House who would disagree with what we have so frequently declared to be the main aim of the Government's foreign policy, namely, the establishment and the maintenance of peace and the removal, as far as that may be practicable, of all causes of possible conflict in the amelioration of grievances between one country and another.

" It pleases the right hon. Gentleman sometimes to suggest that our attitude towards certain countries in Europe is one of continued concession, and although from time to time he gives instances which go to prove the opposite, they are to be excepted. Let not the right hon. Gentleman or anyone, either in this country or elsewhere, imagine for one moment that, although we seek peace, we are willing to sacrifice, even for peace, British honour and British vital interests. We are making rapid progress with our great rearmament programme, and day by day the armed strength of this country becomes more formidable. While that tremendous power which we are accumulating remains there as a guarantee that we can defend ourselves if we are attacked, we are not unmindful of the consideration that although it is good to have a giant's strength, it is tyrannous to use it like a giant. Our aims are not the less peaceful because no one can imagine that we have reason to fear any opponent.

" The right hon. Gentleman moved over a very wide field and put to me a great number of questions. I am not sure that I remember all his questions, much less the answers, but in the course of what I am to say I shall be able to take up, at any rate, a portion of them as I pass from one part of the subject to another. In the brief speech which I propose to make upon the more salient points in the international situation, I shall hope to make clear in each case that what the Government have kept constantly before them is that main fundamental aim and that policy which I began by describing to the House. The right hon. Gentleman paid an eloquent tribute to the magnificent response which was recently accorded to the King and Queen on their visit to France. I would like to associate myself with what the right hon. Gentleman said. I do not think I recall such unanimity among all classes and all parties in France as was displayed on that occasion, and while no doubt it was largely due to the personal bearing and charm of the Royal guests, one may ascribe it in large measure to the consciousness that our two democratic nations are united closely together by common interests and common ideals.

" The unity which exists between France and ourselves is the more happy because I think it is generally recognised that it is not directed against any other nation or combination of Nations. It is in itself a solid buttress of peace. That unity was strengthened and confirmed by conversations which took place between my Noble Friend and the French Ministers in Paris. The right hon. Gentleman asked me to tell him what took place in those conversations. An official communiqué has been issued which gives the substance of them, and I really do not think there is anything more that I can tell the House, because there is no mystery about them. There has been no new undertaking, no new commitment on either side. There was a general discussion of all matters of common interest to the two countries, and there was general and complete agreement upon them. With that, I think, the House may be fairly satisfied.

" If I may turn to France's unhappy neighbour it is a matter of profound regret that one cannot see the prospect of a speedy termination of that terrible struggle which is daily destroying the best of Spain's life and dissipating the resources which will be so sorely needed when the combatants lay down their arms. There is no need for any appeal to be made to this

Government to take advantage of any opportunity which may occur for mediation, or an armistice, or anything that would bring to a close the military operations which, I think, must shock us daily. In all these cases there are moments when it is not only futile but, indeed, mischievous for third parties to try to intervene. I hope the House will believe that, if we do not intervene at this particular moment, it is only because we are convinced that the moment has not come when we can intervene with success."

MISS WILKINSON : " Why did you close the frontier ? "

THE PRIME MINISTER : " The House is aware that the non-intervention plan—the British plan for the withdrawal of volunteers which was agreed upon by the Non-Intervention Committee—has now been submitted to the two parties in Spain. I understand that the Non-Intervention Committee are not yet in receipt of replies from both sides, though I hope that those replies will not be long delayed."

MISS WILKINSON : " Have they not had a reply from the Government ? "

THE PRIME MINISTER : " I believe that they have had a reply from the Spanish Republican Government, but that they have not yet received a reply from General Franco. Perhaps, however, the House might like to have the latest information about the communications which have been passing between His Majesty's Government and the Burgos authorities about the bombing of British ships in Spanish ports. We sent a communication to the Burgos authorities, who have, the House will remember, declared that it was no part of their policy to make deliberate attacks upon British ships. We sent a communication to them proposing that an immediate investigation should be made into certain cases to which we had already drawn their attention, and in which it appeared to us that the attack had been, in fact, a deliberate one. We proposed that this investigation should be carried out by two naval officers, one appointed by His Majesty's Government and the other by the Burgos authorities. If they agreed that the attack was deliberate, then the Burgos authorities would make the necessary arrangements to pay immediate compensation to those concerned. If, on the other hand, the two officers were unable to agree, then our proposal was that the matter should be referred to a third party, not of British or Spanish nationality, but who should be agreed upon between the Burgos authorities and ourselves, and that he should make the final decision. We have now received a reply from the Burgos authorities in which they say that, in pursuance of their desire to meet the wishes of His Majesty's Government, they accept this formula, and they agree that the investigation we propose should be carried out. We are now considering whether it would not be advisable to send Sir Robert Hodgson back to Spain with instructions which would cover, among other things, the detailed working out of this proposal.

" There is another matter which is bound up with the situation in Spain, and that is the position in regard to the Anglo-Italian Agreement. The Agreement was to come into force upon a date to be determined by agreement between the two Governments, but on 16th April, that is to say, the date upon which the Agreement was signed, Lord Perth addressed a Note to the Italian Foreign Minister in which he reminded him that His Majesty's Government regarded the settlement of the Spanish question as a pre-requisite of the entry into force of the Agreement made between the two Governments. I should like to explain, because I am not sure that it is generally apprehended, why it was that we put in that stipulation. We never regarded this Agreement as simply a bilateral arrangement between Italy and ourselves. When we entered into negotiations, we did so because we thought then, and we are still of the same opinion, that the restoration of the relations between Italy and this country to their old terms of friendship and confidence would bring us appreciably nearer to our ultimate aim, which is a general European appeasement. We felt at the time that the moral justification for our recognition of the Italian position in Ethiopia would be the knowledge that that recognition had brought with it a real contribution to the peace of Europe. We felt that, while this conflict was going on in Spain under the sort of conditions in which it has been waged, the Spanish situation was a perpetual menace to the peace of Europe, and it was for that reason that we said that it must be removed from that category before our Agreement was brought into force. It is not our fault, and it is not the fault of the Italian Government, that that condition has not been brought about. They have kept faith with us——"

MISS WILKINSON : " Would you like to send some troops to help them ? "

THE PRIME MINISTER : " They kept full faith with us in the reduction of their troops in Libya, in the cessation of anti-British propaganda, and in collaboration on the Non-Intervention Committee. We on our side have carried out our engagement——"

MR. JAGGER : " To starve the Republic."

THE PRIME MINISTER : " It is very difficult to give a connected account, which I am trying to do, of the state of affairs in Europe, if I am subjected to these constant interruptions. Hon. Members will surely have plenty of opportunity later on of criticising what I am saying, and I think they might at least allow me to finish my sentences. I was saying that we have fulfilled our engagement to take steps at the Council of the League to clarify the position of Member States in regard to the Italian sovereignty over Ethiopia. The right hon. Gentleman stated that the recruiting of Somalis by the Italian forces was taking place in British Somaliland. My information is that he is mistaken. Recruiting has not taken place in British Somaliland——"

MR. JAGGER : " They have taken them out."

THE PRIME MINISTER : " Perhaps I may be allowed just to finish this sentence—but a certain amount of recruiting has taken place, not in British Somaliland, but among people whose home is in British Somaliland but who crossed the frontier for purposes of grazing. The Government of British Somaliland have taken all possible steps to prevent recruiting, and it has recently been agreed with the Italian authorities that no such recruiting shall take place."

SIR A. SINCLAIR : " Have the men been discharged ? "

THE PRIME MINISTER : " I do not think any undertaking has been given to discharge the men. Of course, they ought never to have been recruited. There, for the present, the matter of the Anglo-Italian Agreement must rest. We cannot abandon the position we have taken up about the settlement of the Spanish——"

SIR A. SINCLAIR : " Before the right hon. Gentleman leaves

the subject, will he answer the point about material going through from British Somaliland and up the Nile through the Sudan and Gambela ? "

THE PRIME MINISTER : " I am sorry I cannot answer that question. I have had no notice of it, and have not the slightest idea to what the right hon. Gentleman is referring. I never heard of it before. I will ask my hon. Friend to make inquiries and, if possible, give the right hon. Gentleman an answer later on. I was saying that we cannot abandon the position we have taken up in regard to the settlement of the Spanish question which we have over and over again declared to the House. But, on the other hand, we profoundly regret this unforeseen delay which has taken place in the completion of the Agreement, and we shall do all that we possibly can to facilitate the withdrawal of the foreign volunteers from Spain, in order that that country may cease to offer any threat to the peace of Europe."

MR. ATTLEE : " Do I gather from the right hon. Gentleman's present statement that what he means by a settlement in Spain is the volunteers' withdrawal agreement ? Hitherto we have not known what he meant by a settlement in Spain. Do I understand now that it is merely a question of volunteers being withdrawn ? "

THE PRIME MINISTER : " I would like to see what happens when the volunteers are withdrawn. If His Majesty's Government think that Spain has ceased to be a menace to the peace of Europe, I think we shall regard that as a settlement of the Spanish question.

" In recent weeks the attention of His Majesty's Government has necessarily been particularly directed to two areas in Europe. One is that with which I have been dealing ; the other is Czechoslovakia. In dealing with Czechoslovakia it is very difficult for people in this country, with the exception of a comparatively small number who have made a special study of the position, to arrive at a just conclusion as to the rights and wrongs of the dispute between the Czechoslovakian Government and the Sudeten Germans. Many of us would have been very glad if we could have left this matter to be decided by the two parties concerned ; but, unfortunately, here again we are only too conscious that there are all the materials present for a breach of the peace, with incalculable consequences, if the matter is not handled boldly and with a reasonable amount of speed. Therefore, in accordance with our general policy, and in close association with France, we have done everything that we could to facilitate a peaceful solution of the dispute. It is a problem which, in one form or another, has existed for centuries, and it would perhaps be unreasonable to expect that a difficulty which has been going on so long should be capable of solution in a few short weeks.

"The right hon. Gentleman spoke of one of the many rumours which he has collected, without very much authority behind them. This was to the effect that we were hustling the Czech Government. It is a little difficult to know what one is to do about these rumours. If you deny them when they are untrue, then when you cannot deny them people assume that they are true. You get into a difficulty when you eliminate one rumour after another, and thus allow the skilful journalist to find out the thing you wish him not to know. With regard to this rumour, I should like to assure the right hon. Gentleman that there is no truth in it. Indeed, the very opposite is the truth. Our anxiety has been rather lest the Czechoslovakian Government should be too hasty in dealing with a situation of such delicacy that it was most desirable that the two sides should not get into a position where they were set, and unable to have any further give-and-take between them.

"Perhaps I might say, with regard to the rumour to which the right hon. Gentleman referred when he inquired whether we had urged on the Czechoslovakian Government to submit their proposals to Herr Henlein before putting them to their Parliament, that we did so, and we did so for that very reason, that if by any chance an agreed settlement could be come to between Herr Henlein and the Czechoslovakian Government before any statute was put before the Czech Parliament, obviously that would be the best solution of all. But I do not think that any great amount of pressure need be applied from us to induce the Czechoslovakian Government to do what they were anxious to do all along, and that was to give the fullest opportunity for a full and frank discussion of any proposals they might wish to make. Hitherto we have ourselves abstained from making suggestions as to the particular method of trying to solve this Czechoslovakian question, although, of course, in this country we have had a certain amount of experience of the difficulty of trying to provide for local government without endangering the stability of the State. We have, perhaps, in that respect had as much experience as any country in the world.

" But while we have felt that an agreement voluntarily come to, if it could be reached between the Sudeten Germans and the Czech Government, would be the best solution, nevertheless, as time has gone on, it has begun to appear doubtful whether, without some assistance from outside, such a voluntary agreement could take place. In those circumstances, His Majesty's Government have been considering whether there were some other way in which they could lend their help to bring the negotiators together, and, in response to a request from the Government of Czechoslovakia, we have agreed to propose a person with the necessary experience and qualities to investigate this subject on the spot and endeavour, if need be, to suggest means for bringing the negotiations to success. Such an investigator and mediator would, of course, be independent of His Majesty's Government—in fact, he would be independent of all Governments. He would act only in his personal capacity, and it would be necessary, of course, that he should have all the facilities and all the information placed at his disposal in order to enable him to carry through his task.

" I cannot assert that a proposal of that kind will necessarily bring about a solution of this problem, but I think it may have two valuable results. First of all, I think it would go far to inform public opinion generally as to the real facts of the case, and, secondly, I hope that it may mean that issues which hitherto have appeared intractable may prove, under the influence of such a mediator, to be less obstinate than we have thought. But it is quite obvious that the task of anyone who undertakes this duty is going to be a very exacting, very responsible, and very delicate one, and His Majesty's Government feel that they are fortunate in having secured from Lord Runciman a promise to undertake it, provided he is assured of the confidence of the Sudeten Germans—I hope he will be—as well as the assistance of the Czechoslovakian Government. Lord Runciman was a Member of this House so long that he is well known to many hon. Members. I think they will agree with me that he has outstanding personal qualifications for the task he has undertaken. He has a long experience of public affairs and of men of all sorts and conditions. He is characterised by fearlessness, freedom from prejudice, integrity and impartiality, and I am quite certain that everyone here will wish him all success."

MR. BELLENGER : " The right hon. Gentleman has stated that Lord Runciman will go in quite a personal capacity, entirely unconnected with His Majesty's Government. Do I understand that his position is only acceptable as long as both sides agree to accept him as an arbitrator, or adviser—the Czechoslovakian Government and the Henlein party ? "

THE PRIME MINISTER : " I think the hon. Gentleman is under a misapprehension. Lord Runciman is not in any sense an arbitrator."

MR. BELLENGER : " An adviser."

THE PRIME MINISTER : " He is an investigator and mediator —that is what I called him. He will try to acquaint himself with all the facts and the views of the two sides, and he will no doubt see them separately, and perhaps later on he will be able to make some proposals to them which will help them. He is in the position, so well known to the hon. Member, of a man who goes down to assist in settling a strike. He has to see two sides who have come to a point when they cannot go any further. He is there as an independent, impartial person."

MR. BELLENGER : " Acceptable to both sides in the dispute ? "

THE PRIME MINISTER : " That is Lord Runciman's stipulation, and obviously a necessary one. If one side declare that they will have nothing to do with him, it will be quite impossible for him to undertake the task."

MR. CHURCHILL : " Have both sides agreed ? "

THE PRIME MINISTER : " We have not heard from the Sudeten Germans."

MISS WILKINSON : " Could we hear that personal exchange ? "

I

THE PRIME MINISTER : " My right hon. Friend asks whether both sides have agreed, and my reply was that we have not heard from the Sudeten Germans. We have impressed upon the Government of Czechoslovakia, and also upon the German Government, our own sense of the desirability of restraint. We have noted with satisfaction the efforts which the Czech Government have made, and we have also been very happy to receive assurances, only recently renewed, from the German Government of their own desire for a peaceful solution. The right hon. Gentleman asked me what assurances I had given to the German Ambassador. I was not myself responsible for the exact wording of the communiqué to which the right hon. Gentleman has referred ; but it does not mean anything more than I have already told the House of our action in urging the Czechoslovakian Government to try to do all they possibly can, consistent with what they consider essential to their own State, to come to an agreement. On the other side, too, we have continually urged the need for patience in a very delicate and difficult situation.

" If only we could find some peaceful solution of this Czechoslovakian question, I should myself feel that the way was open again for a further effort for a general appeasement—an appeasement which cannot be obtained until we can be satisfied that no major cause of difference or dispute remains unsettled. We have already demonstrated the possibility of a complete agreement between a democratic and a totalitarian State, and I do not myself see why that experience should not be repeated. When Herr Hitler made his offer of a Naval Treaty under which the German fleet was to be restricted to an agreed level bearing a fixed ratio to the size of the British fleet, he made a notable gesture of a most practical kind in the direction of peace, the value of which it seems to me has not ever been fully appreciated as tending towards this general appeasement. There the treaty stands as a demonstration that it is possible for Germany and ourselves to agree upon matters which are vital to both of us. Since agreement has already been reached on that point, I do not think that we ought to find it impossible to continue our efforts at understanding, which, if they were successful, would do so much to bring back confidence.

" I agree very much with the right hon. Gentleman (Sir Archibald Sinclair) in the value that he attaches to our relations with the United States of America. I am happy to think that they have never been better than they are at the present moment. With regard to the debt, I am not quite sure what the right hon. Gentleman meant by cauterising it. The settlement of the debt has to be a settlement between two parties and cannot be settled by one alone. As for the attitude of the British Government, I would like to refer the right hon. Gentleman to the Debate which took place on this subject only a few days ago in another place, when the spokesman of His Majesty's Government made it perfectly clear what our attitude was.

" Coming to the trade agreement, I regard that not merely as an attempt to come to a commercial agreement, which if we could find a fair settlement, would be of benefit to both countries, but as an effort to demonstrate the possibility of these two great countries working together on a subject which, if they can come to terms, may prove to be the forerunner of a policy of wider application. I hope that the right hon. Gentleman will not feel that it is necessary to display impatience, because of the length of time which has been taken over this matter. To begin with, a commercial treaty of that kind deals with an enormous schedule of articles, every one of which has to be the subject of discussion and conversation, and he knows very well that the constitutional procedure in the United States, however admirably it may be adapted to a thorough sifting of the question, is not one which lends itself to expedition. At the present time we have gone through this great schedule and we have agreed upon a great part of it, but, as always happens in these cases, we have come down after a time to certain particular instances which offer exceptional difficulties, and those are not yet entirely resolved. All that I can say is, that I know there is good will on both sides, and I hope that we shall not have to wait too long before we are able to announce that we have finally come to an agreed conclusion.

" I have only one other part of the world upon which I now need touch, and that is the Far East, where war is still being carried on with all the horrors which seem inseparable from modern warfare. The Brussels Conference last November showed clearly enough that no proposals which would involve intervention in the conflict on the part of the Members of the League of Nations would have any chance of acceptance. Of course, His Majesty's Government could not alone undertake that great burden. The right hon. Gentleman asked me, Can we show what we are doing to carry out our obligations under the League resolutions? and he made special reference to the request of China for a loan. We considered long and anxiously whether we should be justified in introducing the special legislation which would have been necessary if this Government had granted or guaranteed such a loan, and we came finally to the definite conclusion that we should not be so justified in the case of a loan, which would have been based upon security of hypothetical value, and as to which it was by no means certain that, if it were granted, it would achieve the objects which were intended. The fact that we have not been able to grant or guarantee a loan to China does not exclude all forms of assistance, financial or otherwise, and there are various proposals which have come to us from China for assistance in another way, which are not open to the objections at any rate which we found to a loan, and which are now under examination by the Government Departments concerned.

" It cannot be said that we are disinterested as a country in the position in the Far East, because for a hundred years our interests in China have been of great importance, and when the Japanese Government claim that they are protecting their interests in China, I am sure they must recognise that we too have our interests in China and that we cannot stand by and see them sacrificed in the process. But there again, in the Far East, we should be very glad to offer our services to bring about the cessation of hostilities if ever and whenever we can see an opportunity which presents a favourable prospect of success. In the meantime we are resolved to do our utmost to see that British interests shall not suffer in a conflict for which we have no responsibility and in which we have no direct concern.

" I think that I have touched on all matters which are of special interest to the House, but in this survey, which has included a glance at two ferocious wars, and an area which is the subject of dispute which is a potential threat to the peace of Europe, situated as it is in the very heart of the Continent, it is as much a matter of regret to others as it is to His Majesty's Government that we cannot record any effective or active intervention by the League of Nations. We know well enough what is the cause of this ineffectiveness, and it is ineffectiveness which is likely to persist as long as some of the most powerful nations in the world are outside the League. We regard the present position of the League as temporary, and even if it is necessary for the time being that the League should renounce the idea of the use of force, there still remains a wide field of usefulness for the League, in pursuing which, as it seems to us, the League may well be able to build up a fresh position of confidence and of approval, with the result that in time we may find that those nations who have left the League, because they did not agree with the use of force by the League, may come back to it and take part in this other work, and, who knows what further developments may then take place once the League can be considered more representative of the world as a whole than it is to-day ?

" I would only say that with that view of the future of the League we intend to give the League all the support and encouragement in our power. In the meantime, in the critical situation in which we find ourselves, we have to fall back upon the ordinary methods of diplomacy. At the beginning of this year I think that many of us must have felt that it was likely to be critical, for good or for evil, in the history of the world, and now that more than half of it has gone, I believe we all feel that the atmosphere is lighter, and that throughout the Continent there is a relaxation of that sense of tension which six months ago was present. To that lightening of the atmosphere and slackening of the tension, we believe that the policy of His Majesty's Government has made its contribution. We intend to pursue it and we believe that in the end we shall succeed in bringing back security and confidence to Europe."

THE SEPTEMBER CRISIS

1938

During the Parliamentary vacation events in Czechoslovakia became increasingly grave. Lord Runciman's efforts to find a solution acceptable to Czechs and Sudeten Germans, though welcomed by both parties, proved unavailing : concessions which might have been received with relief a little earlier, before feelings had become acerbated by delay, were, when at last made, no longer acceptable. The Czech army had been partially mobilised since the end of May : in August the German army was put on what was virtually a war footing for autumn manœuvres of unprecedented size. Nor were these war-like preparations confined to the two countries directly concerned. On 27th August, following urgent representations of the consequences of using force made by the British Ambassador in Berlin to the German Minister for Foreign Affairs, the Chancellor of the Exchequer, speaking at Lanark, had repeated the Prime Minister's warning of 24th March that, if war broke out over the question of Czechoslovakia, it would be unlikely to be confined to those who had assumed direct obligations. These warnings were repeated by the British Ambassador on 31st August and in the early days of September. Meanwhile French reservists had been called up to man the Maginot Line. Though by this time no doubt could have been left in Herr Hitler's mind as to the gravity with which Britain would regard a resort to force and the determination of France, if not of Russia, to honour her treaty obligations to Czechoslovakia, Germany's resolve to support the demands of the Sudeten Germans showed no sign of abating. On 12th September, in his long-awaited address to the Nuremberg Conference, Herr Hitler spoke with passionate conviction of the rights of his fellow Germans in Czechoslovakia and promised them the aid of the Reich if they could obtain these rights in no other way.

On 13th September, following a succession of serious incidents in the unhappy Sudetenland and the declaration of martial law by the Czech Government, the Sudeten leaders broke off negotiations and declared their unalterable desire to return to the Reich. By this time Lord Runciman, despairing of establishing any permanently satisfactory co-operation between two peoples *who now cordially hated one another, had come to the conclusion that cession to Germany of the predominantly German areas of Czechoslovakia was the only solution left. These conclusions he reported to the British Government, urging that the transfer on an approved ethnological basis should take place at the earliest possible moment and condemning even the idea of a plebiscite on the ground that such a " formality," in a case where the ethnological issues were so clear, would by causing delay " serve to excite popular feelings with perhaps dangerous results." Lord Runciman's general opinion, as expressed in his formal letter to the Prime Minister of 21st September, was that, though the Sudeten leaders were responsible for the final break, Czech rule of the German areas granted to them in 1919, " while not actively oppressive and certainly not terroristic" (as the Nazi Press was maintaining), " has been marked by tactlessness, lack of understanding, petty intolerance and discrimination to a point where the resentment of the German population was inevitably moving in the direction of a revolt."*

British public opinion, however, long accustomed to the promulgation of very different views, was not yet ready to accept so novel an idea. On 7th September The Times *had first mooted it in a leading article, that " it might be worth while for the Czechoslovak Government to consider the project, which has found favour in some quarters, of making Czechoslovakia a more homogeneous State by the secession of that fringe of alien populations who are contiguous to the nation with which they are united by race." This suggestion of post-war frontier revision by peaceful means found little apparent support in any other section of the Press. The second week of September saw a return even in peaceful Britain to the rising passions of 1914. The outbreak of a general European War was imminent, and every successive and seemingly inevitable act of the Chancellories and War Offices concerned brought it hourly nearer.*

Such was the situation when on the afternoon of the 14th *September the Prime Minister came to a momentous decision and put into effect a plan which he had long contemplated as a last resort to save the world from the shameful tragedy of another war. He sent to Herr Hitler the following message :*

" In view of increasingly critical situation, I propose to come over at once to see you with a view to trying to find peaceful

solution. I propose to come across by air and am ready to start
to-morrow. Please indicate earliest time at which you can see me
and suggest place of meeting. Should be grateful for very early
reply."

*The announcement of this step, together with Herr Hitler's
cordial reply to it, was made on the wireless the same night.
It was received by the British public, and indeed by the entire
world, with intense relief.*

*At 8.35 a.m. next morning Mr. Chamberlain left Heston
aerodrome for Munich, arriving at Berchtesgaden after seven
and a half hours' continuous travelling at 4.5 p.m. that afternoon. Here, in the course of a three-hours' conversation, he
learned from the German leader's own lips his resolve to give
the Sudeten Germans their right to self-determination without further delay even if the cost of doing so should be
a European war with Britain aligned with France and Russia
against the Reich. Obtaining from Herr Hitler an assurance
that, if the British Government were to give its immediate
approval to the principle of self-determination for the Sudeten
Germans, he would be prepared to discuss peaceful ways and
means of carrying it out, Mr. Chamberlain set out for London
early next morning to consult his colleagues and the French
Government. On landing at Heston at 5.30 that afternoon he
made a brief statement to the assembled representatives of the
Press and Public :*

" I have come back again rather quicker than I expected,
after a journey which, had I not been so preoccupied, I should
have found thoroughly enjoyable. Yesterday afternoon I had
a long talk with Herr Hitler. It was a frank talk, but it was
a friendly one, and I feel satisfied now that each of us fully
understands what is in the mind of the other.

" You will not, of course, expect me to discuss now what
may be the results of these talks. What I have got to do is
to discuss them with my colleagues, and I would advise
you not to accept prematurely any unauthorised account of
what took place in the conversations. I shall be discussing
them to-night with my colleagues and others, especially Lord
Runciman. Later—perhaps in a few days—I am going to
have another talk with Herr Hitler ; only this time he has

told me that it is his intention to come half-way to meet me. That is to spare an old man such another long journey."

Six days later, on Thursday, 22nd September, Mr. Chamberlain again flew to Germany to meet Herr Hitler at Bad Godesberg, having first obtained the unanimous agreement of his colleagues in the Cabinet and of the French Prime Minister and Foreign Minister (who, in their desire to find a solution that would not compel France to take military action in accordance with her obligations, had already warmly approved the flight to Berchtesgaden) and the consent of the Czech Government to the principle of the transfer of the predominantly German areas of Czechoslovakia to the Reich. But the German Chancellor, asserting acts of oppression and terrorism against the Sudeten Germans, was impatient at further delay and insistent on an immediate transfer of all predominantly German areas. On the following day Mr. Chamberlain refused to renew the conversations until the situation had been clarified, and the following letters passed between the two statesmen :

Mr. Chamberlain to Herr Hitler

" GODESBERG,

" *September* 23, 1938.

" I think it may clarify the situation and accelerate our conversation if I send you this note before we meet this morning.

" I am ready to put to the Czech Government your proposal as to the areas, so that they may examine the suggested provisional boundary. So far as I can see, there is no need to hold a plebiscite for the bulk of the areas, i.e., for those areas which (according to statistics upon which both sides seem to agree) are predominantly Sudeten German areas. I have no doubt, however, that the Czech Government would be willing to accept your proposal for a plebiscite to determine how far, if at all, the proposed new frontier need be adjusted.

" The difficulty I see about the proposal you put to me yesterday afternoon arises from the suggestion that the areas should in the immediate future be occupied by German troops. I recognise the difficulty of conducting a lengthy investigation under existing conditions and doubtless the plan you propose would, if it were acceptable, provide an immediate easing of the tension. But I do not think you have realised the impossibility of my agreeing to put forward any plan unless I have reason to suppose that it will be considered by public opinion in my country, in France and, indeed, in the world generally, as carrying out the principles already agreed upon in an orderly fashion and free from the threat of force. I am sure that an attempt to occupy forthwith by German troops areas which will become part of the Reich at once in principle, and very shortly afterwards by formal delimitation, would be condemned as an unnecessary display of force.

" Even if I felt it right to put this proposal to the Czech Government, I am convinced that they would not regard it as being in the spirit of the arrangement which we and the French Government urged them to accept and which they have accepted. In the event of German troops moving into the areas as you propose, there is no doubt that the Czech Government would have no option but to order their forces to resist, and this would mean the destruction of the basis upon which you and I a week ago agreed to work together, namely, an orderly settlement of this question rather than a settlement by the use of force.

" It being agreed in principle that the Sudeten German areas are to join the Reich, the immediate question before us is how to maintain law and order pending the final settlement of the arrangements for the transfer. There must surely be alternatives to your proposal which would not be open to the objections I have pointed out. For instance, I could ask the Czech Government whether they think there could be an arrangement under which the maintenance of law and order in certain agreed Sudeten German areas would be entrusted to the Sudeten Germans themselves—by the creation of a suitable force, or by the use of forces already in existence, possibly acting under the supervision of neutral observers.

" As you know, I did last night, in accordance with my understanding with you, urge the Czech Government to do all in their power to maintain order in the meantime.

" The Czech Government cannot, of course, withdraw their forces, nor can they be expected to withdraw the State Police so long as they are faced with the prospect of forcible invasion ; but I should be ready at once to ascertain their views on the alternative suggestion I have made and, if the plan proved acceptable, I would urge them to withdraw their forces and the State Police from the areas where the Sudeten Germans are in a position to maintain order.

" The further steps that need be taken to complete the transfer could be worked out quite rapidly.

" I am,

" Yours faithfully,

" NEVILLE CHAMBERLAIN."

Herr Hitler to Mr. Chamberlain

" GODESBERG,

" September 23, 1938.

" A thorough examination of your letter, which reached me to-day, as well as the necessity of clearing up the situation definitely, lead me to make the following communication :

" For nearly two decades the Germans, as well as the various other nationalities in Czechoslovakia, have been maltreated in the most unworthy manner, tortured, economically destroyed, and, above all, prevented from realising for themselves also the right of the nations to self-determination. All attempts of the oppressed to change their lot failed in the face of the brutal will to destruction of the Czechs. The latter were in possession of the power of the State and did not hesitate to employ it ruthlessly and barbarically. England and France have never made an endeavour to alter this situation. In my speech before the Reichstag of February 22, I declared that the German Reich would take the initiative in putting an end to any further oppression of these Germans. I have in a further declaration during the Reich Party Congress given clear and unmistakable expression to this decision. I recognise gratefully that at last, after twenty years, the British Government, represented by your Excellency, has now decided for its part also to undertake steps to put an end to a situation which from day to day, and, indeed, from hour to hour, is becoming more unbearable. For if formerly the behaviour of the Czechoslovak Government was brutal, it can only be described during recent weeks and days as madness. The victims of this madness are innumerable Germans. In a few weeks the number of refugees who have been driven out has risen to over 120,000. This situation, as stated above, is unbearable, and will now be terminated by me.

" Your Excellency assures me now that the principle of the transfer of the Sudeten territory to the Reich has, in principle, already been accepted. I regret to have to reply to your Excellency that as regards this point, the theoretical recognition of principles has also been formerly granted to us Germans. In the year 1918 the Armistice was concluded on the basis of the 14 points of President Wilson, which in principle were recognised by all. They were, however, in practice broken in the most shameful way. What interests me, your Excellency, is not the recognition of the principle that this territory is to go to Germany, but solely the realisation of this principle, and the realisation which both puts an end in the shortest time to the sufferings of the unhappy victims of Czech tyranny, and at the same time corresponds to the dignity of a Great Power. I can only emphasise to your Excellency that these Sudeten Germans are not coming back to the German Reich in virtue of the gracious or benevolent sympathy of other nations, but on the ground of their own will based on the right of self-determination of the nations, and of the irrevocable decision of the German Reich to give effect to this will. It is, however, for a nation an unworthy demand to have this recognition made dependent on conditions which are not provided for in treaties nor are practical in view of the shortness of the time.

" I have, with the best intentions and in order to give the Czech nation no justifiable cause for complaint, proposed —in the event of a peaceful solution—as the future frontier, that nationalities frontier which I am convinced represents a fair adjustment between the two racial groups, taking also into account the continued existence of large language islands. I am, in addition, ready to allow plebiscites to be taken in the whole territory which will enable subsequent corrections to be made, in order—so far as it is possible—to meet the real will of the peoples concerned. I have undertaken to accept these corrections in advance. I have, moreover, declared myself ready to allow this plebiscite to take place under the control either of international commissions or of a mixed German-Czech commission. I am finally ready, during the days of the plebiscite, to withdraw our troops from the most disputed frontier areas, subject to the condition that the Czechs do the same. I am, however, not prepared to allow a territory which must be considered as belonging to Germany, on the ground of the will of the people and of the recognition granted even by the Czechs, to be left without the protection of the Reich. There is here no international power or agreement which would have the right to take precedence over German right.

" The idea of being able to entrust to the Sudeten Germans alone the maintenance of order is practically impossible in consequence of the obstacles put in the way of their political organisation in the course of the last decade, and particularly in recent times. As much in the interest of the tortured, because defenceless, population as well as with regard to the duties and prestige of the Reich, it is impossible for us to refrain from giving immediate protection to this territory.

" Your Excellency assures me that it is now impossible for you to propose such a plan to your own Government. May I assure you for my part that it is impossible for me to justify any other attitude to the German people. Since, for England, it is a question at most of political imponderables, whereas, for Germany, it is a question of primitive right of the security of more than three million human beings and the national honour of a great people.

" I fail to understand the observation of your Excellency that it would not be possible for the Czech Government to withdraw their forces so long as they were obliged to reckon with possible invasion, since precisely by means of this solution the grounds for any forcible action are to be removed. Moreover, I cannot conceal from your Excellency that the great mistrust with which I am inspired leads me to believe that the acceptance of the principle of the transfer of Sudeten

Germans to the Reich by the Czech Government is only given in the hope thereby to win time so as, by one means or another, to bring about a change in contradiction to this principle. For if the proposal that these territories are to belong to Germany is sincerely accepted, there is no ground to postpone the practical resolution of this principle. My knowledge of Czech practice in such matters over a period of long years compels me to assume the insincerity of Czech assurances so long as they are not implemented by practical proof. The German Reich is, however, determined by one means or another to terminate these attempts, which have lasted for decades, to deny by dilatory methods the legal claims of oppressed peoples.

" Moreover, the same attitude applies to the other nationalities in this State. They also are the victims of long oppression and violence. In their case, also, every assurance given hitherto has been broken. In their case, also, attempts have been made by dilatory dealing with their complaints or wishes to win time in order to be able to oppress them still more subsequently. These nations, also, if they are to achieve their rights, will, sooner or later, have no alternative but to secure them for themselves. In any event, Germany, if—as it now appears to be the case—she should find it impossible to have the clear rights of Germans in Czechoslovakia accepted by way of negotiation, is determined to exhaust the other possibilities which then alone remain open to her.

" ADOLF HITLER."

Mr. Chamberlain to Herr Hitler

" GODESBERG,

" *September* 23, 1938.

" I have received your Excellency's communication in reply to my letter of this morning and have taken note of its contents.

" In my capacity as intermediary, it is evidently now my duty—since your Excellency maintains entirely the position you took last night—to put your proposals before the Czechoslovak Government.

" Accordingly, I request your Excellency to be good

enough to let me have a memorandum which sets out these proposals, together with a map showing the area proposed to be transferred, subject to the result of the proposed plebiscite.

"On receiving this memorandum, I will at once forward it to Prague and request the reply of the Czechoslovak Government at the earliest possible moment.

"In the meantime, until I can receive their reply, I should be glad to have your Excellency's assurance that you will continue to abide by the understanding, which we reached at our meeting on the 14th September and again last night, that no action should be taken, particularly in the Sudeten territory, by the forces of the Reich to prejudice any further mediation which may be found possible.

"Since the acceptance or refusal of your Excellency's proposal is now a matter for the Czechoslovak Government to decide, I do not see that I can perform any further service here, whilst, on the other hand, it has become necessary that I should at once report the present situation to my colleagues and to the French Government. I propose, therefore, to return to England.

"Yours faithfully,

"NEVILLE CHAMBERLAIN."

At half-past ten on the same night, a further interview took place between the Prime Minister and the German Chancellor. In the course of it news arrived of the mobilisation of the Czech Army and consequently of all Sudeten Germans of military age. The three hours conversation between the two statesmen, though friendly, was exceedingly frank and direct, Mr. Chamberlain describing the Memorandum in which Herr Hitler presented the detailed German demands as an ultimatum, and severely criticising his proposal to send troops into the ceded territory without waiting for an agreed plan of peaceful and orderly evacuation.

Next day Mr. Chamberlain returned to London fully cognisant of the gravity of the situation, but still refusing to abandon hope. Before taking off from Cologne he issued the following statement to the Press :

" I am returning to London, where I shall at once consult with my colleagues. During the next few days there is a grave responsibility upon everybody concerned to consider very carefully the issues that are at stake. We must still make great efforts to save the peace of Europe."

Mr. Chamberlain made a further statement on landing early that afternoon at Heston, speaking into the microphone and by means of B.B.C. transmission to anxious listeners all over Britain :

" My first duty now that I have come back is to report to the British and French Governments the result of my mission, and until I have done that, it would be difficult for me to say anything about it.

" I will only say this. I trust all concerned will continue their efforts to solve the Czechoslovakia problem peacefully, because on that turns the peace of Europe in our time."

During the week-end the gravity of the situation increased hourly. The German ultimatum to Czechoslovakia was due to expire on 1st October and all countries prepared themselves for a war over a question already agreed in principle but whose dispute by arms would probably have resulted in the total destruction of the civilised world. On Monday night, in a speech listened to by the whole world, Herr Hitler told the German people that his patience was at an end. Immediately afterwards the Prime Minister issued a statement to the Press.

" I have read the speech of the German Chancellor and I appreciate his references to the efforts I have made to save the peace.

" I cannot abandon those efforts since it seems to me incredible that the peoples of Europe who do not want war with one another should be plunged into a bloody struggle over a question on which agreement has already been largely obtained.

" It is evident that the Chancellor has no faith that the promises made will be carried out. These promises were made, not to the German Government direct, but to the British and French Governments in the first instance.

"Speaking for the British Government we regard ourselves as morally responsible for seeing that the promises are carried out fairly and fully, and we are prepared to undertake that they shall be so carried out with all reasonable promptitude, provided that the German Government will agree to the settlement of terms and conditions of transfer by discussion and not by force.

"I trust that the Chancellor will not reject this proposal, which is made in the same spirit of friendliness as that in which I was received in Germany and which, if it is accepted, will satisfy the German desire for the union of Sudeten Germans with the Reich without the shedding of blood in any part of Europe."

NATIONAL BROADCAST

But though further exchanges took place between Berlin and London, Tuesday and Wednesday morning brought no ray of hope. In Britain the Fleet was mobilised, gas-masks distributed and trenches dug in the Park, while the people set themselves with resolution but with infinite sadness to the terrible task before them. On Tuesday night the Prime Minister broadcast to the nation.

"To-morrow Parliament is going to meet, and I shall be making a full statement of the events which have led up to the present anxious and critical situation.

"An earlier statement would not have been possible when I was flying backwards and forwards across Europe, and the position was changing from hour to hour. But to-day there is a lull for a brief time, and I want to say a few words to you, men and women of Britain and the Empire, and perhaps to others as well.

"First of all I must say something to those who have written to my wife or myself in these last weeks to tell us of their gratitude for my efforts and to assure us of their prayers for my success. Most of these letters have come from women —mothers or sisters of our own countrymen. But there are countless others besides—from France, from Belgium, from Italy, even from Germany, and it has been heart-breaking to read of the growing anxiety they reveal and their intense relief when they thought, too soon, that the danger of war was past.

" If I felt my responsibility heavy before, to read such letters has made it seem almost overwhelming. How horrible, fantastic, incredible it is that we should be digging trenches and trying on gas-masks here because of a quarrel in a far-away country between people of whom we know nothing. It seems still more impossible that a quarrel which has already been settled in principle should be the subject of war.

" I can well understand the reasons why the Czech Government have felt unable to accept the terms which have been put before them in the German memorandum. Yet I believe after my talks with Herr Hitler that, if only time were allowed, it ought to be possible for the arrangements for transferring the territory that the Czech Government has agreed to give to Germany to be settled by agreement under conditions which would assure fair treatment to the population concerned.

" You know already that I have done all that one man can do to compose this quarrel. After my visits to Germany I have realised vividly how Herr Hitler feels that he must champion other Germans, and his indignation that grievances have not been met before this. He told me privately, and last night he repeated publicly, that after this Sudeten German question is settled, that is the end of Germany's territorial claims in Europe.

" After my first visit to Berchtesgaden I did get the assent of the Czech Government to proposals which gave the substance of what Herr Hitler wanted, and I was taken completely by surprise when I got back to Germany and found that he insisted that the territory should be handed over to him immediately, and immediately occupied by German troops without previous arrangements for safe-guarding the people within the territory who were not Germans, or did not want to join the German Reich.

" I must say that I find this attitude unreasonable. If it arises out of any doubts that Herr Hitler feels about the intentions of the Czech Government to carry out their promises and hand over the territory, I have offered on the part of the British Government to guarantee their words, and I am sure the value of our promise will not be underrated anywhere.

" I shall not give up the hope of a peaceful solution, or abandon my efforts for peace, as long as any chance for peace remains. I would not hesitate to pay even a third visit to Germany if I thought it would do any good. But at this moment I see nothing further that I can usefully do in the way of mediation.

" Meanwhile there are certain things we can and shall do at home. Volunteers are still wanted for air raid precautions, for fire brigade and police services, and for the Territorial units. I know that all of you, men and women alike, are ready to play your part in the defence of the country, and I ask you all to offer your services, if you have not already done so, to the local authorities, who will tell you if you are wanted and in what capacity.

" Do not be alarmed if you hear of men being called up to man the anti-aircraft defences or ships. These are only precautionary measures such as a Government must take in times like this. But they do not necessarily mean that we have determined on war or that war is imminent.

" However much we may sympathise with a small nation confronted by a big and powerful neighbour, we cannot in all circumstances undertake to involve the whole British Empire in war simply on her account. If we have to fight it must be on larger issues than that. I am myself a man of peace to the depths of my soul. Armed conflict between nations is a nightmare to me ; but if I were convinced that any nation had made up its mind to dominate the world by fear of its force, I should feel that it must be resisted. Under such a domination life for people who believe in liberty would not be worth living ; but war is a fearful thing, and we must be very clear, before we embark on it, that it is really the great issues that are at stake, and that the call to risk everything in their defence, when all the consequences are weighed, is irresistible.

" For the present I ask you to await as calmly as you can the events of the next few days. As long as war has not begun, there is always hope that it may be prevented, and you know that I am going to work for peace to the last moment. Good night."

LIGHT AFTER DARKNESS

Next day, 28th September, 1938, at five minutes to three in the afternoon, the Prime Minister rose to make a statement to the House of Commons which had been hastily summoned to meet the emergency. At that time the outbreak of a general European war seemed a question of hours.

" SHORTLY before the House adjourned at the end of July I remember that some questions were addressed to me as to the possibility of summoning the House before the time arranged, and during the Recess, in certain eventualities. Those eventualities referred to possible developments in Spain. But the matter which has brought us together to-day is one which even at that time was already threatening, but which, I think, we all hoped would find a peaceful solution before we met again. Unhappily those hopes have not been fulfilled. To-day we are faced with a situation which has had no parallel since 1914.

" To find the origins of the present controversy it would be necessary to go back to the constitution of the State of Czechoslovakia with its heterogeneous population. No doubt at the time when it was constituted, it seemed to those then responsible that it was the best arrangement that could be made in the light of conditions as they then supposed them to exist. I cannot help reflecting that if Article XIX of the Covenant providing for the revision of the Treaties by agreement had been put into operation, as was contemplated by the framers of the Covenant, instead of waiting until passion became so exasperated that revision by agreement became impossible, we might have avoided the crisis. For that omission all Members of the League must bear their responsibility. I am not here to apportion blame among them.

" The position that we had to face in July was that a deadlock had arisen in the negotiations which had been going on between the Czechoslovak Government and the Sudeten Germans and that fears were already entertained that if it were not speedily broken, the German Government might presently intervene in the dispute. For His Majesty's Government there were three alternative courses that we might have adopted. Either we could have threatened to go to war with Germany if she attacked Czechoslovakia, or we could have stood aside and allowed matters to take their course, or,

279

finally, we could attempt to find a peaceful settlement by way of mediation. The first of those courses we rejected. We had no treaty liabilities to Czechoslovakia. We always refused to accept any such obligation. Indeed, this country, which does not readily resort to war, would not have followed us if we had tried to lead it into war to prevent a minority from obtaining autonomy, or even from choosing to pass under some other Government.

" The second alternative was also repugnant to us. However remote this territory may be, we knew, of course, that a spark once lighted there might give rise to a general conflagration, and we felt it our duty to do anything in our power to help the contending parties to find agreement. We addressed ourselves to the third course, the task of mediation. We knew that the task would be difficult, perhaps even perilous, but we felt that the object was good enough to justify the risk, and when Lord Runciman had expressed his willingness to undertake our mission, we were happy to think that we had secured a mediator whose long experience and well-known qualities of firmness, of tact, and of sympathy gave us the best hopes of success. That in the end Lord Runciman did not succeed was no fault of his, and we, and indeed all Europe, must ever be grateful to him and to his staff for their long and exhausting efforts on behalf of peace, in the course of which they gained the esteem and the confidence of both sides.

" On 21st September Lord Runciman addressed a letter to me reporting the results of his mission. That letter is printed in the White Paper—it is document No. 1—but perhaps I may conveniently mention some of the salient points of his story. On 7th June the Sudeten German Party had put forward certain proposals which embodied the eight points of Herr Henlein's speech at Carlsbad on 24th April. The Czechoslovak Government, on their side, had embodied their proposals in a draft Nationality Statute, a Language Bill, and an Administrative Reform Bill. By the middle of August it had become clear to Lord Runciman that the gap between these two proposals was too wide to permit of negotiations between the parties on that basis. In his capacity as mediator, he was successful in preventing the Sudeten German Party from closing the door upon further negotiations, and he was largely instrumental in inducing Dr. Benes to put forward new proposals on 21st August, which appear to have been regarded by the Sudeten Party leaders as a suitable basis for the continuance of negotiations. The prospects of negotiations being carried through to a successful conclusion were, however, handicapped by the recurrence of incidents in Czechoslovakia, involving casualties both on the Czech and Sudeten German side.

" On 1st and 2nd September Herr Henlein went to Berchtesgaden to consult with Herr Hitler about the situation. He was the bearer of a message from Lord Runciman to Herr Hitler, expressing the hope that he would give his approval and support to the continuance of the negotiations going on in Prague. No direct reply was communicated to Lord Runciman by Herr Henlein, but the latter returned convinced of Herr Hitler's desire for a peaceful solution, and after his return it became clear that the Sudeten leaders insisted upon complete satisfaction of the eight Carlsbad points, so-called, in any solution that might be reached. The House will see that during August Lord Runciman's efforts had been directed, with a considerable degree of success, towards bringing the Sudeten and Czechoslovak Government negotiators closer together.

" In the meantime, however, developments in Germany itself had been causing considerable anxiety to His Majesty's Government. On 28th July the Secretary of State for Foreign Affairs had written a personal letter to the German Minister of Foreign Affairs, Herr von Ribbentrop, expressing his regret at the latter's statement to Sir Nevile Henderson, our Ambassador in Berlin, that the German Government must reserve its attitude towards Lord Runciman's mission and regard the matter as one of purely British concern. The Secretary of State had gone on to express the hope that the German Government would collaborate with His Majesty's Government in facilitating a peaceful solution of the Sudeten question and so opening the way to establishing relations between Great Britain and Germany on a basis of mutual confidence and co-operation.

" But early in August we received reports of military preparations in Germany on an extensive scale. They included the calling up of reservists, the service of second-year recruits beyond the beginning of October, when they would normally have been released, the conscription of labour for the completion of German fortifications on her Western frontier, and measures which empowered the military authorities to conscript civilian goods and services. These measures, which involved a widespread dislocation of civilian life, could not fail to be regarded abroad as equivalent to partial mobilisation, and they suggested that the German Government were determined to find a settlement of the Sudeten question by the autumn. In these circumstances His Majesty's Ambassador in Berlin was instructed, in the middle of August, to point out to the German Government that these abnormal measures could not fail to be interpreted abroad as a threatening gesture towards Czechoslovakia, that they must therefore increase the feeling of tension throughout Europe, and that they might compel the Czechoslovak Government to take precautionary measures on their side. The almost certain consequence would be to destroy all chance of successful mediation by Lord Runciman's mission and perhaps endanger the peace of every one of the great Powers of Europe. This, the Ambassador added, might also destroy the prospects of the resumption of Anglo-German conversations. In these circumstances it was hoped that the German Government might be able to modify their military measures in order to avoid these dangers.

" To these representations Herr von Ribbentrop replied in a letter in which he refused to discuss the military measures referred to and expressed the opinion that the British efforts in Prague had only served to increase Czech intransigence. In face of this attitude His Majesty's Government, through the Chancellor of the Exchequer, who happened to be speaking at Lanark on 27th August, drew attention again to some words which I had used on 24th March in this House. He declared that there was nothing to add to or to vary in the statement which I had made. Perhaps I may just refresh the memories of hon. Members by reading that statement of 24th March once again :

" ' Where peace and war are concerned, legal obligations are not alone involved, and, if war broke out, it would be unlikely to be confined to those who have assumed such obligations. It would be quite impossible to say where it would end and what governments might become involved. The inexorable pressure of facts might well prove more powerful than formal pronouncements, and in that event it would be well within the bounds of probability that other countries, besides those which were parties to the original dispute, would almost immediately become involved. This is especially true in the case of two countries like Great Britain and France, with long associations of friendship, with interests closely interwoven, devoted to the same ideals of democratic liberty, and determined to uphold them.'

Towards the end of August further events occurred which marked the increasing seriousness of the situation. The French Government, in consequence of information which had reached them about the moving of several German divisions towards their frontier, took certain precautionary measures themselves, including the calling up of reserves to man the Maginot Line. On 28th August Sir Nevile Henderson had been recalled to London for consultation and a special meeting of Ministers was held on 30th August to consider his report and the general situation. On the 31st he returned to Berlin and he gave Baron von Weiszäcker, the State Secretary at the Wilhelmstrasse, a strong personal warning regarding the probable attitude of His Majesty's Government in the event of German aggression against Czechoslovakia, particularly if France were compelled to intervene. On 1st September the Ambassador saw Herr von Ribbentrop and repeated to him, as a personal and most urgent message, the warning he had already given to the State Secretary on the previous day.

"In addressing these personal warnings through Sir Nevile Henderson and in making the reference to Czechoslovakia contained in the Chancellor of the Exchequer's speech on 27th August, His Majesty's Government desired to impress the seriousness of the situation upon the German Government without risking a further aggravation of the situation by any formal representations, which might have been interpreted by the German Government as a public rebuff, as had been the case in regard to our representations on 21st May. His Majesty's Government also had to bear in mind the close approach of the Nazi Party Congress at Nuremberg, which was to open on 5th September and to last until the 12th. It was to be anticipated that the German Chancellor would feel himself compelled to make some public statement regarding the Sudeten question, and it therefore appeared necessary, in addition to warning the German Government of the attitude of His Majesty's Government in the United Kingdom, to make every effort in Prague to secure a resumption of negotiations between the Czechoslovak Government and the Sudeten representatives on a basis which would give hope of a rapid and satisfactory settlement.

"Accordingly, His Majesty's Minister at Prague saw Dr. Benes on 3rd September and emphasised to him that it was vital in the interests of Czechoslovakia to offer immediately and without reservation those concessions without which the Sudeten question could not be immediately settled. His Majesty's Government were not in a position to say whether anything less than the full Carlsbad programme would suffice. They certainly felt that the Czechoslovak Government should go forthwith and unreservedly to the limit of concessions. Lord Runciman strongly supported Mr. Newton's representations to Dr. Benes, but both Lord Runciman and Mr. Newton drew Dr. Benes' attention to the importance of reaching a settlement before Herr Hitler's expected pronouncement at Nuremburg and to the dangerous international situation resulting from the German military preparations. Dr. Benes responded to these representations, which were made in the best interests of Czechoslovakia, by putting forward proposals afterwards known as the Fourth Plan, which were communicated to the Sudeten German representatives on 6th September. In Lord Runciman's opinion this plan embodied almost all the requirements of the eight Carlsbad points and formed a very favourable basis for the resumption of negotiations. In forming this opinion he was guided partly by his own examination of the Czech Government's plan and partly by the favourable reception that was accorded to it by the Sudeten negotiators.

"Since the opening proclamation of the Nuremberg Congress had not contained any reference to the Czechoslovak question, and the recent attitude of Herr Hitler and other leading German personalities indicated that Germany welcomed the continuation of negotiations in Prague, the prospects of a satisfactory solution of the Sudeten question on the basis of autonomy within the Czechoslovak State appeared not unpromising on the publication of the Czechoslovak Government's Fourth Plan on 7th September. The publication of the Fourth Plan was, unfortunately, however, immediately followed by a serious incident at Mährischa-Ostrau. It would appear from the investigations of the British observer that the importance of this incident was very much exaggerated. The immediate result was a decision on the part of the Sudeten leaders not to resume negotiations until this incident had been liquidated. Immediately measures were taken by the Czechoslovak Government to liquidate it, but further incidents took place on 11th September near Eger, and, in spite of Lord Runciman's efforts to bring both parties together, negotiations could not be resumed before Herr Hitler's speech winding up the Nuremberg Congress on 12th September.

" In view of the unsatisfactory development of the situation in Czechoslovakia, and of the danger that Herr Hitler's speech might close the door to further negotiations, His Majesty's Government made further efforts to exercise a restraining influence upon the German Government. The French Government had shown themselves particularly insistent that nothing should be left undone to make the attitude of His Majesty's Government clear to the Chancellor himself. Sir Nevile Henderson was at Nuremberg from 9th September to the 12th, and he took every opportunity to impress upon leading German personalities, such as Field-Marshal Goering, Herr von Ribbentrop, Dr. Goebbels, Baron von Neurath and Baron von Weiszäcker, the attitude of His Majesty's Government as set forth in my speech on 24th March and repeated by my right hon. Friend on 27th August. Our Ambassador reported that there could be no grounds for any doubts in the minds of the German Government as a result of his efforts, and as such action might have had a contrary effect to what was intended, it was decided not to make any personal representations to Herr Hitler himself. The French Government were informed of the warnings which had been conveyed by Sir Nevile Henderson at Nuremberg.

" On 9th September the Cabinet met to consider the situation and decided to take certain precautionary naval measures, including the commissioning of mine-layers and mine-sweepers. On 11th September I made a statement to the Press, which received widespread publicity, stressing in particular the close ties uniting Great Britain and France and the probability in certain eventualities of this country going to the assistance of France. On the morning of 12th September the Cabinet met again, but they decided that no further action could usefully be taken before Herr Hitler's speech at Nuremberg that evening.

" In his speech on 12th September Herr Hitler laid great stress upon the defensive military measures taken on Germany's western frontier. In his references to Czechoslovakia he reminded the world that on 22nd February he had said that the Reich would no longer tolerate further oppression or persecution of the Sudeten Germans. They demanded the right of self-determination, he said, and they were supported in their demand by the Reich. Therefore, for the first time this speech promised the support of the Reich to the Sudeten Germans if they could not obtain satisfaction for themselves, and for the first time it publicly raised the issue of self-determination. He did not, however, close the door upon further negotiations in Prague, nor did he demand a plebiscite. As the speech was also accompanied by pacifying references to Germany's frontiers with Poland and France, its general effect was to leave the situation unchanged, with a slight diminution of the tension.

" The speech, however, and in particular Herr Hitler's reference to German support for the cause of the Sudeten Germans, had an immediate and unfortunate effect among those people. Demonstrations took place throughout the Sudetenland, resulting in an immediate extension of the incidents which had already begun on 11th September. Serious rioting occurred, accompanied by attacks upon Czech police and officials, and by 14th September, according to official Czechoslovak figures, there had been 21 killed and

75 wounded, the majority of whom were Czechs. Martial law was immediately proclaimed in the affected districts. On the evening of 13th September Herr Henlein and other Sudeten leaders assembled at Eger and sent a telegram to the Czechoslovak Government declaring that they could not be responsible for the consequences of martial law and the special Czech emergency measures if they were not immediately withdrawn. Attempts by Lord Runciman's Mission to bring the Sudeten leaders into discussion with the Czechoslovak Government failed, and on 14th September Herr Henlein issued a proclamation stating that the Carlsbad Points were no longer enough and that the situation called for self-determination. Thereupon, Herr Henlein fled to Germany, where, it is understood, he has since occupied himself with the formation of a Sudeten legionary organisation reported to number 40,000 men. In these circumstances Lord Runciman felt that no useful purpose would be served by his publishing a plan of his own.

" The House will recall that by the evening of 14th September a highly critical situation had developed in which there was immediate danger of the German troops now concentrated upon the frontier entering Czechoslovakia to prevent further incidents occurring in Sudetenland, and fighting between the Czech forces and the Sudeten Germans, although reliable reports indicated that order had been completely restored in those districts by 14th September. On the other hand, the Czechoslovak Government might have felt compelled to mobilise at once and so risk provoking a German invasion. In either event German invasion might have been expected to bring into operation French obligations to come to the assistance of Czechoslovakia, and so lead to a European War in which this country might well have been involved in support of France.

" In those circumstances I decided that the time had come to put into operation a plan which I had had in my mind for a considerable period as a last resort. One of the principal difficulties in dealing with totalitarian Governments is the lack of any means of establishing contact with the personalities in whose hands lie the final decisions for the country. So I resolved to go to Germany myself to interview Herr Hitler

K

and find out in personal conversation whether there was yet any hope of saving the peace. I knew very well that in taking such an unprecedented course I was laying myself open to criticism on the ground that I was detracting from the dignity of a British Prime Minister, and to disappointment, and perhaps even resentment, if I failed to bring back a satisfactory agreement. But I felt that in such a crisis, where the issues at stake were so vital for millions of human beings, such considerations could not be allowed to count.

"Herr Hitler responded to my suggestion with cordiality, and on 15th September I made my first flight to Munich. Thence I travelled by train to Herr Hitler's mountain home at Berchtesgaden. I confess I was astonished at the warmth of the approval with which this adventure was everywhere received, but the relief which it brought for the moment was an indication of the gravity with which the situation had been viewed. At this first conversation, which lasted for three hours and at which only an interpreter was present besides Herr Hitler and myself, I very soon became aware that the position was much more acute and much more urgent than I had realised. In courteous but perfectly definite terms, Herr Hitler made it plain that he had made up his mind that the Sudeten Germans must have the right of self-determination and of returning, if they wished, to the Reich. If they could not achieve this by their own efforts, he said, he would assist them to do so, and he declared categorically that rather than wait he would be prepared to risk a world war. At one point he complained of British threats against him, to which I replied that he must distinguish between a threat and a warning, and that he might have just cause of complaint if I allowed him to think that in no circumstances would this country go to war with Germany when, in fact, there were conditions in which such a contingency might arise.

"So strongly did I get the impression that the Chancellor was contemplating an immediate invasion of Czechoslovakia that I asked him why he had allowed me to travel all that way, since I was evidently wasting my time. On that he said that if I could give him there and then an assurance that the British Government accepted the principle of self-determination he would be quite ready to discuss ways and means of carrying it out; but, if, on the contrary, I told him that such a principle could not be considered by the British Government, then he agreed that it was of no use to continue our conversations. I, of course, was not in a position to give there and then such an assurance, but I undertook to return at once to consult with my colleagues if he would refrain from active hostilities until I had had time to obtain their reply. That assurance he gave me, provided, he said, that nothing happened in Czechoslovakia of such a nature as to force his hand. That assurance has remained binding ever since. I have no doubt whatever now, looking back, that my visit alone prevented an invasion, for which everything was ready. It was clear to me that with the German troops in the positions they then occupied, there was nothing that anybody could do that would prevent that invasion unless the right of self-determination were granted to the Sudeten Germans and that quickly. That was the sole hope of a peaceful solution.

" I came back to London next day, and that evening the Cabinet met and it was attended by Lord Runciman, who, at my request, had also travelled from Prague on the same day. Lord Runciman informed us that although, in his view, the responsibility for the final breach in the negotiations at Prague rested with the Sudeten extremists, nevertheless, in view of recent developments, the frontier districts between Czechoslovakia and Germany, where the Sudeten population was in the majority, should be given the full right of self-determination at once. He considered the cession of territory to be inevitable and thought it should be done promptly. Measures for a peaceful transfer could be arranged between the two Governments. Germans and Czechs, however, would still have to live side by side in many other areas of Czechoslovakia, and in those areas Lord Runciman thought that a basis ought to be sought for local autonomy on the lines of the Fourth Plan which had been published by the Czecho-slovak Government on the seventh of this month. Moreover, he considered that the integrity and security of Czecho-slovakia could only be maintained if her policy, internal and external, was directed to enabling her to live at peace with all her neighbours. For this purpose, in his opinion, her policy should be entirely neutral, as in the case of Switzerland. This would involve assurances from Czechoslovakia that in no circumstances would she attack any of her neighbours and it would also mean guarantees from the principal Powers of Europe against aggression.

" Lord Runciman recommended that, in order to carry out the policy he was advocating, an international commission should be invited to deal with the delimitation of the area transferred to Germany and with controversial points arising from the execution of whatever agreement was reached. He also recommended the organisation of an international force to keep order in the transferred districts, so that the Czechoslovak troops and police might be withdrawn as soon as possible.

" Naturally, His Majesty's Government felt it necessary to consult the French Government before they replied to Herr Hitler, and, accordingly, M. Daladier and M. Bonnet were invited to fly to London for conversations with British Ministers on 18th September. Perhaps I may read the communiqué which was issued after those conversations, and which read as follows :

" ' After a full discussion of the present international situation, the representatives of the British and French Governments are in complete agreement as to the policy to be adopted with a view to promoting a peaceful solution of the Czechoslovak question. The two Governments hope that thereafter it will be possible to consider a more general settlement in the interests of European peace.'

During these conversations the representatives of the two Governments were guided by a desire to find a solution which would not bring about a European War, and, therefore, a solution which would not automatically compel France to take action in accordance with her obligations. It was agreed that the only means of achieving this object was to accept the principle of self-determination, and, accordingly, the British and the French Ministers in Prague were instructed to inform the Czechoslovak Government that the further maintenance within the boundaries of the Czechoslovak State of the districts mainly inhabited by Sudeten Germans could not continue any longer without imperilling the interests of Czechoslovakia herself and of European peace. The Czechoslovak Government were, therefore, urged to agree immediately to the direct transfer to the Reich of all areas with over 50 per cent Sudeten inhabitants. An international body was to be set up to deal with questions like the adjustment of frontiers and the possible exchange of populations on the basis of the right to opt.

" The Czechoslovak Government were informed that, to meet their natural desire for security for their future, His Majesty's Government would be prepared, as a contribution to the pacification of Europe, to join in an international guarantee of the new boundaries of the Czechoslovak State against unprovoked aggression. Such a guarantee would safeguard the independence of Czechoslovakia by substituting a general guarantee against unprovoked aggression in place of the existing treaties with France and Soviet Russia, which involve reciprocal obligations of a military character. In urging this solution upon the Czechoslovak Government, the British and French Governments took account of the probability that the Czechoslovak Government would find it preferable to deal with the problem by the method of direct transfer rather than by means of a plebiscite, which would involve serious difficulties as regards other nationalities in Czechoslovakia.

" In agreeing to guarantee the future boundaries of Czechoslovakia against unprovoked aggression, His Majesty's Government were accepting a completely new commitment as we were not previously bound by any obligations towards Czechoslovakia other than those involved in the Covenant of the League.

" The Czechoslovak Government replied on 20th September to these representations by suggesting that the Sudeten dispute should be submitted to arbitration under the terms of the German-Czechoslovak Arbitration Treaty of 1926. The British and French Ministers in Prague were, however, instructed to point out to the Czechoslovak Government that there was no hope of a peaceful solution on this basis, and, in the interests of Czechoslovakia and of European peace, the Czechoslovak Government was urged to accept the Anglo-French proposals immediately. This they did immediately and unconditionally on 21st September. His Majesty's

Minister in Prague was instructed on 22nd September to inform Dr. Benes that His Majesty's Government were profoundly conscious of the immense sacrifices to which the Czechoslovak Government had agreed, and the great public spirit they had shown. These proposals had naturally been put forward in the hope of averting a general disaster and saving Czechoslovakia from invasion. The Czechoslovak Government's readiness to go to such extreme limits of concession had assured her of a measure of sympathy which nothing else could have aroused.

"That Government resigned on 22nd September, but it was immediately succeeded by a Government of National concentration under General Syrovy, Inspector-General of the Army, and it has been emphasised in Prague that this Government is not a military dictatorship and has accepted the Anglo-French proposals. We had hoped that the immediate problem of the Sudeten Germans would not be further complicated at this particular juncture by the pressing of the claims of the Hungarian and Polish minorities. These minorities have, however, consistently demanded similar treatment to that accorded to the Sudeten minority, and the acceptance of the Anglo-French proposals, involving the cession of the predominantly Sudeten German territories, has led to a similar demand for cession of the territory predominantly inhabited by Polish and Hungarian minorities being advanced by the Hungarian and Polish Governments. The Hungarian Minister in London and the Polish Ambassador in London made representations to His Majesty's Government in this sense on 19th and 20th September. Representations were also made in Prague on 21st and 22nd September. His Majesty's Government have taken note of these representations, and have replied that they were at present concentrating all their efforts on the Sudeten problem, on the solution of which the issue of peace and war in Europe depended. They fully appreciated the interest of the Hungarian and Polish Governments in their respective minorities in Czechoslovakia, but hoped they would do nothing in the present delicate situation to extend the scope of the present crisis. The Polish Government have expressed considerable dissatisfaction at this reply, and emphasised that the Polish claims require urgent settlement. Troop movements have taken place in the direction of Teschen and considerable popular feeling has been aroused in Poland. The Hungarian Government has been encouraged by the visits of the Regent to Field-Marshal Goering at Rominten on 20th September and of the Prime Minister, Minister for Foreign Affairs and Chief of the General Staff to Berchtesgaden on 21st September. Mobilisation measures have been taken to double the strength of the Hungarian Army.

" In view of these developments, the task of finding a solution of the Sudeten German problem was still further complicated. However, on the 22nd I went back to Germany to Godesberg on the Rhine, where the Chancellor had appointed a meeting-place as being more convenient for me than the remote Berchtesgaden. Once again I had a very warm welcome in the streets and villages through which I passed, demonstrating to me the desire of the German people for peace, and on the afternoon of my arrival I had my second meeting with the Chancellor. During my stay in London the Government had worked out with the French Government arrangements for effecting the transfer of the territory proposed, and also for delimiting the final frontier. I explained these to Herr Hitler—he was not previously aware of them—and I also told him about the proposed guarantee against unprovoked aggression.

" On the point of a guarantee he made no objection, but said he could not enter into a guarantee unless other Powers, including Italy, were also guarantors. I said, I had not asked him to enter into a guarantee but I had intended to ask him whether he was prepared to conclude a pact of non-aggression with the new Czechoslovakia. He said he could not enter into such a pact while other minorities in Czechoslovakia were still unsatisfied ; but hon. Members will see that he has since put his views in a more positive form, and said that when they are satisfied he will then be prepared to join in an international guarantee. At this particular time, however, no further discussion took place between us on the subject of a guarantee. Herr Hitler said he could not accept the other proposals I had described to him, on the ground that they were too dilatory and offered too many opportunities for further evasion on the part of the Czechs. He insisted that a speedy solution was essential, on account of the oppression and terrorism to which the Sudeten Germans were being subjected, and he proceeded to give me the main outlines of the proposal which he subsequently embodied in a memorandum—except that he did not in this conversation actually name any time limit.

" Hon. Members will realise the perplexity in which I found myself, faced with this totally unexpected situation. I had been told at Berchtesgaden that if the principle of self-determination were accepted, Herr Hitler would discuss with me the ways and means of carrying it out. He told me afterwards that he never for one moment supposed that I should be able to come back and say that the principle was accepted. I do not want hon. Members to think that he was deliberately deceiving me—I do not think so for one moment—but, for me, I expected that when I got back to Godesberg I had only to discuss quietly with him the proposals that I had brought with me ; and it was a profound shock to me when I was told at the beginning of the conversation that these proposals were not acceptable, and that they were to be replaced by other proposals of a kind which I had not contemplated at all.

" I felt that I must have a little time to consider what I was to do. Consequently, I withdrew, my mind full of foreboding as to the success of my mission. I first, however, obtained from Herr Hitler an extension of his previous assurance, that he would not move his troops pending the results of the negotiations. I, on my side, undertook to appeal to the Czech Government to avoid any action which might provoke incidents. I have seen speculative accounts of what happened on the next day, which have suggested that long hours passed whilst I remained on one side of the Rhine and Herr Hitler on the other, because I had difficulty in obtaining this assurance from him about the moving of his troops. I want to say at once that that is purely imaginary. There was no such difficulty. I will explain in a moment what did cause the delay ; but the assurance was given readily, and it has been, as I have said before, abided by right up to the present time.

" We had arranged to resume our conversation at half-past eleven the next morning, but, in view of the difficulties of talking with a man through an interpreter and of the fact that I could not feel sure that what I had said to Herr Hitler had always been completely understood and appreciated by him, I thought it would be wise to put down on paper some comments upon these new proposals of his and let him have them some time before the talks began. Accordingly, I wrote him a letter—which is No. 3 in the White Paper—which I sent to him. I sent that soon after breakfast. It will be seen that in it I declared my readiness to convey the proposals to the Czechoslovak Government, but I pointed out what seemed to me to be grave difficulties in the way of their acceptance. On the receipt of this letter, the Chancellor intimated that he would like to send a written reply. Accordingly, the conversations were postponed. The reply was not received until well into the afternoon.

" I had hoped that this delay might mean that some modification was being worked out, but when I received the letter—which is No. 4—I found, to my disappointment, that, although it contained some explanation, it offered no modification at all of the proposals which had been described to me the night before. Accordingly, I replied as in document No. 5, asking for a memorandum of the proposals and a copy of the map for transmission to Prague, and intimating my intention to return to England. The memorandum and the map were handed to me at my final interview with the Chancellor, which began at half-past ten that night and lasted into the small hours of the morning, an interview at which the German Foreign Secretary was present, as well as Sir Nevile Henderson and Sir Horace Wilson; and, for the first time, I found in the memorandum a time limit. Accordingly, on this occasion I spoke very frankly. I dwelt with all the emphasis at my command on the risks which would be incurred by insisting on such terms, and on the terrible consequences of a war, if war ensued. I declared that the language and the manner of the document, which I described as an ultimatum rather than a memorandum, would profoundly shock public opinion in neutral countries, and I bitterly reproached the Chancellor for his failure to respond in any way to the efforts which I had

K *

made to secure peace. In spite of these plain words, this conversation was carried on on more friendly terms than any that had yet preceded it, and Herr Hitler informed me that he appreciated and was grateful for my efforts, but that he considered that he had made a response since he had held back the operations which he had planned and that he had offered in his proposal to Czechoslovakia a frontier very different from the one which he would have taken as the result of military conquest.

"I think I should add that before saying farewell to Herr Hitler I had a few words with him in private, which I do not think are without importance. In the first place he repeated to me with great earnestness what he had said already at Berchtesgaden, namely, that this was the last of his territorial ambitions in Europe and that he had no wish to include in the Reich people of other races than Germans. In the second place he said, again very earnestly, that he wanted to be friends with England and that if only this Sudeten question could be got out of the way in peace he would gladly resume conversations. It is true he said: ' There is one awkward question, the Colonies.' [HON. MEMBERS : ' Spain.'] (Laughter.) I really think that at a time like this these are not subjects for idle laughter. They are words which count in the long run and ought to be fully weighed. He said: ' There is one awkward question, the Colonies, but that is not a matter for war,' and, alluding to the mobilisation of the Czechoslovakian Army, which had been announced to us in the middle of our conversations and had given rise to some disturbance, he said, about the Colonies : ' There will be no mobilisation about that.'

"I may now briefly recapitulate the contents of the Memorandum. It proposed immediate separation from Czechoslovakia of areas shaded on the map. These areas included all areas in which Sudeten Germans constituted more than 50 per cent of the population, and some additional areas. These were to be completely evacuated by Czech soldiers and officials and occupied by German troops by 1st October. A plebiscite was to be held in November, and according to the results, a definitive frontier was to be settled by a German-Czech or an International Commission ; that is to say, the frontier would be altered according as the majority were either Germans or Czechs on one side or the other. In addition, certain other areas marked in green, were to be the subject of a plebiscite but these were to remain in the occupation of Czech troops. Both German and Czech troops were to be withdrawn from the disputed areas during the plebiscite and all further details were to be settled by a joint German-Czech Commission.

" I returned to London on 24th September, and arrangements were made for the German Memorandum and map to be communicated directly to the Czech Government, who received them that evening. On Sunday, the 25th, we received from Mr. Masaryk, the Czech Minister here, the reply of the Czech Government, which stated that they considered Herr Hitler's demands in their present form to be absolutely and unconditionally unacceptable. This reply was communicated to the French Ministers, M. Daladier and M. Bonnet, who arrived that same evening and exchanged views with us on the situation. Conversations were resumed the next morning, when the French Ministers informed us that if Czechoslovakia were attacked, France would fulfil her Treaty obligations, and in reply we told them that if as a result of these obligations French forces became actively engaged in hostilities against Germany, we should feel obliged to support them.

" Meanwhile, as a last effort to preserve peace I sent Sir Horace Wilson to Berlin on the 26th, with a personal message to Herr Hitler to be delivered before the speech that Herr Hitler was to make in Berlin at eight o'clock that night. The French Ministers entirely approved this initiative and issued a communiqué to that effect at midday. Sir Horace Wilson took with him a letter—No. 9 on the White Paper—from me, pointing out that the reception of the German Memorandum by the Czechoslovak Government and public opinion in the world generally had confirmed the expectation which I had expressed to him at Godesberg. I, therefore, made a further proposal with a view to rendering it possible to get a settlement by negotiation rather than by military force, namely, that there should be immediate discussions between German and Czechoslovak representatives in the presence of British representatives. Sir Horace Wilson arrived in Berlin on the afternoon of the 26th and he presented his letter to Herr Hitler, who listened to him, but expressed the view that he could not depart from the procedure of the memorandum, as he felt conferences would lead to further intolerable procrastinations.

" I should tell the House how deeply impressed on my mind by my conversations with Herr Hitler and by every speech he has made, is his rooted distrust and disbelief in the sincerity of the Czech Government. That has been one of the governing factors in all this difficult story of negotiation.

" In the meantime after reading Herr Hitler's speech in Berlin, in which he, as I say, expressed his disbelief in the intention of the Czech Government to carry out their promises, I issued a statement in which I offered, on behalf of the British Government, to guarantee that the promises they had made to us and the French Government should be carried out. But yesterday morning Sir Horace Wilson resumed his conversations with Herr Hitler, and finding his views apparently still unchanged, he by my instructions repeated to him in precise terms what I said a few minutes ago was the upshot of our conversations with the French, namely, that if the Czechs reject the German Memorandum and Germany attacks Czechoslovakia, we had been informed by the French Government that they would fulfil their obligations to Czechoslovakia, and that should the forces of France in consequence become actively engaged in hostilities against Germany, the British Government would feel obliged to support them.

" The next document in the White Paper refers to a conversation which I had with M. Masaryk as to whether the Czechoslovak Government would take part in such a conference as I had proposed to Herr Hitler, and the Czech Government replied accepting the proposal under certain conditions which are set out in their letter. Now the story which I have told the House brings us up to last night. About 10.30 I received from Herr Hitler a reply to my letter sent by Sir Horace Wilson. It is printed in the White Paper. A careful perusal of this letter indicates certain limitations on

Herr Hitler's intentions which were not included in the Memorandum, and also gives certain additional assurances. There is, for example, a definite statement that troops are not to move beyond the red line, that they are only to preserve order, that the plebiscite will be carried out by a free vote under no outside influence, and that Herr Hitler will abide by the result, and, finally, that he will join the international guarantee of the remainder of Czechoslovakia once the minorities questions are settled. Those are all reassuring statements as far as they go, and I have no hesitation in saying, after the personal contact I had established with Herr Hitler, that I believe he means what he says when he states that. But the reflection which was uppermost in my mind when I read his letter to me was that once more the differences and the obscurities had been narrowed down still further to a point where really it was inconceivable that they could not be settled by negotiations. So strongly did I feel this, that I felt impelled to send one more last letter—the last last— to the Chancellor. I sent him the following personal message :

" ' After reading your letter I feel certain that you can get all essentials without war and without delay. I am ready to come to Berlin myself at once to discuss arrangements for transfer with you and representatives of the Czech Government, together with representatives of France and Italy if you desire. I feel convinced that we could reach agreement in a week. However much you distrust the Prague Government's intentions, you cannot doubt the power of the British and French Governments to see that the promises are carried out fairly and fully and forthwith. As you know, I have stated publicly that we are prepared to undertake that they shall be so carried out. I cannot believe that you will take the responsibility of starting a world war which may end civilisation, for the sake of a few days' delay in settling this long-standing problem.'

" At the same time I sent the following personal message to Signor Mussolini :

" ' I have to-day addressed last appeal to Herr Hitler to abstain from force to settle Sudeten problem, which, I feel sure, can be settled by a short discussion and will give him the essential territory, population and protection for both Sudetens and Czechs during transfer. I have offered myself to go at once to Berlin to discuss arrangements with German and Czech representatives, and if the Chancellor desires, representatives also of Italy and France.

" ' I trust your Excellency will inform the German Chancellor that you are willing to be represented and urge him to agree to my proposal which will keep all our peoples out of war. I have already guaranteed that Czech promises shall be carried out and feel confident full agreement could be reached in a week.'

In reply to my message to Signor Mussolini, I was informed that instructions had been sent by the Duce to the Italian Ambassador in Berlin to see Herr von Ribbentrop at once and to say that while Italy would fulfil completely her pledges to stand by Germany, yet, in view of the great importance of the request made by His Majesty's Government to Signor Mussolini, the latter hoped Herr Hitler would see his way to postpone action which the Chancellor had told Sir Horace Wilson was to be taken at 2 p.m. to-day for at least twenty-four hours so as to allow Signor Mussolini time to re-examine the situation and endeavour to find a peaceful settlement. In response, Herr Hitler has agreed to postpone mobilisation for twenty-four hours.

"Whatever views hon. Members may have had about Signor Mussolini in the past, I believe that everyone will welcome his gesture of being willing to work with us for peace in Europe. That is not all. I have something further to say to the House yet. I have now been informed by Herr Hitler that he invites me to meet him at Munich to-morrow morning. He has also invited Signor Mussolini and M. Daladier. Signor Mussolini has accepted and I have no doubt M. Daladier will also accept. I need not say what my answer will be. [An Hon. Member : ' Thank God for the Prime Minister ! '] We are all patriots, and there can be no hon. Member of this House who did not feel his heart leap that the crisis has been once more postponed to give us once more an opportunity to try what reason and good will and discussion will do to settle a problem which is already within sight of settlement. Mr. Speaker, I cannot say any more. I am sure that the House will be ready to release me now to go and see what I can make of this last effort. Perhaps they may think it will be well, in view of this new development, that this Debate shall stand adjourned for a few days, when perhaps we may meet in happier circumstances."

The end of Mr. Chamberlain's speech was greeted by one of the most tumultous scenes ever witnessed at Westminster. The whole House rose to him and continued to cheer for some minutes, and when the cheering had subsided Mr. Attlee and Sir Archibald Sinclair briefly and warmly expressed their approval and their hopes for Mr. Chamberlain's success.

Next morning at half-past eight the Prime Minister left Heston for Germany for the third time in two weeks. Before he stepped into his aeroplane, he said: " When I was a boy I used to repeat, ' If at first you don't succeed, try, try, try again.' That is what I am doing."

" When I come back, I hope I may be able to say, as Hotspur says in 'Henry IV' : ' Out of this nettle danger we pluck this flower safety.' "

In the course of the same day the Munich Agreement was negotiated by the four international statesmen, Mr. Chamberlain, Herr Hitler, Signor Mussolini and Monsieur Daladier. It was signed at half-past two in the early morning of Friday, 30th September. Its essence was that by reaching an agreed method of evacuation, by which the Sudetenland was to be transferred to Germany in four successive stages while any outstanding questions were left to the arbitrament of a committee of German, Czech, French, Italian and British diplomats, the resort to arms threatened by Herr Hitler was averted and Britain's ally France was thereby relieved from her treaty obligation to march against Germany to prevent the application of a principle to which she had herself already subscribed.

On the morning of Friday, 30th September, Czechoslovakia accepted the conditions agreed on by the statesmen of the four Powers. Before leaving for England, Mr. Chamberlain had a further conversation with Herr Hitler. To this he referred in a

statement delivered before leaving Munich aerodrome that after-
noon, and afterward repeated in a brief speech made into the
microphone after landing at Heston.

" There are only two things I want to say. First of all I
received an immense number of letters during all these anxious
days—and so has my wife—letters of support and approval
and gratitude ; and I cannot tell you what an encouragement
that has been to me. I want to thank the British people for
what they have done. Next I want to say that the settlement
of the Czechoslovak problem which has now been achieved
is, in my view, only a prelude to a larger settlement in which
all Europe may find peace.

" This morning I had another talk with the German
Chancellor, Herr Hitler, and here is a paper which bears his
name upon it as well as mine. Some of you perhaps have
already heard what it contains, but I would just like to read
it to you.

" ' We, the German Führer and Chancellor and the British
Prime Minister, have had a further meeting to-day and are
agreed in recognising that the question of Anglo-German
relations is of the first importance for the two countries and
for Europe.

" ' We regard the agreement signed last night and the
Anglo-German Naval Agreement as symbolic of the desire
of our two peoples never to go to war with one another again.

" ' We are resolved that the method of consultation shall
be the method adopted to deal with any other questions that
may concern our two countries, and we are determined to
continue our efforts to remove possible sources of difference
and thus to contribute to assure the peace of Europe.' "

After being received at Buckingham Palace by the King
Mr. Chamberlain drove to Downing Street amid cheering
crowds. In response to repeated demands he spoke from the
first floor window of No. 10.

" My good friends, this is the second time in our history
that there has come back from Germany to Downing Street
peace with honour."

It was some time before the cheering of the crowds enabled the Prime Minister to continue.

" I believe it is peace for our time. We thank you from the bottom of our hearts."

The response was immediate. " We thank you," came back from the crowd below. " God bless you." Mr. Chamberlain paused for a moment and then said : " And now I recommend you to go home and sleep quietly in your beds."

THE POST-MUNICH DEBATE

On Monday, 3rd October, five days after the dramatic scene described a few pages earlier, the House met to hear the Prime Minister. He was preceded by Mr. Duff Cooper, formerly First Lord of the Admiralty, who, holding that it had been a mistake to address Herr Hitler " through the language of sweet reasonableness " instead of " the language of the mailed fist," had resigned on the ground that, " though the modifications the Prime Minister obtained " at Munich " were important and of great value," they had failed to save Czechoslovakia from " the ignominy and the horror of invasion." Mr. Duff Cooper also disapproved of the joint-declaration renouncing the resort to war as a means of settling disputes between Britain and Germany. " I would suggest," he said, " that for the Prime Minister of England to sign, without consulting with his colleagues and without, so far as I am aware, any reference to his Allies, obviously without any communication with the Dominions and without the assistance of any expert diplomatic advisers, such a declaration with the dictator of a great State, is not the way in which the foreign affairs of the British Empire should be conducted."

The Prime Minister rose to make his statement at 3.30 p.m.

" IT has been my lot to listen to more than one speech by a Minister who came to this House to explain the reasons why he had felt it necessary to resign his office in the Government. I have never been able to listen to such speeches without emotion. When a man gives up, as my right hon. Friend has so eloquently described, a great position, and association with friends in the pursuit of work in which he takes a pride and interest, and gives up these things for conscience' sake, everybody must listen to him with respect. One must feel, too, sympathy for a man struggling to explain the reasons which have separated him from his colleagues conscious that among them, at any rate, he has been in a minority. But I am sure my right hon. Friend (Mr. Duff Cooper) will not think me discourteous if this afternoon I make no attempt to answer him or to defend myself against the strictures which he has made upon the policy which the Government have been pursuing. It is not that I have anything to withdraw or to regret, but that in the course of this Debate there will be, no doubt, other criticisms which can be answered before the Debate closes, along with those of my right hon. Friend, and that I desire to open the discussion with the speech that I would have made if my right hon. Friend had not resigned, in order that I may try and give the House the background, as we see it, for the events that have taken place and for the decisions that have been taken.

" When the House met last Wednesday, we were all under the shadow of a great and imminent menace. War, in a form more stark and terrible than ever before, seemed to be staring us in the face. Before I sat down, a message had come which gave us new hope that peace might yet be saved, and to-day, only a few days after, we all meet in joy and thankfulness that the prayers of millions have been answered, and a cloud of anxiety has been lifted from our hearts. Upon the Members of the Cabinet the strain of the responsibility of these last few weeks has been almost overwhelming. Some of us, I have no doubt, will carry the mark of it for the rest of our days. Necessarily, the weight fell heavier upon some shoulders than others. While all bore their part, I would like here and now to pay an especial tribute of gratitude and praise to the man upon whom fell the first brunt of those decisions which had to be taken day by day, almost hour by hour. The calmness, patience, and wisdom of the Foreign Secretary, and his lofty conception of his duty, not only to this country but to all humanity, were an example to us all, and sustained us all through the trials through which we have been passing.

" Before I come to describe the Agreement which was signed at Munich in the small hours of Friday morning last, I would like to remind the House of two things which I think it is very essential not to forget when those terms are being considered. The first is this : We did not go there to decide whether the predominantly German areas in the Sudetenland should be passed over to the German Reich. That had been decided already. Czechoslovakia had accepted the Anglo-French proposals. What we had to consider was the method, the conditions and the time of the transfer of the territory. The second point to remember is that time was one of the essential factors. All the elements were present on the spot for the outbreak of a conflict which might have precipitated the catastrophe. We had populations inflamed to a high degree ; we had extremists on both sides ready to work up and provoke incidents ; we had considerable quantities of arms which were by no means confined to regularly organised forces. Therefore, it was essential that we should quickly reach a conclusion, so that this painful and difficult operation of transfer might be carried out at the earliest possible moment and concluded as soon as was consistent with orderly procedure, in order that we might avoid the possibility of something that might have rendered all our attempts at peaceful solution useless.

" The House will remember that when I last addressed them I gave them some account of the Godesberg Memorandum, with the terms of which I think they are familiar. They will recollect also that I myself at Godesberg expressed frankly my view that the terms were such as were likely to shock public opinion generally in the world and to bring their prompt rejection by the Czechoslovak Government. Those views were confirmed by the results, and the immediate and unqualified rejection of that Memorandum by the Czecho- slovak Government was communicated to us at once by them. What I think the House will desire to take into consideration first, this afternoon, is what is the difference between those unacceptable terms and the terms which were included in the Agreement signed at Munich, because on the difference between those two documents will depend the judgment as to whether we were successful in what we set out to do, namely, to find an orderly instead of a violent method of carrying out an agreed decision.

"I say, first of all, that the Godesberg Memorandum, although it was cast in the form of proposals, was in fact an ultimatum, with a time limit of six days. On the other hand, the Munich Agreement reverts to the Anglo-French plan, the plan referred to in the Preamble, though not in express terms, and it lays down the conditions for the application, on the responsibility of the four Powers and under international supervision, of the main principle of that Memorandum. Again, under the Munich Agreement evacuation of the territory which is to be occupied by German military forces and its occupation by those forces is to be carried out in five clearly defined stages between 1st October and 10th October, instead of having to be completed in one operation by 1st October. Thirdly, the line up to which German troops will enter into occupation is no longer the line as laid down in the map which was attached to the Godesberg Memorandum. It is a line which is to be fixed by an International Commission. On that Commission both Germany and Czechoslovakia are represented. I take the fourth point. Under the Godesberg Memorandum the areas on the Czech side of this German line laid down in the map which were to be submitted to a plebis- cite were laid down on that map by Germany, whereas those on the German side of the line were left undefined. Under the Munich Agreement all plebiscite areas are to be defined by the International Commission. The criterion is to be the predomi- nantly German character of the area, the interpretation of that phrase being left to the Commission. I am bound to say that the German line, the line laid down in the map, did take in a number of areas which could not be called predominantly German in character.

" Then, Sir, it will be remembered that, according to the Godesberg Memorandum, the occupation of plebiscite areas by German and Czech troops respectively was to be up to the time of the plebiscite. They were then to be withdrawn while the plebiscite was being held. Under the Munich Agreement these plebiscite areas are to be occupied at once by an international force. The Godesberg Memorandum did not indicate on what kind of areas the vote would be based. Accordingly, there were fears entertained on the side of the Czechs that large areas might be selected, which would operate to the disadvantage of the Czechoslovaks. In the Munich arrangement it is stated that the plebiscite is to be based on the conditions of the Saar plebiscite, and that indicates that the vote is to be taken by small administrative areas. Under the Munich arrangement the Czech Government, while it is bound to carry out the evacuation of the territories without damaging existing installations, is not placed under the objectionable conditions of the appendix to the Godesberg Memorandum, to which much exception was taken, in that it was provided that no foodstuffs, cattle or raw material were to be removed. Under the Godesberg Memorandum the detailed arrangements for the evacuation were to be settled by Germans and Czechs alone, and I think there were many who thought that such an arrangement did not give the Czechs much chance of making their voices heard. Well, Sir, under the Munich Agreement the conditions of evacuation are to be laid down in detail by the International Commission.

" Again, the Munich arrangement includes certain very valuable provisions which found no place at all in the Godesberg Memorandum, such as the Article regarding the right of option : that is option to leave the territory and pass into Czech territory, provisions for facilitating the transfer of populations, the supplementary declaration which provides that all other questions arising out of the transfer of territory are to be referred to the International Commission, and, finally, the one which gives the Czechs the period of four weeks for the release of the Sudeten Germans from the army and the police, and for the release of Sudeten German political prisoners instead of demanding that those things should be done by 1st October——"

MISS WILKINSON : " What about the kidnapped Czechs ? "

THE PRIME MINISTER : " The joint guarantee, which is given under the Munich Agreement to the Czechoslovak State by the Governments of the United Kingdom and France against unprovoked aggressions upon their boundaries, gives to the Czechs an essential counterpart which was not to be found in the Godesberg Memorandum, and it will not be unnoted that Germany will also undertake to give a guarantee on the question of Polish and Hungarian minorities being settled. Finally, there is a declaration by the Four Powers that if the problems of the Polish and Hungarian minorities in Czechoslovakia are not settled within three months by agreement between the respective Governments, another meeting of the Four Powers will be held to consider them. (Interruption.) I think that every fair-minded, every serious-minded man who takes into consideration the modifications which I have described—modifications of the Memorandum—must agree that they are of very considerable extent and that they are all in the same direction. To those who dislike an ultimatum, but who were anxious for a reasonable and orderly procedure, everyone of those modifications is a step in the right direction. It is no longer an ultimatum, but it is a method which is carried out largely under the supervision of an international body.

" Before giving a verdict upon this arrangement, we should do well to avoid describing it as a personal or a national triumph for anyone. The real triumph is that it has shown that representatives of four great Powers can find it possible to agree on a way of carrying out a difficult and delicate operation by discussion instead of by force of arms, and thereby they have averted a catastrophe which would have ended civilisation as we have known it. The relief that our escape from this great peril of war has, I think, everywhere been mingled in this country with a profound feeling of sympathy. [HON. MEMBERS : ' Shame.'] I have nothing to be ashamed of. Let those who have, hang their heads. We must feel profound sympathy for a small and gallant nation in the hour of their national grief and loss."

Mr. BELLENGER : " It is an insult to say it."

THE PRIME MINISTER : " I say in the name of this House and of the people of this country that Czechoslovakia has earned our admiration and respect for her restraint, for her dignity, for her magnificent discipline in face of such a trial as few nations have ever been called upon to meet. General Syrovy said the other night in his broadcast :

" ' The Government could have decided to stand up against overpowering forces, but it might have meant the death of millions.'

" The army, whose courage no man has ever questioned, has obeyed the order of their President, as they would equally have obeyed him if he had told them to march into the trenches. It is my hope, and my belief, that under the new system of guarantees, the new Czechoslovakia will find a greater security than she has ever enjoyed in the past. We must recognise that she has been put in a position where she has got to reconstruct her whole economy, and that in doing that she must encounter difficulties, which it would be practically impossible for her to solve alone. We have received from the Czechoslovak Government, through their Minister in London, an appeal to help them to raise a loan of £30,000,000 by a British Government guarantee. I believe that the House will feel with the Government that that is an appeal which should meet with a sympathetic and even a generous response.

" So far as we have been able to ascertain, the Czechoslovak Government has not as yet addressed any similar request to any other Government. It is evident that the terms and conditions of a guaranteed loan and the question of what Governments would participate in it, may raise matters which could not be decided immediately ; but evidently this is one of those cases where the old proverb applies, that ' He who gives quickly gives twice.' [HON. MEMBERS : ' Takes twice.'] Would hon. Members opposite kindly allow me to continue this rather important part of my statement without those continual interruptions, which distract attention and make it difficult for the House to take in what I am saying ? His Majesty's Government are informing the Czechoslovak Government that we are prepared immediately to arrange for an advance of £10,000,000, which would be at that Government's disposal for their urgent needs. How this advance will be related to the final figure which may be decided upon hereafter is for the future. Manifestly, all of this depends upon many factors which cannot now be determined. The precise character of the problem will want expert examination, in which we shall, if desired, be very willing to be associated, and during the coming weeks the resulting situation and its needs can be more fully explored.

" What we feel to be required and justified now is that the action I have mentioned should be taken without any delay, first, to assist the Czechoslovak State in what must be the crisis of its difficulties. The Chancellor of the Exchequer, on behalf of the Government, has addressed a letter to the Bank of England requesting the Bank to provide the necessary credit of £10,000,000 sterling, and when the House resumes its sittings in November Parliament will be asked to pass the necessary legislation to reimburse the Bank from the Exchequer.

" I pass from that subject, and I would like to say a few words in respect of the various other participants, besides ourselves, in the Munich Agreement. After everything that has been said about the German Chancellor to-day and in the past, I do feel that the House ought to recognise the difficulty for a man in that position to take back such emphatic declarations as he had already made amidst the enthusiastic cheers of his supporters, and to recognise that in consenting, even though it were only at the last moment, to discuss with the representatives of other Powers those things which he had declared he had already decided once for all, was a real and a substantial contribution on his part. With regard to Signor Mussolini, his contribution was certainly notable and perhaps decisive. It was on his suggestion that the final stages of mobilisation were postponed for twenty-four hours to give us an opportunity of discussing the situation, and I wish to say that at the Conference itself both he and the Italian Foreign Secretary, Count Ciano, were most helpful in the discussions. It was they who, very early in the proceedings, produced the Memorandum which M. Daladier and I were able to accept as a basis of discussion. I think that Europe and the world have reason to be grateful to the head of the Italian Government for his work in contributing to a peaceful solution.

" M. Daladier had in some respects the most difficult task of all four of us, because of the special relations uniting his country and Czechoslovakia, and I should like to say that his courage, his readiness to take responsibility, his pertinacity and his unfailing good humour were invaluable throughout the whole of our discussions. There is one other Power which was not represented at the Conference and which nevertheless we felt to be exercising a constantly increasing influence. I refer, of course, to the United States of America. Those messages of President Roosevelt, so firmly and yet so persuasively framed, showed how the voice of the most powerful nation in the world could make itself heard across 3000 miles of ocean and sway the minds of men in Europe.

" In my view the strongest force of all, one which grew and took fresh shapes and forms every day was the force not of any one individual, but was that unmistakable sense of unanimity among the peoples of the world that war somehow must be averted. The peoples of the British Empire were at one with those of Germany, of France and of Italy, and their anxiety, their intense desire for peace, pervaded the whole atmosphere of the conference, and I believe that that, and not threats, made possible the concessions that were made. I know the House will want to hear what I am sure it does not doubt, that throughout these discussions the Dominions, the Governments of the Dominions, have been kept in the closest touch with the march of events by telegraph and by personal contact, and I would like to say how greatly I was encouraged on each of the journeys I made to Germany by the knowledge that I went with the good wishes of the Governments of the Dominions. They shared all our anxieties and all our hopes. They rejoiced with us that peace was preserved, and with us they look forward to further efforts to consolidate what has been done.

" Ever since I assumed my present office my main purpose has been to work for the pacification of Europe, for the removal of those suspicions and those animosities which have so long poisoned the air. The path which leads to appeasement is long and bristles with obstacles. The question of Czechoslovakia is the latest and perhaps the most dangerous. Now that we have got past it, I feel that it may be possible to make further progress along the road to sanity.

"My right hon. Friend has alluded in somewhat bitter terms to my conversation last Friday morning with Herr Hitler. I do not know why that conversation should give rise to suspicion, still less to criticism. I entered into no pact. I made no new commitments. There is no secret understanding. Our conversation was hostile to no other nation. The objects of that conversation, for which I asked, was to try to extend a little further the personal contact which I had established with Herr Hitler and which I believe to be essential in modern diplomacy. We had a friendly and entirely non-committal conversation, carried on, on my part, largely with a view to seeing whether there could be points in common between the head of a democratic Government and the ruler of a totalitarian State. We see the result in the declaration which has been published, in which my right hon. Friend (Mr. Duff Cooper) finds so much ground for suspicion. What does it say?

"There are three paragraphs. The first says that we agree

"'in recognising that the question of Anglo-German relations is of the first importance for the two countries and for Europe.'

Does anyone deny that? The second is an expression of opinion only. It says that:

"'We regard the agreement signed last night and the Anglo-German Naval Agreement as symbolic of the desire of the two peoples never to go to war with one another again.'

Once more I ask, does anyone doubt that that is the desire of the two peoples? What is the last paragraph?

"'We are resolved that the method of consultation shall be the method adopted to deal with any other questions that may concern our two countries, and we are determined to continue our efforts to remove possible sources of difference and thus to contribute to assure the peace of Europe.'

Who will stand up and condemn that sentence?

I believe there are many who will feel with me that such a declaration, signed by the German Chancellor and myself, is something more than a pious expression of opinion. In our relations with other countries everything depends upon there being sincerity and good will on both sides. I believe that there is sincerity and good will on both sides in this declaration. That is why to me its significance goes far beyond its actual words. If there is one lesson which we should learn from the events of these last weeks it is this, that lasting peace is not to be obtained by sitting still and waiting for it to come. It requires active, positive efforts to achieve it. No doubt I shall have plenty of critics who will say that I am guilty of facile optimism, and that I should disbelieve every word that is uttered by rulers of other great States in Europe. I am too much of a realist to believe that we are going to achieve our paradise in a day. We have only laid the foundations of peace. The superstructure is not even begun.

"For a long period now we have been engaged in this country in a great programme of rearmament, which is daily increasing in pace and in volume. Let no one think that because we have signed this agreement between these four Powers at Munich we can afford to relax our efforts in regard to that programme at this moment. Disarmament on the part of this country can never be unilateral again. We have tried that once, and we very nearly brought ourselves to disaster. If disarmament is to come it must come by steps, and it must come by the agreement and the active co-operation of other countries. Until we know that we have obtained that co-operation and until we have agreed upon the actual steps to be taken, we here must remain on guard.

"When, only a little while ago, we had to call upon the people of this country to begin to take those steps which would be necessary if the emergency should come upon us, we saw the magnificent spirit that was displayed. The Naval Reservists, the Territorial Army, the Auxiliary Air Force, the Observers' Corps, obeyed the summons to mobilise very readily. We must remember that most of these men gave up their peace time work at a moment's notice to serve their country. We should like to thank them. We should like to thank also the employers who accepted the inevitable inconvenience of mobilisation. I know that they will show the same spirit of patriotic co-operation in taking back all their former employés when they are demobilised. I know that, although the crisis has passed, they will feel proud that they are employing men upon whom the State can rely if a crisis should return.

" While we must renew our determination to fill up the deficiencies that yet remain in our armaments and in our defensive precautions, so that we may be ready to defend ourselves and make our diplomacy effective—(Interruption)—yes I am a realist—nevertheless I say with an equal sense of reality that I do see fresh opportunities of approaching this subject of disarmament opening up before us, and I believe that they are at least as hopeful to-day as they have been at any previous time. It is to such tasks—the winning back of confidence, the gradual removal of hostility between nations until they feel that they can safely discard their weapons, one by one, that I would wish to devote what energy and time may be left to me before I hand over my office to younger men."

In the Debate that followed, the Opposition Socialists and Liberals, who had remained silent during the suspense of the previous week when war was threatening, showed that they had recovered their former fighting spirit. Mr. Attlee declared that the Munich Agreement constituted "one of the greatest diplomatic defeats this country and France have ever sustained," and that the Prime Minister had brought his country into great danger and great anxiety and run the ship of State ashore. Sir Archibald Sinclair said : " We have not only given Sudetenland to Germany, but we have restored Germany to Herr Hitler and Italy to Signor Mussolini. Confronted by his " (Hitler's) " ruthless determination and military power, the Prime Minister wilted, and justice and respect for treaties, and even negotiations were cast to the winds." Mr. Dalton said that the Prime Minister " was unduly hustled, intimidated and out-manœuvred by Herr Hitler." The Socialist Party tabled an Amendment to the effect that the Government's policy had led to "the humiliation of our country and its exposure to grave dangers," and demanded a world conference. Mr. Noel-Baker, *in deploring the loss to our defences* " *of* 1,000,000 *Czechoslovak soldiers,* 1000 *Czechoslovak aircraft,* 3000 *modern Russian aircraft,* 2000 *Russian tanks and a vast Russian mechanised army,*" *went so far as to say that the Pact the Prime Minister had signed with Herr Hitler had* " *committed us never to take part in any collective action against aggression again.*" *At the end of a four-days' Debate, on* 6*th October, Mr. Chamberlain replied for the Government.*

" The Leader of the Opposition remarked a few minutes ago that in his view the four days which have been occupied in these discussions have been fully justified. Although I confess that I did not share his view before the Debate began, that three days was too little, I must say, having listened to a great part of it, that I feel inclined to agree with him and to say that it was worth while to carry on our discussion for another day, if only for this reason. It seems to me that as the Debate has progressed, so has the general tone of it tended to leave more passionate aspects and more partisan aspects of the problems on one side and to approach a more serious and more thoughtful review of the situation. There is a great contrast between the speech to which we have just listened and some of the speeches from the Front Opposition Bench to which we listened only a day or two ago. I suppose that, in discussing recent events in which I have taken a prominent part, it was inevitable that the speeches should take a somewhat personal tone, and, indeed, I do not remember a Debate in which there were so many allusions to a single Minister, some of them complimentary—for which I am sincerely grateful—and some of them which could not be described by that name. I have been charged with cowardice, with weakness, with presumption, and with stupidity. I have been accused of bringing the country to the edge of war, and I have been denied the merit of having snatched it back to safety.

"It seems to me that some of those who threw these accusations across the Floor of the House have very quickly forgotten the conditions of last week, and the thoughts and the emotions which then filled our minds and hearts. Anybody who had been through what I had to go through day after day, face to face with the thought that in the last resort it would have been I, and I alone, who would have to say that yes or no which would decide the fate of millions of my countrymen, of their wives, of their families—a man who had been through that could not readily forget. For that reason alone, I am not yet in a mood to try to see what I can do by way of retort. When a man gets to my age and fills my position, I think he tends to feel that criticism, even abuse, matters little to him if his conscience approves of his actions. Looking back on the events, I feel convinced that by my action—I seek no credit for my action ; I think it is only what anyone in my position would have felt it his duty to do—I say, by my action I did avert war. I feel perfectly sure that I was right in doing so.

" War to-day—this has been said before, and I say it again —is a different thing not only in degree, but in kind from what it used to be. We no longer think of war as it was in the days of Marlborough or the days of Napoleon or even in the days of 1914. When war starts to-day, in the very first hour, before any professional soldier, sailor or airman has been touched, it will strike the workman, the clerk, the man-in-the-street or in the 'bus, and his wife and children in their homes. As I listened, I could not help being moved, as I am sure everybody was who heard the hon. Member for Bridgeton (Mr. Maxton) when he began to paint the picture which he himself had seen and realised what it would mean in war—people burrowing underground, trying to escape from poison gas, knowing that at any hour of the day or night death or mutilation was ready to come upon them. Remembering that the dread of what might happen to them or to those dear to them might remain with fathers and mothers for year after year—when you think of these things you cannot ask people to accept a prospect of that kind ; you cannot force them into a position that they have got to accept it ; unless you feel yourself, and can make them feel, that the cause for which they are going to fight is a vital cause—a cause that transcends all the human values, a cause to which you can point, if some day you win the victory, and say, ' That cause is safe.'

" Since I first went to Berchtesgaden more than 20,000 letters and telegrams have come to No. 10, Downing Street.

L

Of course, I have only been able to look at a tiny fraction of them, but I have seen enough to know that the people who wrote did not feel that they had such a cause for which to fight, if they were asked to go to war in order that the Sudeten Germans might not join the Reich. That is how they are feeling. That is my answer to those who say that we should have told Germany weeks ago that, if her army crossed the border of Czechoslovakia, we should be at war with her. We had no treaty obligations and no legal obligations to Czechoslovakia and if we had said that, we feel that we should have received no support from the people of this country.

" There is something else which I fancy hon. Members are a little too apt to forget. They often speak of the British Empire. Do they always remember how deeply and how vitally the great self-governing nations of the British Empire are affected by the issues of peace and war ? You may say that we are the country that is directly affected in such a case as that which we are considering, but must not the very loyalty of the Dominions to the Empire, their consciousness of their sympathy, make them feel that where the mother country stands they would wish to stand, too. They have a right to be brought into consultation before we take a step which may have incalculable consequences for them. Although it is not for me to speak for them, I say that it would have been difficult to convince them that we should have been justified in giving such an assurance as has been suggested.

" I am told that if you were not prepared to put the issue of peace and war out of the hands of this country and into someone else's hands in that way, you should have told Czechoslovakia long ago that in no circumstances would you help her and that she had better make the best terms she could with the Sudetens or with Germany. Was the issue as simple as that ? Consider France, who was under Treaty obligations to Czechoslovakia to go to her assistance by virtue of her Treaty. Were we to say that we would not go to the assistance of France if in consequence she became involved in conflict with Germany ? If so, we should have been false to our own obligations. Therefore, it would not have been enough for us to tell Czechoslovakia that we would have nothing to do with her and that she must make the best terms she could. It would have been necessary for France also to say that. Is anybody prepared to suggest that France, who was bound by solemn treaty to give aid and assistance to Czechoslovakia if she was the subject of unprovoked aggression, should repudiate this obligation beforehand? I would not have cared to have been the one who made such a suggestion to a French Minister.

" It was impossible for us to take either of these courses, either to say that we would stand by Czechoslovakia if she were attacked, or to say that in no circumstances would we be involved if she were attacked and other countries were involved. What we did do, and it was the only course we could take, was twofold. We advised the Czech Government repeatedly to come to terms with the Sudeten Germans, and when Germany mobilised we uttered no threats, but we did utter a warning. We warned her again and again that if as a consequence of her obligations France was engaged in active hostilities against Germany we were bound to support her. When we were convinced, as we became convinced, that nothing any longer would keep the Sudetenland within the Czechoslovakian State, we urged the Czech Government as strongly as we could to agree to the cession of territory, and to agree promptly. The Czech Government, through the wisdom and courage of President Benes, accepted the advice of the French Government and ourselves. It was a hard decision for anyone who loved his country to take, but to accuse us of having by that advice betrayed the Czechoslovakian State is simply preposterous. What we did was to save her from annihilation and give her a chance of new life as a new State, which involves the loss of territory and fortifications, but may perhaps enable her to enjoy in the future and develop a national existence under a neutrality and security comparable to that which we see in Switzerland to-day. Therefore, I think the Government deserve the approval of this House for their conduct of affairs in this recent crisis which has saved Czechoslovakia from destruction and Europe from Armageddon.

" That is all I want to say of the past. I come to the present and the future. First of all I want to say a word or two about some allusions which have been made, I understand, to

rumours current in a portion of the Press that it is intended
to have a General Election at an early date. It is evident
that some hon. Members do not desire a General Election;
they are anxious, and, if I may say so, suspicious of my
intentions. It is not usual for a Prime Minister to give long
notice of the date when he proposes that a General Election
should take place, but on this occasion I will say this. I do
not want a General Election now, although I cannot agree
with my right hon. Friend, if I may still call him so, the
Member for Epping (Mr. Churchill)——"

MR. CHURCHILL : " If I am not unworthy."

THE PRIME MINISTER : "——that it would be consti-
tutionally indecent; but I have two reasons why I should
prefer not to have a General Election now. One is that that
feeling of relief and thankfulness, which everyone knows has
been so conspicuous, goes far beyond the reach of any party.
I do not at all want to capitalise a feeling of that kind for the
sake of obtaining some temporary party advantage. The
second reason is this. Hon. Members may have noticed the
tendency of a General Election to magnify differences. It is
possible that we may want great efforts from the nation in the
months that are to come, and if that be so, the smaller our
differences the better. There are only two conditions which
I can see that would lead me to change my mind. One is if
some new issue arose which I felt required a new mandate
from the country, and the other would be, of course, if I felt
that I had lost the confidence of my supporters. Neither
condition has arisen yet. I have no reason to suppose that
either will arise.

" As regards future policy, it seems to me that there are
really only two possible alternatives. One of them is to base
yourself upon the view that any sort of friendly relations, or
possible relations, shall I say, with totalitarian States are
impossible, that the assurances which have been given to me
personally are worthless, that they have sinister designs and
that they are bent upon the domination of Europe and the
gradual destruction of democracies. Of course, on that
hypothesis, war has got to come, and that is the view—a
perfectly intelligible view—of a certain number of hon. and
right hon. Gentlemen in this House. I am not sure that it is

not the view of some Members of the party opposite. [An HON MEMBER : ' Yes.'] Not all of them. They certainly have never put it in so many words, but it is illustrated by the observations of the hon. Member for Derby (Mr. Noel-Baker), who spoke this afternoon, and who had examined the Agreement signed by the German Chancellor and myself, which he described as a pact designed by Herr Hitler to induce us to relinquish our present obligations. That shows how far prejudice can carry a man. The Agreement, as anyone can see, is not a pact at all. So far as the question of ' never going to war again ' is concerned, it is not even an expression of the opinion of the two who signed the paper, except that it is their opinion of the desire of their respective peoples. I do not know whether the hon. Member will believe me or attribute to me also sinister designs when I tell him that it was a document not drawn up by Herr Hitler but by the humble individual who now addresses this House.

" If the view which I have been describing is the one to be taken, I think we must inevitably proceed to the next stage—that war is coming, broadly speaking the democracies against the totalitarian States—that certainly we must arm ourselves to the teeth, that clearly we must make military alliances with any other Powers whom we can get to work with us, and that we must hope that we shall be allowed to start the war at the moment that suits us and not at the moment that suits the other side. That is what some right hon. and hon. Gentlemen call collective security. Some hon. Members opposite would walk into any trap if it is only baited with a familiar catchword and they do it when this system is called collective security. But that is not the collective security we are thinking of or did think of when talking about the system of the League of Nations. That was a sort of universal collective security in which all nations were to take their part. This plan may give you security ; it certainly is not collective in any sense. It appears to me to contain all the things which the party opposite used to denounce before the War—entangling alliances, balance of power and power politics. If I reject it, as I do, it is not because I give it a label ; it is because, to my mind, it is a policy of utter despair.

" If that is hon. Members' conviction, there is no future hope for civilisation or for any of the things that make life worth living. Does the experience of the Great War and of the years that followed it give us reasonable hope that if some new war started that would end war any more than the last one did ? No. I do not believe that war is inevitable. Someone put into my hand a remark made by the great Pitt about 1787, when he said :

" ' To suppose that any nation can be unalterably the enemy of another is weak and childish and has its foundations neither in the experience of nations nor in the history of man.'

It seems to me that the strongest argument against the inevitability of war is to be found in something that everyone has recognised or that has been recognised in every part of the House. That is the universal aversion from war of the people, their hatred of the notion of starting to kill one another again. This morning I received a letter not written to me, but written to a friend by a German professor. I cannot give his name, because I have not asked whether I might do so. I think it is typical of feeling in Germany, because I have heard the same from many other sources. I would like to repeat to the House one or two phrases from it. He writes :

" ' " Never again." That is the main idea, not only among the professors, but also among the students who did not share the experience of 1914, but heard enough about it. That is the idea of the rich and of the poor and even of the army themselves. As an officer of the Reserve I know what I am speaking about.'

" Later in the letter he says :

" ' Now peace has been secured, and not only for the moment. Now the end of the period of changes and treaties of 1918 can be foreseen and we all hope that a new era will begin in Anglo-German relations.'

What is the alternative to this bleak and barren policy of the inevitability of war ? In my view it is that we should seek by all means in our power to avoid war, by analysing possible causes, by trying to remove them, by discussion in a spirit of collaboration and good will. I cannot believe that such a pro-gramme would be rejected by the people of this country, even if it does mean the establishment of personal contact with dictators, and of talks man to man on the basis that each, while maintaining his own ideas of the internal government of his country, is willing to allow that other systems may suit better other peoples. The party opposite surely have the same idea in mind even if they put it in a different way. They want a world conference. Well, I have had some experience of conferences, and one thing I do feel certain of is that it is better to have no conference at all than a conference which is a failure. The corollary to that is that before you enter a con-ference you must have laid out very clearly the lines on which you are going to proceed, if you are at least to have in front of you a reasonable prospect that you may obtain success. I am not saying that a conference would not have its place in due course. But I say it is no use to call a conference of the world, including these totalitarian Powers, until you are sure that they are going to attend, and not only that they are going to attend, but that they are going to attend with the intention of aiding you in the policy on which you have set your heart.

" I am told that the policy which I have tried to describe is inconsistent with the continuance, and much more incon-sistent with the acceleration of our present programme of arms. I am asked how I can reconcile an appeal to the country to support the continuance of this programme with the words which I used when I came back from Munich the other day and spoke of my belief that we might have peace for our time. I hope hon. Members will not be disposed to read into words used in a moment of some emotion, after a long and exhausting day, after I had driven through miles of excited, enthusiastic, cheering people—I hope they will not read into those words more than they were intended to convey. I do indeed believe that we may yet secure peace for our time, but I never meant to suggest that we should do that by disarmament, until we can induce others to disarm too. Our past experience has shown us only too clearly that weakness in armed strength means weakness in diplomacy, and if we want to secure a lasting peace, I realise that diplomacy cannot be effective unless the consciousness exists, not here alone, but elsewhere, that behind the diplomacy is the strength to give effect to it.

" One good thing, at any rate, has come out of this emergency through which we have passed. It has thrown a vivid light upon our preparations for defence, on their strength and on their weakness. I should not think we were doing our duty if we had not already ordered that a prompt and thorough inquiry should be made to cover the whole of our preparations, military and civil, in order to see, in the light of what has happened during these hectic days, what further steps may be necessary to make good our deficiencies in the shortest possible time. There have been references in the course of the Debate to other measures which hon. Members have suggested should be taken. I would not like to commit myself now until I have had a little time for reflection, as to what further it may seem good to ask the nation to do, but I think nobody could fail to have been impressed by the fact that the emergency brought out that the whole of the people of this country, whatever their occupation, whatever their class, whatever their station, were ready to do their duty, however disagreeable, however hard, however dangerous it may have been.

" I cannot help feeling that if, after all, war had come upon us, the people of this country would have lost their spiritual faith altogether. As it turned out the other way, I think we have all seen something like a new spiritual revival, and I know that everywhere there is a strong desire among the people to record their readiness to serve their country, wherever or however their services could be most useful. I would like to take advantage of that strong feeling if it is possible, and although I must frankly say that at this moment I do not myself clearly see my way to any particular scheme, yet I want also to say that I am ready to consider any suggestion that may be made to me, in a very sympathetic spirit.

" Finally, I would like to repeat what my right hon. Friend the Chancellor of the Exchequer (Sir John Simon) said yesterday in his great speech. Our policy of appeasement does not mean that we are going to seek new friends at the expense of old ones, or, indeed, at the expense of any other nations at all. I do not think that at any time there has been a more complete identity of views between the French Government and ourselves than there is at the present time. Their objective is the same as ours—to obtain the collaboration of all nations, not excluding the totalitarian States, in building up a lasting peace for Europe. That seems to me to be a policy which would answer my hon. Friends' appeal, a policy which should command the support of all who believe in the power of human will to control human destiny. If we cannot here this afternoon emulate the patriotic unanimity of the French Chamber, this House can by a decisive majority show its approval of the Government's determination to pursue it."

NO DESIRE FOR ENCIRCLEMENT

During the weeks that followed the Opposition speakers kept up an increasingly bitter campaign against the policy that had averted war in September. In a debate on 1st November on the International Situation, Mr. Attlee attacked the Government for the Munich Agreement, for its general policy, for its lack of military preparations and for its failure to defend the economic interests of the country. The Prime Minister again replied.

" I DO not offer any apologies for intervening at this stage of the Debate because I think it would be for the general convenience of the House if I say what I have to say at as early a stage as possible. The speech of the right hon. Gentleman (Mr. Attlee) was divided into two very well marked parts, the second of which appeared to me to have very little relation to international affairs and to be rather more suitable for an election platform than for the Debate that we are conducting this afternoon. I do not propose to reply to that part of the right hon. Gentleman's speech which, perhaps, had better be dealt with by my right hon. Friend the President of the Board of Trade (Mr. Oliver Stanley) who will be speaking later in the evening. There is, however, one question he addressed to me which I would like to answer at once. He asked me whether it were true that, as reported in the *Daily Herald*, instructions had been sent out from Whitehall to all the Departments dealing with social services to cut down their expenditure in order to pay for armaments. I read the statement in the *Daily Herald* this morning, and it was the first I had heard of it. I have asked my right hon. Friend the Chancellor of the Exchequer whether there was any action which had been taken by the Treasury which might provide the slightest justifiable foundation for such a statement. He informs me that no action of any kind like that suggested has been taken by the Treasury. The whole story, therefore, is entirely an invention.

" To return to the first part of the right hon. Gentleman's speech. He asked a number of questions and made a number of comments upon what he considered to be the consequences of the Munich Agreement. I find myself in agreement with a number of observations made by the right hon. Gentleman, but there was one statement with which he began, to which I must take exception. He described the Munich Agreement as a great defeat for this country and for France and to the cause of law and order. If the right hon. Gentleman really believes that, I am sorry that he should say so publicly. It is not one of the characteristics of totalitarian States, at any rate, that they are accustomed to foul their own nests. I do strongly deprecate all the statements made by persons in responsible, or even in irresponsible positions, who take opportunities of broadcasting to the world or in other countries in particular that their own country is in a state of decadence."

MR. ATTLEE : " I never suggested that."

THE PRIME MINISTER : " I was not referring to the right hon. Gentleman in what I said then." (Interruption.)

MR. SPEAKER : " If the hon. Member for West Fife (Mr. Gallacher) continues to interrupt I shall have to ask him to leave the House."

THE PRIME MINISTER : " Others have gone a great deal further than the right hon. Gentleman, but the observation which he has made gave me an opportunity of expressing an opinion which I think is very widely held. I do not regard the Munich Agreement as a defeat either for the democracies or for the cause of law and order. On the contrary, the Munich Agreement was an attempt to carry out by discussion between two Powers representing democracies and two Powers representing totalitarian States an agreed solution of a problem for which the only other solution appeared to be the use of force. Instead of using force the Agreement has been carried out in an orderly manner. It is quite true that there have been many things which none of us would approve of, which all of us would wish to have done differently—that is quite true—but hon. Members should consider that, as my Noble Friend the Foreign Secretary (Lord Halifax) said on another occasion, we had to choose between hard alternatives, and when you find fault, as you may justly find fault, with the solution which has in fact been carried out, do not forget what the alternative was and what the effect of the alternative would have been upon Czechoslovakia."

MR. ATTLEE : " The right hon. Gentleman says that the solution has been carried out. The whole of my point was that the solution was not carried out."

THE PRIME MINISTER : " That may have been the whole of the right hon. Gentleman's point, but I hope I shall be able to say something which will refute that point of view. After all, the Munich Agreement, which was come to in the course of a comparatively short time, measured by hours, could not be expected to deal in itself with every detail of the operation which was contemplated. All that we could do at Munich was to lay down certain general outlines, leaving to an International Commission the task of filling in details. The right hon. Gentleman (Mr. Attlee) criticises the International Commission in the carrying out of that task. I say again that though we may not like the solution I would ask the right hon. Gentleman not to forget what the alternative was, and if he was not prepared to accept the alternative use of force—[An HON. MEMBER: 'Why not?']—we must recognise that we had to accept the alternative, disagreeable though it may be in many respects.

"The right hon. Gentleman spoke among other things about the boundaries which are to be laid down between the new State of Czechoslovakia and Germany. By the fourth Article of the Munich Agreement there was imposed on the International Commission the duty of determining the extent of the territories outside the four zones which were to be occupied by German troops by 7th October—territories outside those which, being preponderantly German in 1918, should be occupied by Germany by 10th October. The time was short, and the International Commission decided that in order to ascertain the limits of that territory they must get as near as they could to the position in 1918. That was in accordance with the methods under the plebiscite in the Saar district. The right hon. Gentleman says that they went back much further than 1918, that they went back to 1910, and that no justification has ever been given for going back to a period so long ago as that. I do not know that there has been any opportunity on any previous occasion of giving that justification, but, of course, the answer is very simple. There was no census in 1918, and as there were no reliable figures for that date the International Commission were obliged to go back to the last date for which there were reliable figures, and that was 1910. That was the reason why the census of 1910 was taken as a basis."

SIR ARCHIBALD SINCLAIR: "Why were they obliged to go back to that time and not to take later figures?"

MR. HERBERT MORRISON : " Has there been no census since 1910 ? "

MR. CHAMBERLAIN : " The reason was because the position in 1918 was to be taken as the basis, the argument being—I am not saying this is my view, I am only explaining the position —that the position had been deliberately changed since 1918 by the introduction of Czechs into areas which in 1918 were predominantly German, and therefore if a census had been taken later than 1918 it would not have met that particular objection. Once the Czechoslovakian Government had accepted that decision of the International Commission, which they did on 13th October, it became apparent that there was no longer any need for plebiscites. The Czechs agreed that the lines which had been determined in accordance with that basis should be the provisional frontier, but that it should be subject to examination and modification not only in accordance with strictly ethnographical lines but also taking into account the economic considerations, and it will be observed that in consequence of that agreement the line may be modified not only in those areas in which, under the original Agreement, there would have been a plebiscite, but the whole line from one end to the other may be reconsidered. As it had been decided not to have any plebiscite there was, of course, no occasion for any international force to occupy the plebiscite areas, and therefore His Majesty's Government were not able to avail themselves of the very public-spirited offer which had been made by the British Legion for this purpose. I should like, on behalf of the Government, to express our very warm appreciation of the offer and our confidence that had the need materialised members of the British Legion would have distinguished themselves as much in peace as they formerly did in war.

" Another point to which the right hon. Gentleman addressed himself referred to the rights of optants. He said the clause referring to optants was entirely illusory. I do not know by what right he said that. I do not know whether he is aware of the present position. Under Article 7 of the Munich Agreement it is provided that a German-Czech Commission was to settle the details of this right of option. They were to determine ways of facilitating the transfer of those individuals who wished to exercise the right, and also any question of principle which arose out of the transfer. This is a subject of considerable magnitude, because we are informed that there are something like 580,000 Czechs now in German territory and something like 250,000 Germans in Czech territory. That is a matter which is left to this German-Czech Commission, and they have not yet, I understand, formulated any conclusions, but when they do they will bring them to the notice of the International Commission.

" Then I come to the question of the refugees. Here, at any rate, I do not think I need quarrel with the right hon. Gentleman. All of us, I think, are at one in approaching this problem of the refugees with a very sincere sympathy, not only on account of the ordinary humanitarian principles which are common to everybody but because it has always been a tradition of British policy to offer asylum, as far as possible, to persons who, on account of racial or political or religious reasons were not able any longer to live in their own country. At the beginning of October it was represented to the Government that there were in Czechoslovakia a certain number of individuals who were in danger if they remained where they were, and accordingly we authorised the temporary admission to this country of those individuals up to the number of 350, on the undertaking, given to us, that means would be found to maintain these individuals, if necessary, during their stay here."

Miss Rathbone : " Why only 350 ? "

The Prime Minister : " Permission to enter was given only to the actual individual in danger and not to his family, but the Government are willing to admit the families of those individuals also if similar undertakings about their maintenance are provided. I agree with the right hon. Gentleman in the welcome which he paid to the initiative of the Lord Mayor of London in issuing an appeal for the relief of refugees. As he said, a considerable sum of money has been raised, and the Government are giving all the assistance they can to the Lord Mayor and to his representatives in Prague ; and we have given similar assistance to other British subjects who have interested themselves in the evacuation or the relief of refugees. The House will remember that we have placed at the disposal of the Czechoslovakian Government a sum of £10,000,000 for their urgent needs. We told them, when we announced this decision to them, that we had particularly in mind the demands which they would have to meet in respect of the maintenance and settlement of refugees from the transferred areas, and we expressed the view that if it were thought necessary for some of those refugees to emigrate, their transfer elsewhere should be assisted by the Czechoslovakian Government by funds derived from this £10,000,000.

" With regard to the guaranteed loan out of which this £10,000,000 will be repaid, that is a matter which we shall have to lay before Parliament in due course. We have not yet got sufficient information as to the necessary details, nor have we yet been able to ascertain what is likely to be the attitude of the French Government in joining with us in a loan of this kind. Therefore, we are not in a position to carry the matter any further at this moment, but in due course we shall have to lay before the House the proposals we shall have to make. In the meantime, we have been informed by the Czechoslovak Government that they would welcome any arrangement by which we could be informed of the methods and the progress of expenditure out of those funds. We at once appointed as our liaison officer in Prague Mr. R. J. Stopford, who was a member of the Runciman Commission, to obtain such information as may be available from time to time as to the number and types of refugees in Czechoslovakia and the conditions in which those who might have to emigrate might be enabled to do so.

" I think that the right hon. Gentleman (Mr. Attlee) rightly pointed out that we are here in the presence of a comparatively new problem which goes much beyond that of the Czechoslovak refugees. We are face to face with the difficulty that more and more persons are to-day finding themselves Stateless. They are being driven out of the countries in which they had settled, and other countries have not shown any great willingness to take them in. The inter-governmental committee, over which my right hon. Friend the Chancellor of the Duchy of Lancaster (Lord Winterton) presides, has the duty of dealing with this question and has made it clear that involuntary emigrants of German origin, whose emigration has arisen out of the transfer of Sudetenland, will be put in the same position as other involuntary emigrants from Germany with whom the committee is already concerned. As to whether it may be possible in the future to initiate a project of the dimensions which the right hon. Gentleman fore-shadowed, that is evidently a matter with which I could not deal here. It is not one for this country alone. This is not a country which has the area or the opportunity for settling a large number of emigrants. The question concerns the world as a whole. I am sure that we shall all join in hoping that a solution may be found which will mitigate the sufferings of these unfortunate people. The right hon. Gentleman drew a gloomy picture of what might be called the economic consequences of the Munich Agreement, and he suggested that there was some sinister political motive behind the economic activities of Dr. Funk."

MR. DALTON: " Has not the right hon. Gentleman for-gotten that my right hon. Friend asked him to make a state-ment as to the guarantees of the new Czechoslovakian frontier ? "

THE PRIME MINISTER: " I am very much obliged to the hon. Gentleman. I had forgotten the question, but, as a matter of fact, I have a note to come back to the question later on ; but I will deal with it at once and say that I am not yet in a position to add anything, on the subject of guarantees, to what has already been said by my right hon. Friend the Minister for the Co-ordination of Defence. The position remains exactly the same and it cannot be cleared up until the whole question of minorities in Czechoslovakia has been settled. The House will remember that it was stated that Germany and Italy would be ready to enter into a guarantee on the question of Czechoslovakia when the question of minorities had been settled. Our original offer was to enter into an international guarantee, but what the terms of that guarantee will be and who will be the partakers in that guaran-tee is not a question on which I can give the House any further information to-day. Of course, before anything were settled, the terms of such a guarantee and the names of those who are taking part in it would be brought before this House."

MR. WEDGWOOD BENN: " In dealing with the frontiers

the right hon. Gentleman has not dealt with the Hungarian frontier. Many people are asking why we are to guarantee a frontier *vis-à-vis* Hungary in the determination of which we and the French are excluded."

THE PRIME MINISTER : " In speaking of a guaranteed frontier the right hon. Gentleman is mistaken. We never guaranteed the frontiers as they existed. What we did was to guarantee against unprovoked aggression—quite a different thing. That did not mean that we gave our seal to the existence of frontiers as they were then or at any other time. Our guarantee was against unprovoked aggression and not the crystallisation of frontiers. The right hon. Gentleman alternates between violent indignation and insuppressible amusement, but I do not think that my answer could give rise to either of those expressions.

" I was dealing with the economic consequences of Dr. Funk's activities. Again, I am sorry that the right hon. Gentleman thought it necessary to suggest that the activities of Dr. Funk, who is the Minister concerned with economic questions, should be concealing some political motive. It is this attitude of constant suspicion—nothing can be done by anybody but what somebody or other finds concealed in it something sinister or evil—which is very largely the cause of the want of confidence existing in Europe to-day. What, taking an economic view, is the position of Germany in relation to the States of Central and South-Eastern Europe ? Geographically, she must occupy a dominating position there. She does now. As a matter of fact, in so far as those States are agricultural in character, the nature of the trade between them and Germany is complementary. They can supply Germany with raw materials and foodstuffs in return for articles of manufacture which Germany is so well fitted to supply, but I do not see any reason why we should expect that a fundamental change is likely to take place in those regions. So far as Czecho-slovakia is concerned, the industries in the ceded regions were industries mainly exporting in character, and they suffered a good deal in competition from Germany. It is quite true that she has ceded also valuable supplies of raw materials, such as coal, lignite, and timber, but so long as she is able to import those raw materials, there is no reason, so far as I can see, why her industrial position should be worsened. Exchanges of goods over the frontier between Germany and Czechoslovakia are likely to be mutually beneficial. I do not imagine that there will be difficulty put in the way of importing raw materials."

MR. E. J. WILLIAMS: "Will it not affect the coal trade in this country?"

THE PRIME MINISTER: "I am talking of the industrial position of Czechoslovakia. So far as this country is concerned, we have no wish to block Germany out from those countries or to encircle her economically. It is true that we have certain trade interests there ourselves, and of course, we mean to maintain those trade interests; and indeed, in that respect, we shall have the good will of the countries themselves. Although, as I have said, their natural market is to be found chiefly in Germany, nevertheless, they can, as a rule, only obtain payment from Germany either in the form of goods—a barter arrangement—or in the form of blocked marks. That does not suit them. They want free currency so that they may import other materials and things which they cannot get in Germany. Therefore, they do desire at least a certain proportion of their trade to be done with other countries, and for that reason we shall have their assistance and good will in our efforts to maintain our trade.

Do not let us suppose that there necessarily must be economic warfare between Germany and ourselves. There must be some competition. Competition is a thing that we thrived on in the past. It is not in our interest to see any part of the world remain poor. If by means of international trade between Germany and these countries the economic position of these countries is improved, you may be quite certain that we shall get our share of the trade. They may not buy exactly the same things from us as they buy from Germany, but they will buy from us those articles which we are most fitted to supply. I finish what I have to say on this subject by the general observation that, in my view, there is room both for Germany and for us in trade with those countries and that neither of us ought to try to obtain exclusive possession of their markets.

With regard to the other minorities, the right hon. Gentleman (Mr. Attlee) appeared to indicate that it was very wrong that any further encroachment should be made upon the territory of Czechoslovakia. Surely that is not a position that we can take up. What we are doing now, as was pointed out by my Noble Friend the Foreign Secretary, is witnessing the readjustment of frontiers laid down in the Treaty of Versailles. I do not know whether the people who were responsible for those frontiers thought they would remain permanently as they were laid down. I doubt very much whether they did. They probably expected that from time to time the frontiers would have to be adjusted. It is impossible to conceive that those people would be such supermen as to be able to see what would be the right frontiers for all time. The question is not whether those frontiers should be readjusted from time to time but whether they should be readjusted by negotiation and discussion, or be readjusted by war. Readjustment is going on and, in the case of the Hungarian frontier, arbitration by Germany and Italy has been accepted by Czechoslovakia and Hungary for the final determination of the frontier between them. I think I have said enough about Czechoslovakia.

" I do not propose to talk about Spain, following the example of the right hon. Gentleman. As to China, I can only say that there again the right hon. Gentleman appears to me to be taking an unnecessarily gloomy view of the future. He spoke of China as one of the largest potential markets in the world. Potential—what does that mean? China cannot be developed into a real market without the influx of a great deal of capital, and the fact that so much capital is being destroyed during this war means that even more capital will have to be put into China in the future, when the war is over. Who is going to supply the capital? It is quite certain that it cannot be supplied by Japan. Therefore, when the right hon. Gentleman appears to contemplate a future in which Japan will have the monopoly of Chinese trade, and we shall be excluded from it altogether, I say that that is flying in the face of the facts. It is quite certain that, when the war is over and the reconstruction of China begins, she cannot possibly be reconstructed without some help from this country. (Interruption.) That is a matter for those who are asked to invest their money to consider at the time.

" I want to turn to another aspect of the consequences that flow, I will not say from the Munich Agreement, but from the events which led up to it. The House will remember that when I spoke last, on 6th October, I told hon. Members that I was proposing to make a thorough and complete review of our civil and military defences, in order to see what errors and deficiencies might have been revealed and to take the necessary steps to make them good. On the civil side that review has been made, and, of course, it has shown what, indeed, was well known before, that our preparations were far from complete. All the same, I am of opinion that, if they had been put to the test, they would have been shown to have worked a great deal better than many people seem to suppose from the accounts of the deficiencies which were in fact shown up. This country, sometimes, is rather slow to get to work, but, when it does get to work, it works in double quick time ; and the amount of work which was actually carried out, and efficiently carried out, during the crisis, is, I think, an indication that these air-raid precautions would not have been the complete and utter failure which some seem to think they would have been. I need not go further into that matter now, since it is to be the subject of a Vote of Censure, I understand, in a couple of days' time. What seems to me to be of much more interest to the general public than the question as to what blame should be attributed and where, is what is going to be done now, in order that there may be no cause for blame in the future. We had our warning ; we had some sort of rehearsal ; and we are in a position now to get a better picture of the whole situation than we were before. I think the House will probably like me to give them some short account of the measures by which we are proposing to deal with air-raid precautions in the future.

" We have come to the conclusion that the whole subject of air-raid precautions has assumed such gigantic proportions, and has developed such complexity, that the burden is really too great to be imposed upon the Home Office in addition to its ordinary duties. We want a separate Minister with special administrative and organising experience, who could devote his whole attention to this subject. Accordingly, I invited my right hon. Friend the Member for the Scottish Universities

(Sir J. Anderson) to undertake this task, and, as the House will be aware, his appointment as Lord Privy Seal has been approved by His Majesty the King. He will hold the office of Lord Privy Seal, but the duties of that office are not very onerous, and, in fact, this Minister will be the Minister of Civilian Defence. In that capacity he will have direct charge of air-raid precautions, and he will also be responsible, in consultation with the Departments concerned, for determining arrangements for national voluntary service.

" With reference to air-raid precautions, hon. Members will appreciate that a large number of Departments are concerned in this work, and that they must be responsible in an emergency for functions which have to be exercised through their existing organisation. We have the Home Office, dealing with, perhaps, the major part of the work, especially police work, as well as fire brigades, gas-masks and so forth. Then we have the Ministry of Health, which is in close touch with local authorities, and is also responsible for the medical services, including nursing and ambulance provision. Then there is the Board of Trade, which must be responsible for the storage and distribution of food, and, of course, for the distribution of shipping and the decision as to where shipping is to be embarked and disembarked. There is the Board of Education, which must marshal the children in case of evacuation; there is the Ministry of Transport, which has to provide that railways or other forms of transport shall be available to carry out evacuation; there is the Post Office, which is responsible for communications and for the repair of such things as telephone or telegraph services in case of damage; and finally, of course, there is the Ministry of Labour, which has to see that labour is available for all the services as it is wanted. These services in Scotland are, of course, under the Secretary of State for Scotland. The House will see, therefore, that, in addition to the Home Office and the Scottish Office, all these other Departments have to play their part, and it is necessary that their activities should be co-ordinated, so that each of them may know beforehand exactly what is going to be expected of it in an emergency. For that purpose we shall set up committees of the Ministers of these various Departments and also of the senior officials.

Over both these committees, for the time being at any rate, while the organisation is being perfected, my right hon. Friend the Minister for Civilian Defence will preside. These committees will be part of the organisation of the Committee of Imperial Defence, and their purpose will be to ensure a proper co-ordination between the civilian Services and the needs of the Defence Services."

MR. H. MORRISON: " Is it intended that the Lord Privy Seal shall be a member of the Committee of Imperial Defence?"

THE PRIME MINISTER: " Oh, yes, certainly. That is a brief outline of the arrangement, which can be further developed. I feel confident that this arrangement will produce the results we require in the shortest possible time."

MR. ATTLEE: " Will the Lord Privy Seal be the responsible Minister in charge, or will he be merely a co-ordinating Minister, running round and bringing other people together ? "

THE PRIME MINISTER: " He will be both ; he will be the responsible Minister in charge and also the co-ordinating Minister. With regard to national voluntary service, it will be one of the first duties of my right hon. Friend to examine, with his colleagues, what will be the best way of availing ourselves of the general desire on the part of the public to help the nation. While the House is already aware that we have no intention of imposing compulsion in any form, we are satisfied that it is both desirable and practicable to meet the needs of civilian defence by voluntary action, provided that that action is suitably guided and organised.

" With regard to the review of our military, naval, and air defences, the right hon. Gentleman has mentioned again to-day the question of a Ministry of Supply, which, he says, he and his friends have long demanded. We have considered once more whether the time had come when it would be useful and desirable to set up a Ministry of Supply. In forming a judgment on that question, it is necessary to think very clearly what a Ministry of Supply would be expected to do which is not already done by the Service Departments with the assistance of my right hon. Friend the Minister for the Co-ordination of Defence, whose title, of course, includes co-ordination of supply, and with the assistance also of my right hon. Friend the Minister of Labour. If a Minister of Supply

were appointed merely to take over the designing and con-
tracting staffs of the Defence Departments, without any
additional powers, I cannot resist the conclusion that the first
effect must be a dislocation to some extent of the existing
arrangements, and that must necessarily result, not in an
acceleration, but in a slowing down of the progress of our
armaments. If you are really to produce any substantial
result—and even then it would not come at once—you would
have to arm such a Minister with compulsory powers, with
powers of compulsion upon individual firms, and also upon
individual men and women. I venture to say that, while you
can easily persuade people to accept compulsion of that kind
in time of war, it is quite another thing to ask them to do so in
time of peace ; and it would be all the more difficult to obtain
agreement because those powers, if given now, would not
require to be exercised universally, but would have to be
exercised with discrimination. You would have to dis-
criminate between one firm and another, and between one
individual and another, and you would have to justify yourselves every time you proposed to put compulsion upon
Firm A instead of Firm B, or upon Ben Smith instead of
Tom Jones.

" It must be remembered that we are not to-day in the same
position as we were in 1914, in this respect : that we are not
now contemplating the equipment of an army on a continental
scale. Our requirements to-day are limited ; our difficulties
are chiefly concerned with the supply of certain classes of
specially skilled labour. I am not satisfied that in order to
obtain that supply of labour where we want it, or, alternatively, in order to put the work where that labour is—I am
not satisfied that it is necessary to introduce compulsion. I am
not satisfied that we cannot get what we want by voluntary
co-operation of employers and trade unionists. When we
have done everything that we can on voluntary lines, if we find
that we still cannot fill our requirements, then it will be time
enough to talk about a Ministry of Supply with compulsory
powers. But up to then I am convinced that the most satisfactory course is to perfect and accelerate the methods we have
been pursuing, and which have given a very large measure
of success."

MR. ATTLEE : " May I ask the right hon. Gentleman to bear in mind that those who advocate a Ministry of Supply do not accept for a moment the idea that it must have compulsory powers ? "

THE PRIME MINISTER : " I said that it must involve compulsory powers if it was to produce an appreciable effect. If the right hon. Gentleman does not accept that, perhaps he will say, when he again intervenes in the Debate, in what way it will produce an appreciable effect without compulsory powers. I have never yet been able to discover how it can be done. Generally, on the military side we have not yet completed the consideration of the review which we have made, but, as I stated in answer to a question, there will be an opportunity in the new Session of Parliament to have a full debate on this subject. I would like, however, to make two general observations on the subject now. The first is this. I want hon. Members to remember that our programme of rearmament is a five-year programme, and we are now only in the third year of that programme. To argue that because everything had not been completed in the third year the programme had broken down is to lose sight altogether of the fact that it was never intended to be completed in three years. I doubt whether it would have been possible, if we had endeavoured to do so at the beginning of the programme, to squeeze a five-year programme into three years. But, to conclude, our review does bring up the special urgency of certain parts of that programme and the necessity for reinforcement of certain weak spots, which, if they were allowed to continue, might jeopardise the effectiveness of the whole system which we have built up. Therefore, we have to address ourselves to this point. The measures which it will be necessary to take will undoubtedly add to the total cost of armaments as we had hitherto contemplated.

" That brings me to my second observation, which concerns the use which is to be made of these armaments. I tried on 5th October to give as clear an exposition as I could of the Government's policy ; but I regret to observe that since then doubts have been expressed in some quarters, both at home and abroad, as to whether this review, this bringing up to standard, of the scale of our armaments, is consistent with the peaceful professions which we are expressing at the same time. I do not know why any different standards should be applied to this country and to other countries in that respect. But I do repeat here categorically what I have so often said, that we have no aggressive intentions against Germany or any other country. Our sole concern is to see that this country and her Imperial communications are safe, and that we shall not be so weak relatively with other countries that our diplomacy cannot enter upon discussions upon an equal footing. There is nothing further from our minds than entry upon a new armaments race.

" In talking about the Munich results, it seems to me that the right hon. Gentleman (Mr. Attlee) forgot the last act at Munich, which, after all, is not the least important one. That declaration which was signed by Herr Hitler and myself, and in which we recorded our belief in the desire of our two peoples never to go to war with one another again, and expressed our own intention that the method of consultation should be the method adopted to deal with other questions which might concern us, and our intention also to continue our efforts to remove every possible source of difference— that declaration signed by us seems to have dropped out of sight lately. I myself feel that in that declaration, if it is properly and suitably followed up, lies the chance of a new era of peace in Europe. When I signed that document I meant what was in the document. I am convinced that Herr Hitler meant it too when he signed it ; and I am equally convinced that those views are the views of the majority of the people both in Germany and in this country. Let there be no mistake, let there be no doubts as to our policy and our intentions ; as to the desire, the firm determination, that there shall be no sitting still and waiting for peace to come, but that we must take firm and practical steps towards that end. The right hon. Gentleman asked whether we were to wait always until war threatened before we thought the time was ripe for discussion. No, Sir. That is the whole point of the policy which we are pursuing, that we should not wait. Too often delays have taken place in the past. We should not wait until a crisis becomes acute before we try to settle it, but we should try to consolidate the good will of the four Powers when they assembled at Munich, and we should endeavour to restore European confidence by the removal of fears and suspicions.

" The ultimate aim of this Government, as I believe it must be the ultimate aim of every Government, whatever its complexion may be, is the improvement of the standard of living of the people. It is difficult to reconcile that with the continued piling up of armaments. We should always have that in mind. What we are aiming at is, first, the limitation of armaments by agreement—for unilateral disarmament will help nobody—and, in the end, the practical abolition. That is looking very far ahead : I shall not see it ; but I do not see why we should not get the first stages of it if we pursue a consistent and persistent policy. We shall never get far unless we can accustom ourselves to the idea that the democracies and the totalitarian States are not to be ranged against one another in two opposing blocs, but that they can, if they choose, work together not merely for the settlement of differences after they have arisen, but also for the operation of a constructive programme, a programme which will facilitate the international exchange of goods and the regulation of international relations in various ways for the good of all. That is the policy which is sometimes called the policy of appeasement. That is the policy to which this Government intends whole-heartedly to devote itself."

A CONTRIBUTION TO GENERAL
APPEASEMENT

*On the following afternoon, Wednesday, 2nd November,
Mr. Chamberlain rose again in the Commons to move the
House's approval of the Government's intention to bring into
force the Anglo-Italian Agreement, concluded in the previous
April (see pp. 181-4). Since the Munich Agreement, following
a decision of the Spanish Government to disband the International Brigades—a decision not then actually implemented—
the Italians had withdrawn 10,000, or roughly half their remaining effective legionaries, from Spain. In view of this fact, as well
as of General Franco's declaration of neutrality during the
international crisis of September, the Government had come to
the conclusion that the Spanish Civil War no longer constituted
a menace to the peace of Europe and that, this preliminary
condition having been satisfied, the time had come to put the
long-delayed Anglo-Italian Agreement into force.*

"I BEG to move:

"'That this House welcomes the intention of His Majesty's Government to bring the Anglo-Italian Agreement into force.'

"Yesterday, in speaking of the Declaration signed at Munich by Herr Hitler and myself, I said I thought that if it were suitably followed up it might well be found to contain the seed which would ultimately develop into a new era of confidence and peace in Europe. Somewhat the same idea was expressed, in different language, by the right hon. Gentleman the Leader of the Opposition (Mr. Attlee) when he asked whether we must always wait for subjects of difference between nations to give rise to threats of war before we considered them ripe for peaceful discussion and negotiation. Since we made an Agreement with Italy on 16th April last, I am glad to think that there are no differences between our two countries [An Hon. Member: 'What about Spain?'] but it is clear that if the improvement in our relations which so markedly followed upon the conclusion of that Agreement is to be maintained, the delay in putting the Agreement into force, which had already lasted for more than six months, cannot be indefinitely prolonged.

"It is not necessary for me this afternoon to discuss the merits of the Agreement itself. The terms of the Agreement were debated in this House last May, and on the 2nd of that month, a Motion, which was moved by me, of approval of the Agreement was carried by a large majority. Of course, I am well aware that the Opposition resisted the Motion then, and naturally I do not expect them to have changed their views, but the question we have to consider to-day is not whether this is a good Agreement or not. That has already been settled as far as this House is concerned. The question we have to consider is whether the time has now come to put it into force, and whether the preliminary condition which I laid down as essential before the Agreement could be put into force has now been fulfilled. The House will remember very well what that condition was. It was that we should be able to consider that the Spanish question was settled, and I explained last July why we had thought it necessary to make that condition. I said then that in our view the justification for the formal recognition of Italian sovereignty over Ethiopia was to be found if we could feel that that recognition would constitute an important advance towards the general appeasement of Europe, and it was because we felt at that time that the conflict which was going on in Spain under the then existing conditions did constitute a perpetual menace to the peace of Europe that we felt that it must be removed from that category before we could ask Parliament to agree to the Agreement being put into force.

" Since that time a good many efforts have been made by various Members of the Opposition to get me to say exactly what I meant by a settlement in Spain. I have always refused to give any such definition, not because I wanted to evade any proper duty which fell upon me, but because I did not feel that I could give such a definition in the absence of more knowledge than I possessed of what might be the future developments in the Spanish situation. But perhaps hon. Members may recollect that on 26th July last, in answer to an interruption by the Leader of the Opposition relating to the withdrawal of volunteers from Spain, I used these words :

" ' I would like to see what happens when the volunteers are withdrawn. If His Majesty's Government think that Spain has ceased to be a menace to the peace of Europe, I think we shall regard that as a settlement of the Spanish question.'—[OFFICIAL REPORT, 26th July, 1938; col. 2965, Vol. 338.]

Since then a great deal has happened. Already, even at that date, all the Powers represented on the Non-Intervention Committee, including Italy, of course, had accepted the British plan for the withdrawal of volunteers, and if that plan is not in operation to-day, it cannot be said that that is the fault of Italy. (Interruption.) It cannot properly be said. Again, since then the Spanish Government have announced their intention of withdrawing the International Brigade. [An Hon. Member: 'They have done it!'] When I was at Munich, Signor Mussolini volunteered me the information that he intended to withdraw 10,000 men, or about half the Italian infantry forces, from Spain, and since then those men have in fact been withdrawn.

"I have no doubt that hon. Members will represent that Italian men, pilots, aircraft and other material still remain in Spain, and so also there remain men and material of other than Italian nationality in Spain on one side or the other; but we have received from Signor Mussolini definite assurances, first of all that the remaining Italian forces of all categories will be withdrawn when the non-intervention plan comes into operation; secondly, that no further Italian troops will be sent to Spain; and thirdly—in case this idea had occurred to anybody—that the Italian Government have never for a moment entertained the idea of sending compensatory air forces to Spain in lieu of the infantry forces which have now been withdrawn. These three assurances, taken in conjunction with the actual withdrawal of this large body of men, in my judgment constitute a substantial earnest of the good intentions of the Italian Government. They form a considerable contribution to the elimination of the Spanish question as a menace to peace.

"But these are not the only considerations which weigh with His Majesty's Government. Some hon. Members, with that eternal tendency to suspicion which, I am afraid, only breeds corresponding suspicions on the other side, persist in the view that Germany and Italy have a design of somehow permanently establishing themselves in Spain, and that Spain itself will presently be setting up a Fascist State. I believe both those views to be entirely unfounded. When I was at Munich, I spoke on the subject of the future of Spain with Herr Hitler and Signor Mussolini, and both of them assured me most definitely that they had no territorial ambitions whatever in Spain. I would remind hon. Members that when, in September, Europe was apparently faced with the prospect of a new major war, General Franco made a declaration of his neutrality and stated that he would not violate the French frontier unless he was attacked from that quarter. It seems to us that the events which took place in September put the whole Spanish conflict into a new perspective, and if the nations of Europe escaped a great catastrophe in the acute Czechoslovakian crisis, surely nobody can imagine that, with that recollection fresh in their minds, they are going to knock their heads together over Spain. In my own mind I am perfectly clear that the Spanish question is no longer a menace to the peace of Europe, and, consequently, that there is no valid reason why we should not take a step which, obviously, would contribute to general appeasement.

" In the realm of international affairs one thing generally leads to another, and if any justification were required for the policy of the Government in closing our differences with Italy, it surely can be found in the action of Signor Mussolini, when, at my request, he used his influence with Herr Hitler in order to give time for the discussion which led up to the Munich Agreement. By that act, the peace of Europe was saved. Does anybody suppose that my request to Signor Mussolini to intervene would have met with a response from him, or, indeed, that I could even have made such a request if our relations with Italy had remained what they were a year ago ?

" There is one other point which I ought to mention because it seems to me to weigh heavily, although I think unnecessarily, upon certain minds. That is the propriety of the recognition of Italian sovereignty over Ethiopia. I wonder how far those who hold that view are prepared to carry their reluctance. Are they prepared to withhold recognition in perpetuity ? Because, if that really were so, I am afraid they would very speedily find themselves in complete isolation. I would like to remind them that, in the first place, the Council of the League of Nations, by a large majority, last May, expressed the unqualified view that it was for each nation to decide for itself whether it should or should not accord this formal recognition. Further, I would remind them that, of all the countries in Europe, there are only two, namely, ourselves and the Government of Soviet Russia, which have restricted themselves to *de facto* recognition. The latest country to recognise formally Italian sovereignty in Ethiopia is France, and their new Ambassador is to be accredited to the King of

Italy and the Emperor of Ethiopia. We propose to follow the same course as France, and, accordingly, new credentials will be issued to our Ambassador in Italy on similar lines, thereby according legal recognition to Italian sovereignty.

" Perhaps the House may like to know that on being informed of our intention to take this course the French Government not only raised no objection but stated that they welcomed generally anything which could contribute to the improvement of Anglo-Italian relations. It is, perhaps, unnecessary to tell the House that, in accordance with what has now become the usual routine, the Dominions have been kept fully informed of all our intentions, and I am very glad to be able to read to the House a message which I have received from the Prime Minister of Australia who says as follows :

" ' The Commonwealth Government are convinced that the Anglo-Italian agreement should be brought into operation forthwith as a contribution to peace and *de jure* recognition accorded to the Italian conquest of Abyssinia. The withdrawal of 10,000 Italian troops from Spain seems a real contribution. In our opinion, a peaceful and friendly Mediterranean is essential to the present condition of the world. To refuse *de jure* recognition would seem to us to ignore the facts and to risk danger for a matter which is now immaterial.'

" I have also received the following message from the Prime Minister of South Africa :

" ' General Hertzog has noted the contents of this telegram '—
that is the telegram informing him of our intention to bring the Anglo-Italian Agreement into force—
' with much satisfaction, and he feels that the steps that His Majesty's Government in the United Kingdom propose taking are wise and necessary and will materially contribute to appeasement in Europe.'

It will be observed how, in both those messages, the Prime Ministers of Australia and South Africa respectively have gone to what, I think, is the root of the matter, and have recognized that, in the action which His Majesty's Government propose to take they are not concerned solely with the relations between ourselves and Italy, but that the step we are taking must be regarded as a step in the policy which I have described to the House on so many occasions."

MR. STEPHEN: "Will the right hon. Gentleman say whether he has had any message from the Prime Minister of New Zealand?"

THE PRIME MINISTER: "No, Sir, I have not any message either way."

MR. STEPHEN: "Or Canada?"

MR. MAXTON: "Is there any from Ireland?"

THE PRIME MINISTER: "I ask the House to approve this Motion, and in doing so I am satisfied that the House will be definitely increasing the prospect of peace as a whole. I say, let us put an end here and now to any idea that it is our desire to keep any State at arm's length, and let us remember that every advance which we may make towards removing possible causes of friction upon one subject, makes it easier and more probable that we can deal satisfactorily with those which remain still unsettled."

A "GO-GETTER" FOR PEACE

On the day after the opening of the new Session of Parliament, on 9th November, the Prime Minister spoke as usual at the Lord Mayor's Banquet at the Guildhall.

"YOU, my Lord Mayor, with that courtesy which is traditional among the holders of your great office, have proposed the health of His Majesty's Ministers in terms which are all the more gratifying to our ears because they form a marked contrast to the valuation which has been put upon our services by some less partial observers. It is not for me to say which is the truer estimate, but I may at least thank you, my Lord Mayor, for the discrimination with which you have dwelt upon our achievements and passed over our shortcomings—if we have any. And I must express my unqualified gratitude to this company for the magnificent response which they have given to the toast. I recognised in that demonstration just now a more than usual warmth and enthusiasm, and I think I know what it meant, for it expressed a spirit which has been manifested throughout the many thousands of letters which I have received during recent weeks—the spirit of England, thankful to have been spared the ordeal which came so close, but ready now to answer any call which their country may make upon them in order that she may face the future with equanimity.

" It is customary on these occasions for the Prime Minister to present a general review of foreign affairs, but I hope I shall not be thought discourteous to any nation, or unmindful of those with whom we have especially friendly relations, if to-night I depart from this practice and confine myself to a strictly limited field ; for unless I did that I should be unable to deal as I should wish with the subject which is uppermost in the minds of most of us, and perhaps in the minds of those who are listening to me in different parts of the world—I mean the significance of the events which culminated at Munich.

" Now I am speaking to-night to an audience vastly greater than that I see in front of me. There may be among them many who approve of what I have been trying to do ; there may be many who think I ought to have done something quite different. There will be many who think that they have sufficient knowledge to form a sound and considered judgment upon these events. But I think probably the great majority do not fully understand the situation and would welcome a little guidance, because they feel that what has happened, and still more what is going to happen, must vitally affect their interests and those of the generations which are going to come after them. It is to those people in particular that I want to speak to-night. Since, as I am not infrequently reminded, I am no orator, I shall use such plain and simple language as I can command.

" First of all I should like to get rid of the idea that at Munich there was a clash between different systems of government and that the result was a victory for one side or the other. Now of course you always get enthusiasts who are more royalist than the King, and who make claims which are in no way sponsored by their leaders. They are like the claims which are put forward in war time when, as you may read any time now in our newspapers, both sides declare that in the same action they inflicted a crushing defeat upon their adversaries. By a curious perversion sometimes we get an equally extravagant claim that it was the speaker's own side that suffered defeat and humiliation. I confess that, for my part, I do not understand a state of mind which desires to advertise the defeat of its own country. At any rate I, who happened to be there, can tell you that at Munich there was no clash—there was no question of a victory or defeat for either side. And I think if we are wise we shall find that one of the most gratifying features about Munich was that four Great Powers, owning different systems of government, were able to sit down together to agree without quarrelling upon the main outlines of a settlement of one of the most thorny and dangerous international problems of our time.

" If we are able to do that, does it not encourage us to think that it must be possible for such Powers to agree on other things as well—to agree, not only on preventing disaster, but on creating happiness and prosperity for all their peoples by mutual aid ? For every leader in every country, whatever may be his political creed, must surely put as the first of his aims the improvement of the lot of his fellow-creatures. In such meetings personal contacts are made which may prove of the greatest value.

" In the days before the date at which most of our modern history books begin it was possible for a nation to live in isolation and to develop its civilisation without interference from outside. But to-day we must all of us take account of our neighbours, and unless we can find some understanding of their ways of thought we shall never make real progress or secure stability for ourselves. For my part I prefer our British political system, with the wide extent of freedom which it gives to the individual to any form of government which subjects the will of the individual completely to the authority of the State, which means, of course, to the authority of those who for the time being represent the State. But it does seem to me entirely contrary to the spirit of democracy to attempt to deny to any other nation the right to adopt any form of government they may prefer. It seems to me all the more inappropriate to do so because history shows us that forms of government do not remain unchanged. Alterations, modifications, even reversals, have taken place in every generation in some country or another, and there is no reason to suppose that even to-day any of us have reached the final and unalterable stage.

" After those preliminary observations I should like to turn to the foreign policy of his Majesty's Government, and I shall make no apology for repeating things that have often been said before, because there are some people who persist in saying that they have never been told what the foreign policy of the Government is. In the first speech that I made after I became Prime Minister I summed up the aims of His Majesty's Government under four heads. The first was to maintain peace ; the second, to make this country so strong that she should be treated everywhere with respect ; the third was to promote the prosperity of industry, and thus provide employment for our people ; and the fourth was to work steadily for the improvement of the conditions of the people. Those still remain the aims of the Government, and the policy of the Government must be adapted from time to time to existing conditions in order to achieve them. I can only deal to-night with the first two, but I may say in passing that they are essential to the others. We shall secure neither prosperity nor welfare unless we have peace and the strength to maintain it.

"I want to emphasize this point. To lay down an aim is one thing; to achieve it is something quite different. If you want peace you have got to do something more than sit down and hope for it. The Americans have an expression —doubtless you are familiar with it—which, as American terms so often do, conveys its meaning without explanation. They talk of a ' go-getter.' Well, I want this Government to be a go-getter for peace. That does not mean that we want to go and interfere with other people's business or to undertake the role of policemen-in-ordinary to the world. But if we see peace threatened we shall use any influence that we may possess to save it, and if war breaks out we shall take any opportunity that we can to stop it. For in these days it is difficult to confine war to the source of its origin, and once it begins to spread it is harder still to control its boundaries.

"I feel all the more convinced of the soundness of this policy because I believe that the influence which this country can exert for peace is more powerful than that of any other that I can think of. It arises partly from our geographical position, lying a little apart from Europe; partly from our widespread connexions through the Empire with the whole world; partly, no doubt, from the vastness of the resources at our disposal; but, above all, because there is a general recognition that, fundamentally, what we are seeking is peace, security, and justice for all under the rule of law and order, reason and good faith. It is with these considerations in mind that I have sought to make this country an active agent for peace, and I would like now to turn to the example of that policy in practice which has lately been engaging our attention.

"This is not the place, and I have not the time, to recite the whole history of the Czechoslovak question. But in order that I may illustrate to you the method by which our foreign policy has been carried on, I must first of all go back to the time when, realizing the grave results that might follow upon a continuance of friction and discord, we used our persuasive powers with the two parties in Czechoslovakia in the hope of inducing them to settle their differences. When that failed, still pursuing our policy of conciliation, we suggested to them that they should make use of the services of Lord Runciman as mediator, and thereafter Lord Runciman devoted all his time and his great gifts to the task of bringing the two parties together.

"No doubt you recollect the incidents which brought Lord Runciman's mission to a standstill. From that moment the situation became one of increasing gravity till at last not only His Majesty's Government, but all the peoples of the world found themselves on the very brink of the abyss. It is needless to relate now the steps that were taken, even at the eleventh hour, to avert disaster. What I want to stress to you is this : Peace was not saved by words, not even by Notes ; it was saved by action.

"Now that the crisis is over, it is very easy to find fault with the solution, but the fact is that in the situation with which we had to deal, it was not possible to present the ideal solution as the alternative to force. We were dealing with a situation which had arisen from forces which had been set in motion nearly twenty years before, and the surgeon who has to deal with long-neglected wounds or disease must cut more swiftly and more deeply than he who is dealing with the first symptoms. If the settlement at Munich imposed upon Czechoslovakia a fate which arouses our natural sympathy for a small State and for a proud and brave people, yet we cannot dismiss in silence the thought of what the alternative would have meant to the peoples not only of Czechoslovakia, but of all the nations that would have been involved. I have no shadow of doubt in my mind that what we did was right. In doing it we have earned the gratitude of the vast majority in Europe and even in the world.

"Now you would make a great mistake if you thought that Munich began and ended with a settlement of the Czecho-slovak question. On the day after the conference was ended I had a long conversation with the German Chancellor, at the close of which we issued a joint declaration, and I should like, with your permission, to read to you the three paragraphs of which it was composed, because it does not seem to me that even now they have received sufficient attention. And I may say that, although the Munich settlement has been freely criticized, I think it would be very difficult for even the most determined war-at-any-price man to find much fault with the paragraphs which I am going to recall to your memory.

" In the first one we agreed in recognising that the question of Anglo-German relations was of the first importance for the two countries and for Europe. I do not think anyone would deny that. The second one expresses an opinion—namely, that ' we regard the agreement signed last night and the Anglo-German Naval Agreement as symbolic of the desire of our two peoples never to go to war with one another again.' Again I ask, can anybody, knowing the feeling here, and knowing the feeling of the people in Germany, can anybody doubt that these words express the heartfelt desire of the two peoples ?

" Then I come to the third paragraph. ' We are resolved that the method of consultation shall be the method adopted to deal with any other questions that may concern our two countries, and we are determined to continue our efforts to remove possible sources of difference, and thus to contribute to assure the peace of Europe.' Is anybody going to condemn that statement of policy ? And yet there are some minds so saturated with suspicion that they see even in such a blameless document as that some loosening of our ties with France. What a fatuous proposition, based on the false assumption that Europe must for ever be ranged in two opposing *blocs* and that it is impossible to make friends of one without becoming the enemy of the other. Our relations with France are too long-standing, too intimate, too highly prized by both of us to allow such suspicions to be entertained for one moment.

" It is with the utmost pleasure that Lord Halifax and I are looking forward to the visit which we shall shortly be paying, accompanied by our respective ladies, to Paris in response to the cordial invitation of the French Government.

" There is just one other matter I should like to mention before passing from the subject, because, if not the result of Munich, it is certainly connected with it. As part of this active policy of peacemaking, which involves searching out and removing causes of suspicion and antagonism wherever they exist, I attempted soon after I became Prime Minister to improve our relations with Italy, and last April we were able to make an agreement with the Italian Government. Although that agreement did not immediately come into full operation, yet it was at once followed by a return of the old feelings of cordiality and friendship between our two peoples. And subsequently this change for the better had the happiest result in enlisting the powerful aid of Signor Mussolini for a peaceful solution of the Czechoslovak question. Now, since we need no longer regard the Spanish conflict as a menace to the peace of Europe, that agreement will soon be coming into force, and I am confident that it will be found to be a further advance towards that general appeasement of Europe at which we are aiming.

" My Lord Mayor, to some people this policy of conciliation and appeasement which I have been describing may seem to forbid that at the same time we should be completing and accelerating the programme of rearmament to which we are simultaneously devoting ourselves, but there is really no inconsistency between the two. Ultimately, if we can get rid of suspicion, and if we can enter upon a new era of confidence, we shall all be ready to disarm together ; and the sooner that time comes the better. But meantime we should not be serving the cause of peace by unilateral disarmament. On the contrary, we must maintain our forces at a level commensurate with our responsibilities and with the part we want to play in maintaining peace. The British Commonwealth of Nations has traditions of freedom which make it a steadying factor in a world which has not yet regained its former stability. We in this country are vitally interested in preserving it, and we must be ready to play our part in its military protection. That is a fact which always comes to the front in the reviews which are made from time to time of our Defence requirements by our Service advisers. I myself for a number of years have been concerned directly or indirectly in these reviews, and I cannot remember any paper of major importance coming to us from the Chiefs of Staffs which did not direct our attention to our oversea commitments and to responsibilities for helping to defend this or that part of the Empire. Therefore, when we speak of our Defence Forces, and say they must be adequate, it is upon that word defence that we lay stress.

" We do not need to build armaments in order to take from anybody else anything that they now have, but we should be failing in our duty to our own people if we were to leave them without the means of resisting aggression from any nation less peacefully disposed than our own. And I would venture to add this : That it is the man who is conscious of his own weakness who can least afford to be generous in his dealings with others because he will always recoil from yielding to the claims of justice lest his action should be attributed to his fear of the consequences of resistance.

" Now it was inevitable that an experience such as that which we have lately passed through should reveal shortcomings in our defensive system. Such defects, depend upon it, exist in the defensive systems of other countries, although they are not always advertised as publicly as they are here. But it would be a profound error to think that if war had come we should not have given a good account of ourselves. Our task now is to remedy those defects, and the further measures which we think necessary will in due course be laid before Parliament in main outline, if not in all the details ; and if that should entail further efforts and further sacrifices upon the nation, I have no doubt of the willingness of the nation to undertake them, whether they be in services or in money.

" I think it is unnecessary for me to repeat here what I have said on other occasions, that the whole business of piling up armaments is utterly distasteful to me. It seems to me the height of human folly to be thus dissipating resources which can and should be used for purposes conducive to the health and happiness of mankind. But for the time being I regard it as an inevitable, but I hope only a temporary accompaniment of that other half of the policy to which I can turn all my energies without qualification and without misgiving— the policy of understanding and good will which is desired by all the peoples, the policy to which I invite the co-operation of all the nations.

" The aims that I have described are not to be achieved

within a few minutes. They require untiring patience, prolonged effort in the face of misunderstanding, of criticism, of disappointment; they require the vision to seize every opportunity as it comes. It is an end which is worthy to inspire that spirit of England of which I spoke earlier in the evening, for it alone can save the generation which is coming from the nightmare which has hung over us for so long.

" Just one last word. Christmas is coming, and I see no reason why we should not prepare ourselves for the festive season in a spirit of cheerfulness and confidence. You here in this great centre of trade and commerce are accustomed to watch very closely the signs of the times. No doubt you have noted those favourable features to which I directed the attention of the House of Commons yesterday—improvement in employment in this country, the check in the downward trend in commodity prices, the healthier condition of business in the United States, where transactions are on such a vast scale that they must always exercise a powerful influence on the world. I would add to that one other consideration perhaps more important than all. It is that in my judgment, after the disturbance in September, political conditions in Europe are now settling down to quieter times. I say, in this brightening atmosphere, let us not conjure up troubles which may never arise. Let us rather set about our several tasks with a determination that the New Year shall be more prosperous and happier than the old."

NO EASY ROAD

Throughout November and December the Government, in the face of all obstacles, pursued its twin policy of avoiding and diminishing the causes of war and of strengthening the long-neglected defences of the country so as to remove the temptation of aggression provided by a rich nation which had been so rash as to disarm unilaterally. In doing so the Prime Minister, as one of his supporters remarked in the House of Commons, was "persistently and perpetually heckled, harried and abused." His task was rendered more difficult by the angry recriminations of the totalitarian leaders at the jibes of the Left-wing politicians and publicists, the consequent Press war between the Dictatorships and the Democracies, and the natural feelings of horror and indignation aroused throughout the world by the renewal of Jewish persecution in Germany following the murder of Herr Von Rath by a Jewish fanatic on 7th November at the German Embassy in Paris. Throughout these trials and troubles, some of them perhaps inevitable in the reaction of exhaustion that followed the strain of September, the Prime Minister kept his course. He spoke once more of his aims at the jubilee dinner of the Foreign Press Association at Grosvenor House on 13th December.

"AS you have reminded us, Mr. President, we are cele-
brating the fiftieth anniversary of the Foreign Press
Association in London, and I count myself honoured indeed
to be your guest on such an interesting occasion. I am
more than honoured, I am flattered by your generous words
and by the cordiality of the response which this distinguished
company has made to the toast you have just proposed. But
if I am to lay bare my secret soul to this audience, and that,
of course, is what you will naturally expect of me to-night, I
must confess that I would face all the dictators in the world
with less apprehension than that nameless power which we call
the Press and which can convey our words to every quarter
of the globe with unimpeachable accuracy and yet with such
variation in effect that no two reports seem alike.

" This is a formidable power that you wield ; yet I frankly
admit that we who carry the responsibilities of State administration can no more dispense with your services than you can
dispense with ours, who furnish you with so much of your
daily food. And I gratefully acknowledge that, if at times your
zeal for providing the public with stimulating information
sometimes causes us some embarrassment, I have hardly ever
known a case where a confidence has been deliberately
betrayed.

" To-night I have nothing startling to say to you and
nothing confidential. On the contrary, I welcome an opportunity of saying to you and to the much larger audience which
I am told is listening to me things which I have said before
on other occasions, but which I think will bear repeating,
since memories are short in days when great events succeed
one another with such rapidity that it is difficult to view them
in proper perspective. What I have to say concerns, as is
natural in speaking to the foreign Press, the aims and actions of
the British Government in relation to foreign affairs since I
entered upon my present office in the summer of last year.

" With the exception of the period of the Great War, I

doubt if any of my predecessors during the last hundred years has had to contend with more trying and anxious conditions than we have encountered during the last eighteen months, and it would be too much to expect that anyone in my position, forced by circumstances to walk continually through dark and perilous ways, should escape criticism from some who think they see further or clearer than I. But since for the time being the responsibility for guidance rests on my shoulders, I am bound to discharge it to the best of my ability in the light of the conditions as I see them, for if I were ultimately to fail it would afford little consolation to me or to anyone else to be able to say that I had followed the advice of others instead of relying on my own judgment.

" My aim has been consistently the same from beginning to end. Faced with a situation in which relations between this country on the one hand and Germany and Italy on the other were rapidly deteriorating and in so doing steadily destroying the confidence in Europe in the maintenance of peace, it seemed to me that only two alternatives were open to us. One was to make up our minds that war was inevitable and to throw the whole energies of the country into preparation for it. The other was to make a prolonged and determined effort to eradicate the possible causes of war and to try out the methods of personal contact and discussion, while at the same time proceeding steadily with such rearmament as was necessary to restore the power of defence which we had voluntarily abandoned for a period of many years.

" There are some who sincerely believe that the first course was the one we should have taken. I believe that in this country they are in a small minority. I did not take that view myself and I do not take it now. War to-day differs fundamentally from all the wars of the past, inasmuch as to-day its first and its most numerous victims are not the professional fighters but the civilian population, the workman and the clerk, the housewife and, most horrible of all, the children. And when the war is over, whoever may be the victor, it leaves behind a trail of loss and suffering which two generations will not obliterate, and it sows the dragon's teeth which are the seeds of fresh quarrels, fresh injustices, and fresh conflicts.

" Such consequences are not to be lightly incurred ; they ought never to be incurred unless we can be satisfied, and our peoples are satisfied, that every honourable alternative has been tried and found to be impossible. It was with these considerations in mind that I chose the second course, and my aim has never wavered. The goal is not only peace, but confidence that peace can be maintained. I never imagined that the goal could be attained in the twinkling of an eye or without checks, disappointments, and setbacks. I have had them all, perhaps in greater measure than I had anticipated, but I am neither disheartened nor deterred by these passing phases. It has been well said that failure only begins when you leave off trying to succeed. As long as I am where I am, I will never leave off trying.

" And when I look back over this past year and consider the record of our actions I confess I am astonished at the pessimism which seems to possess some of our critics. They profess, and I am sure their profession is made in all sincerity, that they too desire peace above all things. But if you want peace you must seek and ensue it. You must find out what threatens it and you must take active positive steps to remove that threat. In pursuit of our aim the British Government has been active, and it has not been unsuccessful. Let me remind you of the agreements which stand up like milestones to mark our progress as the year has gone by.

" In April we made the agreement between the United Kingdom and Eire—an agreement which brought to an end the long and bitter struggle between our two countries. In that same month we concluded the Anglo-Italian Agreement and thereby closed the breach which had unhappily for a time interrupted the old friendship between us. In September came the Munich Agreement, followed by the Anglo-German declaration. In due course that has led to the complementary Franco-German declaration signed a few days ago. And lastly let me mention the Anglo-American Trade Agreement, because, while it is primarily a commercial treaty, I regard that agreement as symbolic of the good relations happily existing between the United States and ourselves.

" Here, then, in something less than twelve months are five major international agreements, three of which have been concluded between democratic and authoritarian States. Surely that is an achievement which calls for satisfaction rather than pessimism, and one which should encourage us to persist in a policy which has given such remarkable results.

" Of course, I am well aware that the Munich Agreement has been described in some quarters not as an example of co-operation but as a defeat for democracies. The curious thing is that that description comes from men who are proud to call themselves democrats. I cannot help thinking that such pronouncements do no service to democracy or to the chances of further international co-operation. In my view we should not try to assess the results of such meetings in terms of victory or defeat. We should rather remember what was the alternative which the Munich Agreement averted— namely, an attempt to effect a revision of the Treaty of Versailles by force instead of by discussion, an attempt which would certainly have resulted in a condition of affairs very different from the peaceful atmosphere in which we are dining here to-night.

" Moreover, other results followed the Munich Agreement besides the settlement of the Czechoslovak frontiers. Last September the peoples of four great countries, Great Britain, France, Germany, and Italy, were brought face to face with the imminent horrors of war. In imagination they saw husbands, brothers, and sons torn from their families, perhaps never to return ; they saw their homes wrecked, their children terrified or mutilated, their happiness and peace of mind gone for ever. When the news of the Munich Agreement was known, a sigh of relief and thankfulness went up from the whole world, which felt a load lifted from its heart.

" Do you think those days are forgotten ? I do not believe it. I must deplore the recent attitude of the German Press, which, in one case, has not scrupled to pour its vituperation against our most respected statesman, himself only recently the Prime Minister of this country, and in few cases has shown much desire to understand our point of view. Nevertheless, I am convinced that the wish of our two peoples remains still as it was recorded in the Munich Declaration— namely, that never again should we go to war with one another, but that we should deal with any differences between us by the method of consultation.

" In the days when the League of Nations was at the height of its prestige, I always used to think that one of its most valuable features was the opportunity it gave of personal contacts between the Ministers of the various members of the League at their periodical meetings in Geneva. To-day such opportunities are sadly limited, and if these personal contacts, so indispensable to good understanding, are to be effected, other means must be sought. Next month Lord Halifax and I have planned a visit to Rome for the purpose of discussing with the head of the Italian Government and his Ministers all matters of common interest and concern. It may be that some will once again be speculating upon who is the winner and who the loser in these talks. That is not the spirit in which we propose to undertake our journey. Rather has it been our hope that we might find an atmosphere in which it could be possible by personal interchange of thought better to understand each other's point of view and by establishing a greater mutual confidence to co-operate in one way or another in further steps towards the general sense of stability and security.

" That brings me to another point. All my political life I have been a party man and I have taken my full share of the knocks that accompany party conflict. But no one can go through such experiences as have fallen to my lot in recent months without feeling that the narrower aspects of internal party controversy have lost much of their savour and much of their importance. And so, too, I find it difficult to rouse much excitement over different systems of government apart from particular actions which may not necessarily be inherent in the system. I am told that in some quarters it is supposed that because I advocate coming to an understanding with dictator countries I must therefore favour the system of Nazism or Fascism. If that means that I should favour such a system for my own country, the contrary is the case.

" To me, as I believe to the vast majority of my countrymen, the complete subordination of individual independence to something which is called the State but which really only means those who for the time being rule the State, would be insupportable, because it runs counter to all our most fundamental conceptions of the framework of human society. But I fully recognize that these ideas are not held universally, and it seems to me neither useful nor desirable to criticize others because they prefer systems which would not suit us but do suit them.

" One other observation I would make on this subject, and it is this : History teaches us that no form of government ever remains the same. The change may come by slow degrees or it may come suddenly like an explosion. But change in one form or other is inevitable and it would seem to follow, therefore, that we should be careful not to shut ourselves off from contact with any country on account of a system which in the course of time may well undergo such modifications as to render it very different from what it is to-day.

" Let me now turn to another aspect of British policy, that which is concerned with our military preparations. You whose business it is to watch and report upon the trend of opinion in this country cannot fail to have noticed that, though there may be differences about the methods of carrying out the aims of our foreign policy, there is practical unanimity about the necessity of pushing forward the progress of our armament programme. That programme was originally designed to be carried out in ' five ' years, three of which have now gone by. From the beginning we made it clear that the programme was flexible and must be modified from time to time in the light of changing circumstances.

" In fact the programme has been modified in two directions ; it has been accelerated and it has been expanded, and those modifications have demanded very considerable efforts on the part of industry, of labour, of the taxpayer, and of the individual whose time and services have been called for. So far from resenting these demands the people of this country have shown that they are ready to make even greater efforts if they should be demanded. Is that to be considered as evidence that our people are war minded ? Not in the least. Their hope is that these armaments may never be required ; certainly they will not be required for aggressive purposes.

" But while we hear so much talk about the advantages of force, while we see others accumulating force and making no response to any suggestion for disarmament, we are bound to take all steps necessary to fill up any deficiencies there may be in our defences. For, while I hope we shall always be ready to discuss in a reasonable spirit any grievances or any injustices that may be alleged to exist, it is to reason that we are prepared to listen and not to force. Nor can we forget that we have obligations not only to our own people at home, but to those for whom we are responsible in the British Empire and to the allies who are bound to us by treaty.

"Those obligations we must be ready to fulfil, and our preparations have now proceeded far enough for us to say with confidence that we are in a position to do so. But let me once again repeat this. No one recognizes more fully than I that the process of piling up armaments for whatever cause must in time exhaust the resources of any nation, resources which should properly be devoted to the advancement of the prosperity and happiness of its own people. No one, therefore, would more gladly than I join in any international arrangement that would limit or reduce armaments all round by mutual agreement.

"More than once in recent weeks I have sustained a certain shock in seeing myself described as 'that old man.' Certainly I am not conscious of the approach of old age either in my mental or physical powers. But in one respect, perhaps, the passage of years has left its mark upon me, and that is in the recognition of the futility of ambition, if ambition leads to the desire for domination. For once again history teaches that attempts at domination are never long successful and have never added to the happiness of nations which have attempted it. Past experience has shown that there is an innate resistant force arising out of fear for the loss of liberty, combined with the ever-present passion for national self-expression, which makes domination difficult and precarious.

"It seems to me, therefore, that happiness must be sought in other directions. Something depends upon our material condition, upon our ability to command a standard of comfort which each sets for himself. But even more are we dependent for our happiness upon our mental condition, upon our freedom from apprehension, upon the possession of that peace of mind without which no material comforts can bring satisfaction. It is the absence of that peace of mind which to-day weighs upon the world, and in its turn by destroying confidence prevents us from reaping the material advantages to which human progress in mastering the forces of nature should entitle us. And I would conclude by appealing through you to all the nations you represent to realize that our aim should be the happiness of all our peoples and that that happiness can only be attained if we are willing to lay aside suspicion and prejudice, to cease looking for points of differences, and to search instead for points of agreement.

" Not many generations ago we were at war with the United States of America ; to-day such a conflict has passed beyond the bounds of possibility. In my own lifetime we were within an ace of war with France ; to-day such a catastrophe seems as remote as war with America. In fact, our relations with France are so close as to pass beyond mere legal obligations, since they are founded on identity of interest. If we have succeeded, then, in reducing the field of possible wars thus far, is there any reason why we should not carry it further until we can attain such a general sense of security that all of us can lay aside our weapons and devote ourselves to the benefit of the human race ? For my part, great as may be the obstacles, discouraging as may appear the outlook in certain respects, I believe it to be possible to attain our goal provided we can keep our purpose firm, our courage undaunted, and our faith untarnished."

AFTER THE ROME VISIT

In January, 1939, Mr. Chamberlain, accompanied by Lord Halifax, the Foreign Secretary, paid a visit to Rome at the invitation of Signor Mussolini with whom he had first established contact—after a period of intense Anglo-Italian strain—by his letter of eighteen months before, and whose goodwill, secured by the Anglo-Italian Agreement of April, 1938, had made peace possible when all other hope had failed in September. The situation was still clouded—by the continuance of Civil War in Spain, by Franco-Italian misunderstanding, by the problem of the refugees and the bitter feelings to which it gave rise. But, though there was no lack of plain speaking, the visit to Rome showed the degree of goodwill that existed not only between the leaders but between the British and Italian peoples. Mr. Chamberlain received a welcome of whose spontaneous warmth there could be no doubt.

Shortly after his return to England Mr. Chamberlain spoke in his native city at a dinner of the Birmingham Jewellers' Association

"WHAT am I to say in response to such a demonstration of loyalty and affection which goes so far beyond anything that I can have done to deserve it? But it is only a continuation of the favours you have always accorded to members of my family. Once more I find myself in these familiar surroundings repeating the practice of my father and brother before me, and once more receiving from the Jewellers' Association a welcome no less cordial than you always gave to them.

"I wish I could find words adequate to express to you how deeply I value your support and goodwill, and how much I am encouraged and fortified in my tasks by the knowledge that I have the sympathy and approval of so many of my fellow-citizens in the work I am trying to do. For I need not tell you that the burden of responsibility which rests upon His Majesty's Ministers, and particularly upon the one who in the last resort has to take the final decision in the solution of every major problem, is as great or greater than it has ever been in our history, and only a young fellow like myself with a good conscience and a cast-iron digestion can stand the strain for very long.

"It is a particular satisfaction to me to reflect that my native city, which has long played such an important part in the industrial life of the country, has now in these strenuous days acquired a new importance by reason of the contribution she is making to the defence programmes. With her unrivalled supplies of skilled labour, her wealth of highly equipped technicians and managers, and her ample resources of power, water, and other necessary services, Birmingham acts like a magnet to industrial enterprise, and I suppose no town can show a greater record in recent years of new factories and extensions of old ones very largely in connexion with the rearmament programme.

"It is, of course, not to be expected that this activity in the production of the weapons and the equipment of war will remain a permanent feature of our life. For the time being it is a grim necessity, but we may hope it is only a preliminary to a return to greater sanity in Europe, when we can devote ourselves once more to the arts of peace, and I feel confident that those who are responsible for the direction of industry in Birmingham are not losing sight of the importance to this country of our export trade, which, in the past, has been the source of so much of our economic and financial strength.

" In a few weeks we shall see the reopening of the Birmingham section of the British Industries Fair, which this year is to receive the much-prized honour of a visit from Their Majesties the King and Queen. It was a great disappointment that Their Majesties had to postpone the visit they were to have paid to the city last year, and we are all the more gratified on that account that they should have given us this early opportunity of showing our loyalty and affection to our Sovereigns.

" If it were not for one consideration, I should be disposed to take a rosy view of the prospects of business during this current year, for until quite lately there were a number of features, such as a rise in the price of primary commodities and the improvement of trading in the United States, which seemed to show that the recession of last year had passed its peak. But I am bound to record that at the present time there exists a certain amount of political tension in international affairs which may or may not be well founded, but which is undoubtedly holding back enterprise.

" That shows how closely politics are entwined with economics and finance apart from any other consideration. I think that fact would justify the efforts which the Government are continuously making to ease that political tension and bring about a better understanding between the nations.

" Lord Dudley has said something about the events of last September which culminated in the Munich Agreement. A great deal of criticism, mostly, I think, in this country, has been directed against that agreement and against the action I took in attempting, by personal contact, to obtain a peaceful solution of a problem which very nearly involved the world in a catastrophe of the first magnitude.

" The criticism has come from various quarters which are perhaps only unanimous in one respect, namely, that they take a less favourable view of the actions of His Majesty's present Ministers than you have been good enough to indicate. But there is one feature common to all the critics. None of them carries the responsibilities that I do, and none of them has that full knowledge of all the circumstances which is only open to the members of the Government. A combination of ignorance and irresponsibility may conduce to a freedom of mind which may be cheerful or gloomy according to the temperament, but I rather doubt whether it constitutes a satisfactory foundation on which to build a sound judgment. For myself, looking back, I see nothing to regret nor any reason to suppose that another course would have been preferable.

" War to-day is so terrible in its effects on those who take part in it, no matter what the ultimate outcome may be ; it brings so much loss and suffering even to the bystanders that it ought never to be allowed to begin unless every practicable and honourable step has been taken to prevent it. That has been the view of this Government from the beginning, and the Munich Agreement, though it is the most important illustration of its practical working, was only an incident in a consistent unwavering policy of peace.

" I go further and say that peace could not have been preserved if it had not been for the events which had preceded it, by the exchange of letters between myself and Signor Mussolini in the summer of 1937, and by the conclusion of the Anglo-Italian Agreement in February of last year, because without the improvement in the relations between this country and Italy I could never have obtained Signor Mussolini's co-operation in September, and without his co-operation I do not believe peace could have been saved.

" Quite recently, as you know, the Foreign Secretary and I paid a visit to Rome and for that, too, we have been criticized by those who seemed determined to obstruct and resist every attempt to improve international relations. There are some who are so blinded by prejudice and partisanship that they do not scruple to attempt to besmirch and belittle the representatives of this country.

" They declared before the visit that we were going to Rome to surrender British interests, that we were going to

N

grant belligerent rights to General Franco, that we were going to betray our friends and allies in France ; and when we came back without having done any of these things they changed their complaint and they said it was not worth while to have made the visit at all because nothing had come of it. Evidently if it is necessary to please them we have got our work cut out over it.

" It is not true that nothing came out of it. We did not go to Rome to make bargains, but to get to know Italian statesmen better, to ascertain by personal discussion what was their point of view, and to make sure that they understood ourselves. We accomplished all that, and, although there was complete frankness of speech on both sides, although we did not convert or attempt to convert one another to our own point of view on any subject on which we might differ, yet I can say that we came away better friends than we were when we went there.

" And something more than that came out of it. From the moment we entered upon Italian soil till the moment we left it, we were the objects of the most remarkable, spontaneous, universal demonstration of welcome that I have ever witnessed.

" It was a demonstration which, it seemed to me, signified two things. In the first place, it brought out the genuine friendliness of the Italian people for the people of this country. Nobody could make any mistake about that. In the second place, it demonstrated as clearly as possible the intense, the passionate desire of the Italian people for peace—a desire which is matched by an equal feeling in this country.

" That feeling is not confined to the peoples of Great Britain and Italy. You find exactly the same thing in France. You find it again in Germany, and you find it, I believe, in every country in the world. I do not exclude the possibility that these feelings of the peoples may not always be shared by their Governments, and I recognize that it is with Governments and not peoples that we have to deal.

" Nevertheless, let us cultivate the friendship of the peoples, and that can be done by individuals and by traders as well as by more official representatives. Let us make it clear to them that we do not regard them as potential foes, but rather as human beings like ourselves with whom we are always prepared to talk on terms of equality, with an open mind, to hear their point of view and to satisfy so far as we can any reasonable aspirations that they cherish and which do not conflict with the general rights of others to liberty and justice.

" In that way alone we shall remove these eternal suspicions that poison the international atmosphere and get back our security of mind and that confidence which is the life-blood of successful enterprise.

" We like to have our grumbles, but sometimes it is a good rule to ' count your blessings.' Anyone who does so in this country—whether employer, worker, man or woman—will find that there is very much to be grateful for in the conditions here as compared with the conditions in most other countries.

" We should like to see their conditions improved ; we should be ready to talk with their representatives to see how best to bring about such a result. But, of course, it is in times of peace alone that attention can be directed to improving the standard of living of the people, war must have the opposite effect, and I am confident therefore that all thoughtful people in all countries will join with me in working for the avoidance of war, so that we and they may equally share in the higher wages, shorter hours, better food, and better clothes which the development of science and industry has rendered possible.

" I wish I could stop there and turn at once to other fields in which you and we could work together for the benefit of the nations. But there is another side to international relations on which I must say a few words.

" We cannot forget that though it takes at least two to make a peace, one can make a war. And until we have come to clear understandings in which all political tension is swept away we must put ourselves in a position to defend ourselves against attack, whether upon our land, our people, or the principles of freedom with which our existence as a democracy is bound up and which to us seem to enshrine the highest attributes of human life and spirit. It is for this purpose, for the purpose of defence and not of attack, that we are pursuing the task of rearmament with unrelenting vigour and with the full approval of the country.

" It has taken us a long time, so low had our defences fallen in the vain hope that others would follow our example, to get going the machinery that had run down. But progress is now being made more rapidly every day in all directions. It is now nearly three years since we started on a very large programme for rebuilding and modernizing the Fleet. To give you some idea of the extent of this programme I may tell you that during the 12 months ending on the 31st of next March some sixty new ships, with a tonnage of about 130,000 tons, will have been added to the Navy. And for the ensuing twelve months the addition will be even larger—namely, about seventy-five ships of 150,000 tons.

" The Royal Air Force is also going ahead at an equally remarkable rate. Large factory extensions have been made and huge new factories have been or are being erected in different parts of the country. You can see for yourselves what has been done here in the Austin factory and the immense new works being erected in record time under the direction of Lord Nuffield. To show you that the results of all this activity are no longer reserved for the future you may like to know that in the last few months we have actually doubled the rate of aircraft production.

" On the recruiting side also good progress is being made, and whereas in 1937, between April and the end of the year, we obtained 9000 new entrants into the R.A.F., this year the corresponding number is 25,000.

" In regard to the Army, I propose only to say a word about the part of our programme which is most frequently referred to by critics—I mean our anti-aircraft defences. Everyone knows that last September certain deficiencies were disclosed in these defences. We were well aware that those deficiencies existed, for we were engaged on a programme which was only planned for completion at a considerably later date. But the programme has now been accelerated and the deficiencies which were apparent last September have largely been removed.

" It would not be in the public interest to give actual figures, but I may tell you that a few days ago I was examining the position as it is to-day and as it will be in the course of the next few months, and you may take it that it is very greatly improved not only as regards the increase in guns and accessories, but also in the organization for directing and manning them.

" A few nights ago I broadcast a message to the nation to initiate the recruiting campaign for National Voluntary Service, and I want to say a few more words on the same subject this evening. It would be superfluous for me to impress on this audience the need for building up what I may call the fourth arm of our National Defence. If we should ever be involved in war we may well find that if we are not all in the firing line we may all be in the line of fire. And in meeting that danger there is a new opportunity of service for the civil population in the various branches of civil defence.

" We are not seeking to build up a vast civil defence force to be embodied like a professional army in war-time, relieving the citizens in general of their responsibilities for their own defence. Our task is to find people for certain definite jobs, not to find jobs for the whole of the people. What we are looking for is men and women who will volunteer now to give their service for certain definite purposes, as air raid wardens, or fire fighters, for first aid and rescue parties, or for those services of a more domestic kind which any scheme of evacuation must demand. And we want them to be ready to undergo training now so that they may be able to give that service efficiently if ever the need for it arises.

" I am not afraid of the result of an appeal for volunteers. The spirit of service has always been strong in our people, and it never was stronger than it is to-day. Our motto is not defiance, and, mark my words, it is not, either, deference. It is defence, and we confidently count on the response of the nation to make that defence invincible.

" Of course, the enrolment of volunteers would be useless without the provision of the civil defence organization which they are to man, and this part of our task is now well in hand. We have considerably extended the facilities for the training of instructors in civil defence in the Government schools. Steps have been taken to accelerate the production of equipment and supplies, and the local authorities are being pressed to overhaul and expand their own local arrangements for the training of volunteers.

" Protection against the effects of air raids is another matter which has engaged our urgent attention. No doubt you have read of the steel air-raid shelters which are to be provided to give protection to those who live in vulnerable areas and cannot be expected to provide them for themselves. These steel shelters will give adequate protection against splinters, blast and falling debris. A first order for 100,000 tons of steel for these shelters has already been placed, and in the course of the next few weeks we expect to begin the distribution of shelters in some of the most vulnerable areas.

" Further progress has also been made in working out the plans for evacuation from our large, congested cities. If evacuation is to be carried out effectively it must be done in an orderly manner, and I think it will be generally agreed that we must consider the children first. Accordingly, the Minister of Health has asked the local authorities concerned to make a comprehensive survey of the accommodation available for the reception of children and, where necessary, their mothers, and to ascertain which householders are able and willing to receive them. This work is now proceeding rapidly, and meanwhile we are examining the possibility of making use of camps to supplement the other accommodation available.

" In all these plans we shall take fully into our confidence the authorities on whose co-operation we are relying, and, except where matters cannot be made public without prejudice to the national safety, we shall disclose fully our revised plans for civil defence to all who would be affected by them.

" I have devoted the greater part of my remarks to-night to foreign affairs and defence because these are the subjects which, as it seems to me, are uppermost in the public mind. But I cannot help once more registering my regret that it should be necessary to devote so much time and so vast a proportion of the revenue of the country to warlike preparations instead of to those more domestic questions which brought me into politics, the health and housing of the people, the improvement of their material conditions, the provision of recreation for their leisure, and the prosperity of industry and agriculture. None of these subjects is indeed being neglected, but their development is necessarily hampered and slowed up by the demands of national security.

" Thinking over these things, I recall the fate of one of the greatest of my predecessors, the younger Pitt. His interests lay at home in the repair of the financial system and in domestic reforms. But events abroad cut short his ambitions and, reluctantly, after long resisting his fate, he found himself involved in what was up to then the greatest war in our history. Worn out by the struggle, he died before success had crowned our efforts, to which his own steadfast courage had contributed so much.

" I trust that my lot may be happier than his, and that we may yet secure our aim of international peace. We have so often defined our attitude that there can be no misunderstanding about it, and I feel that it is time now that others should make their contribution to a result which would overflow with benefits to all.

" To-day the air is full of rumours and suspicions which ought not to be allowed to persist. For peace could only be endangered by such a challenge as was envisaged by the President of the United States in his New Year message— namely, a demand to dominate the world by force. That would be a demand which, as the President indicated, and I myself have already declared, the democracies must inevitably resist. But I cannot believe that any such challenge is intended, for the consequences of war for the peoples on either side would be so grave that no Government which has their interests at heart would lightly embark upon them.

" Moreover, I remain convinced that there are no differences, however serious, that cannot be solved without recourse to war, by consultation and negotiation, as was laid down in the declaration signed by Herr Hitler and myself at Munich.

" Let us then continue to pursue the path of peace and conciliation, but until we can agree on a general limitation of arms let us continue to make this country strong. Then, conscious of our strength, avoiding needless alarms equally with careless indifference, let us go forward to meet the future with the calm courage which enabled our ancestors to win through their troubles a century and a quarter ago."

THE ORGANISATION OF DEFENCE

On 21st February, 1939, the Prime Minister spoke in the House of Commons on the growing strength of the country and the plans which had been made for organising the nation's defence. These had just been reinforced by the appointment of a distinguished naval officer, Lord Chatfield, as Minister for the Co-ordination of Defence, assisted by the new Chancellor of the Duchy of Lancaster, Mr. W. S. Morrison.

" I DO not think it will be necessary for me to trouble the Committee with any very long observations this afternoon. During the Debate which took place yesterday the House was never uncomfortably crowded, and those who listened to it must, I think, have been very much impressed by the contrast in the general atmosphere in which the discussions were conducted, as compared with that which has prevailed when we have considered these defence questions on previous occasions. I, myself, felt that there was an absence of those strong feelings of controversy or of those symptoms of anxiety which I had noticed before, and I have derived the general impression that Members in all parts of the Committee were being forced by the pressure of facts and by the realisation of the realities of the situation, towards something like general agreement as to the necessity for the armaments programme which we are carrying through, as to the manner in which it is being conducted and, particularly, as to the way in which it is to be financed. That is a considerable change from the past.

" I recall, for example, that last year when the House was asked to approve of the proposals in the White Paper on defence, the party opposite expressed the view that it was only by collective security through the League of Nations that the safety of the country could be ensured and the maintenance of peace secured. I was very much struck by the fact that during the whole of the speech of the hon. Member for Bishop Auckland (Mr. Dalton), who led off for the Opposition, there was no mention of either collective security or of the League of Nations, and that seemed to me to indicate that the Party opposite had, at any rate, come to a realisation of the fact that it was of no use in present circumstances to appeal to the League of Nations to obtain collective security for us, but that we had to trust to other means of maintaining peace and keeping this country safe."

AN HON. MEMBER: " You destroyed it."

THE PRIME MINISTER: " The hon. Member says ' You destroyed it.' Of course it is part of the old political stock-in-trade of his Party to say that the League of Nations has been killed by the action of the present Government, but I think that the historian of the future, who will perhaps look upon events with a somewhat more impartial eye, will recall that in the crisis of the League of Nations there was no country which sacrificed so much, which took such risks, which incurred such obloquy and which made such efforts to carry out the methods which were contemplated by the constitution of the League, as did this country. He will remember that striking phrase which was used by my right hon. Friend the Home Secretary (Sir Samuel Hoare) when he said that no country but this had moved a ship, or a gun, or a man. Perhaps the historian will come to the conclusion that if the League failed to carry through the policy of sanctions, then it was not due to the action or inaction of this country, and indeed that blame cannot be attached to any one country or any group of countries in that connection, but the real explanation was that it had been sought to impose upon the League a task which was completely beyond its powers. I do not despair of the view that the Party opposite may presently arrive at the conclusion that the only chance that the League has of becoming again an effective factor in the preservation of peace will be when it has abandoned the idea that peace can be imposed by force.

" The change I observed, however, was not confined to the Opposition. The change was visible in all parts of the Committee, and certainly it was very remarkable that when my right hon. Friend the Chancellor of the Exchequer was putting before the Committee the amazing figures which are contemplated in the defence expenditure of the coming year, the attitude of hon. Members appeared almost to show an indifference, an apparent indifference, to the tremendous significance of the figures, and it was only when he came to that part of his speech in which he told the Committee how he proposed to divide the expenditure between revenue and borrowing that what used to be called ' a certain liveliness ' became apparent. I am aware that conclusions have been drawn from what my right hon. Friend then said about this proposed division, conclusions which, perhaps, did not take full account of the warning with which he ended his remarks. What I have called apparent indifference did not arise from the relief of hon. Members at the notion that my right hon. Friend was not likely to contemplate major increases in taxation in the next financial year. I think this changed attitude to which I have referred is due to the sense which, I believe, was prevalent not only in the House but generally throughout the country, that the long period of effort and preparation and organisation of our programme of defence is now at last beginning to bear visible fruit, and that we are conscious, all of us, that even in the last few months the output of weapons and equipment and munitions of all kinds has shown a marked increase, and, more than that, has shown that the great care, the great amount of thought and the great amount of work which had been put into this programme have been wisely expended and are now giving us the fruits of our labour.

" We are not in these two days proposing to devote any great amount of attention to the subject of civil defence ; that is reserved for a later occasion. We all know that the provision for civil defence has somewhat lagged behind the preparations that have been made in the three more active branches of defence. But in the case of civil defence, under the hand of my right hon. Friend the Lord Privy Seal, the organisation of the necessary measures is now falling into place, and I think it will not be very long before we are able to say of air-raid precautions and kindred measures that they, too, are giving us the results we desire to see.

" The hon. Member for Bishop Auckland (Mr. Dalton) made one criticism upon the White Paper which, perhaps, I should notice. He said that it contained nothing new about Co-ordination of Defence. If I may say so, I think that that criticism is based upon a misunderstanding, because if hon. Members will look at the introductory paragraph they will see it explained there that each statement on defence which has been published in successive years has dealt with some aspects of His Majesty's Government's general policy in defence methods, and in the second paragraph the introduction points out that :

" ' This present statement is presented to Parliament at the same time as the introduction of the Defence Loans Bill, and it is appropriate therefore that the statement should deal with the cost of the defence programme.'

A previous White Paper dealt with the subject of Co-ordination of Defence, and I do not think there is very much more to be said upon that subject than was said then. There is, of course, one new feature about this particular aspect of defence, and that is that we have a new Minister. The hon. Member suggested that it was inappropriate that my Noble Friend (Lord Chatfield), who is known to all the world as a most distinguished sailor, should be appointed to a position in which his duties are to co-ordinate the work not only of the Admiralty but of the other Defence Services as well. I do not think that that is a criticism which will be felt to be valid by the majority in this House or in the country.

" I might remind the House that my Noble Friend served for some considerable time as chairman of the Chiefs of Staffs Committee, being senior officer on that committee. Quite apart therefore from anything else, his experience in that office gave him an opportunity of surveying defence problems as a whole which perhaps is unexampled and which in my judgment makes it peculiarly fitting that he should now be entrusted with the work of Co-ordination of Defence. I believe that every one will feel an added sense of security in the knowledge that we have a man with his particular gifts and his particular knowledge installed now in the very heart of our defence system, and able to give us the benefit of his special knowledge. [An Hon. Member : ' Did you say that about his predecessor ? '] I could not say that, because the qualifications of Lord Chatfield are peculiar to himself.

" Associated with my noble Friend is my right hon. Friend the Chancellor of the Duchy of Lancaster (Mr. W. S. Morrison). If there were any objection to the appointment of my noble Friend as Minister for Co-ordination of Defence it is not that suggested by the hon. Member for Bishop Auckland, but the fact, which he cannot help, that my noble Friend is a Member of the other House ; and it was to correct that difficulty, to enable this House to feel that it was in close personal touch with the work of this Department, that I asked my right hon. Friend the Chancellor of the Duchy to represent him in this House, and also to take over the task of assisting him in his administrative duties.

" The Committee will observe that the Chancellor of the Duchy is the Chairman of the Principal Supply Officers Committee. That does not mean that he is Minister of Supply. It was necessary to make that observation because sometimes I have felt that there was some confusion as to the duties of the Minister for Co-ordination of Defence. His duties in connection with supply are the duties of a co-ordinating Minister. That is not the same thing as a Minister who would himself be executively responsible for supply. But I say this further to the Committee on this occasion, that the immense advance in the output of munitions, and I would particularly say the output of aircraft and other supplies for the Air Ministry, I think shows the wisdom of the course the Government adopted in not appointing a Minister of Supply. The first result of such a change would undoubtedly be to cause a setback to that production just at the very time when it is in full swing, and when it is desirable that it should proceed still further without check.

" I want now to say a few words about the financial aspect of these proposals. It is a curious thing that, while the hon. Member for Bishop Auckland said that in his opinion finance was the easiest part of the work of rearmament, my hon. Friend the Member for East Aberdeen (Mr. Boothby), a little later in the Debate, expressed the view that it was the most difficult part. I would add that for my part I rather agree with my hon. Friend the Member for East Aberdeen, and I wonder whether even now the Committee has grasped the full significance of the scale of the expenditure which is here being contemplated. A sum of £580,000,000 is to be spent in a single year upon the various aspects of defence. That is a figure which does not fall very far short of the whole of the National Debt at the beginning of the Great War, and, of course, that is by no means the end of the story.

" The right hon. Gentleman the Member for East Edinburgh (Mr. Pethick-Lawrence), whom I do not see here to-day, made a very interesting speech last night, in the course of which he pointed out that, when we had spent the £350,000,000 which is the amount that the Chancellor of the Exchequer proposes to borrow next year, we should only have left, out of the £800,000,000 which my right hon. Friend is asking power to borrow, £250,000,000 to cover the last two years of the quinquennium. It will be seen, therefore, that, if we are going to spend £580,000,000 in a single year, £250,000,000 seems a meagre amount to cover the two years that remain, unless the work of rearmament is going to be reduced in a very drastic manner. The right hon. Gentleman suggested that in all probability my right hon. Friend would have to come to the House again and ask for a still further increase in borrowing powers before the last two years had elapsed. He may possibly be right, and, if he should be right, then, if we have to go on borrowing still further after the end of the five-year period, there would, of course, be very little significance in the finding of the sinking fund which was contemplated in the original proposal of the Government. But I cannot help looking even further than that, because, when this process of expansion of our defence forces has been finally completed, we shall not only have to look forward to the finding of the interest and sinking fund upon the amount which we have borrowed, but we shall also have to look forward to the annual cost of the maintenance of those increased forces. It would, of course, be rash at this time to venture upon a prophecy as to what figure the annual cost of maintenance may reach, but when we remember that the Chancellor of the Exchequer, for the purposes of his argument, took the amount which might be expected to be received from revenue next year at £230,000,000, one cannot help wondering whether the annual cost of maintenance of this increased armament, together with the cost of interest and sinking fund, may not be more than it is possible to extract from the taxpayers of this country out of current revenue. That is a serious prospect, to which no one, I think, can look forward with a light heart.

" I am not now going to suggest what the solution of such a problem may be, but I want to make two observations upon it. The first is this : Does it not show up the terrible self-delusion of those who argue that, if we now spend so freely, it cannot hurt us to add a few tens of millions to our annual expenditure, even if those tens of millions produce no return whatever ? My second observation is that in my view it would be criminal to allow the situation to go on developing as it has been developing without making some determined effort to put a stop to it. I listened yesterday to a very eloquent, indeed impassioned speech by the hon. Member for Burslem (Mr. MacLaren). He spoke with great sincerity, which I think appealed strongly to all those who heard it. He begged us not to allow people to slip down this slope like Gadarene swine, and suggested that the leaders of nations ought here and now to call a conference to consider whether the time had not come to agree upon disarmament. If I could believe that such a conference would produce an effective result at this moment—[HON. MEMBERS : ' Have a try.']—I would not hesitate to call it. But a conference that failed would be worse than no conference. I feel that, before it is possible to anticipate success from such a conference, we must be sure that those who came to it would come with good will and with a determination to produce the desired result. I do not feel that we have sufficient confidence established yet to make that conference a practical proposition at this moment."

MR. MAXTON : " Will the Prime Minister allow me to interrupt him for a moment ? I am keenly interested in this part of his speech. He says that no conference would be worth having unless there was a spirit of good will among those who attended it ; but were those conditions present when he went to Berchtesgaden, Godesberg and Munich ? "

THE PRIME MINISTER : " Yes, Sir ; I think that those who went to the conference at Munich went there with the intention of making that conference succeed. (Interruption.) That was the only conference. If I felt the same confidence that a conference for disarmament would come to a satisfactory conclusion now, I should be the first to advocate it. But, as I say, I think we have to be a little further advanced in confidence before the time for such a conference has arrived. Perhaps it would not be a bad thing if we ourselves were to show a little more confidence, and not to allow ourselves to believe every tale that comes to us about the aggressive intentions of others. I am not sure that hon. Members realise how this attitude of suspicion is parallelled elsewhere." (Interruption.)

MR. DAVID GRENFELL: "Were not our suspicions of the German and Italian designs at Munich well founded?"

THE PRIME MINISTER: "I am not making any accusations against any hon. Member; I am merely trying to make an appeal to the House as a whole. I was going on to say that I had sometimes been reproached that I have accused my political opponents of warmongering. I have never thought that my political opponents wanted to go to war. I have thought that the policy which they seemed to be advocating was one which was likely to lead to war, but I do not believe for one moment that, if they occupied the places which my friends and I occupy here now, they would ever think of beginning a preventive war against some other country. Not even my right hon. Friend the Member for Epping (Mr. Churchill), who is Bogy No. 1 in some parts of Europe, has ever thought it would be wise for us as a Government to begin a preventive war against some other country. Our armaments, vast as they are, are armaments for defence, and for defence alone, and if it be true that others have no more intention of aggression than we have, well, then the conclusion that we must come to is that we are all piling up these ruinous armaments under a misunderstanding. I am very much inclined to believe that there is a great deal of truth in that. I would like to remind the Committee of some words used by the late Lord Grey of Fallodon in his book, *Twenty-Five Years*, when he said:

" ' Each Government, while resenting any suggestion that its own measures are anything more than precautions for defence, regards similar measures of another Government as a preparation for attack. Fear begets suspicion and mistrust and evil imaginings of all sorts, till each Government feels it would be criminal and a betrayal of its own country not to take every precaution, while every Government regards every precaution of every other Government as evidence of hostile intent.'

That seems to me to be very much the situation in which we are finding ourselves to-day, so, while I cannot consent that we should relax our armaments in any degree till we can do so by general agreement with others to do the same, I do say that I feel it our duty, the duty of this Government in particular, to watch for every opportunity that may come to try and persuade other Governments of the folly of the course that we are all pursuing, and to induce them to put an end to a situation which, if it is persisted in, must bring bankruptcy to every country in Europe."

THE BREAK-UP OF CZECHOSLOVAKIA

In the second week of March the union between the Czechs and the Slovaks which dated from the last days of the Great War appeared to be coming to an end. On 10th March the Czech President of the Czechoslovak Republic used his powers under the constitution to dismiss the Slovak Government, whose late Prime Minister, Dr. Tiso, the head of the Slovak National Party, thereupon appealed to Herr Hitler for help. Four days after, the Slovak Diet at a special session, proclaimed the independence of Slovakia. On the same day Dr. Hacha, the President of the Czechoslovak Republic travelled to Berlin for an interview with Herr Hitler, which concluded with the issue of a joint signed communiqué stating that in order to secure a final pacification of this part of Europe, Dr. Hacha had placed the destinies of the Czech people and country in the hands of the German Reich. Simultaneously, German forces began a military occupation of the Czech provinces of Bohemia and Moravia, thus bringing to an end not only the short-lived independence of the Czechs, but the Munich Agreement to which the leader of the German State had been a party. On the afternoon of 15th March, the day on which the invasion began, the Prime Minister, though not yet in possession of all the relevant facts, made a statement in the House of Commons.

" I THINK the House will desire that I should begin my
statement this afternoon with a recital of the facts about
the change in the situation in Czechoslovakia, as far as I
know it. On 10th March the President of the Czechoslovak
Republic dismissed certain members of the Slovak Government, including the Prime Minister, Dr. Tiso, on the ground
that certain factors in the Slovak Government had not been
showing sufficient resistance to subversive activities, and that
the Federal interests of the State were thereby threatened.
On 11th March a new Slovak Government was appointed,
under the Premiership of M. Sidor, former Slovak representative in the Central Government at Prague. Dr. Tiso
appealed to Herr Hitler and received an official invitation to
go to Berlin. He had an interview with Herr Hitler on 13th
March, after which he returned to Bratislava to attend a special
session of the Slovak Diet, which had been called for 14th
March. At the conclusion of this session the independence
of Slovakia was proclaimed, with the approval of the Diet,
and a new Slovak Government was constituted under Dr.
Tiso, including M. Sidor.

" Yesterday afternoon the President of the Czechoslovak
Republic and the Foreign Minister left for Berlin. They
had an interview with Herr Hitler and Herr von Ribbentrop,
at the conclusion of which a signed communiqué was issued.
This communiqué stated that the serious situation which
had arisen as the result of events of the past week in what
was hitherto Czechoslovak territory had been closely and
frankly examined. Both sides gave expression to their mutual
conviction that the aim of all efforts in this part of Central
Europe should be the safeguarding of calm, order and peace.
The Czechoslovak President declared that, in order to serve
this purpose, and in order to secure final pacification, he placed
the destinies of the Czech people and country with confidence
in the hands of the German Reich. Herr Hitler accepted this
declaration and expressed his determination to take the

Czech people under the protection of the German Reich and to guarantee to it the autonomous development of its national life in accordance with its particular characteristics.

" The occupation of Bohemia by German military forces began at six o'clock this morning. The Czech people have been ordered by their Government not to offer resistance. The President of the Czechoslovak Republic has returned to Prague. Herr Hitler issued an order to the German armed forces this morning to the effect that German military detachments had crossed the frontier of Czech territory in order to assume impartial control of the safety of the lives and property of the inhabitants of the country. Every German soldier must regard himself not as a foe but as a representative of the German Government to restore a tolerable order. Where opposition was offered to the march it was to be broken down at once by all available methods. The armed forces were to bear in mind that they were treading on Czech soil as the representatives of Great Germany. Meanwhile on 14th March, as a result of incidents on the frontier between Ruthenia and Hungary, Hungarian troops crossed the border and occupied a Czech village. Thereafter the Hungarian Government sent an ultimatum to Prague demanding, among other things, the withdrawal of Czech troops from Ruthenia, the release of Hungarian prisoners, and freedom for persons of Hungarian nationality and race in Ruthenia to arm and to organise. This ultimatum expired this morning, but I have not yet received official reports on the way in which the situation is developing.

" That completes my account of the facts as far as they are known to me. To a large extent the information which I have given to the House is based on Press reports, and while I have very little reason to think that the general effect is not as I have described it to be, final judgment on all the details should await further confirmation. I must deal with three matters which arise out of the circumstances I have described. In the first place, hon. Members will want to know how they affect the guarantee which was described by my right hon. Friend the Secretary of State for the Dominions on 4th October last in the following words :

" ' The question has been raised whether our guarantee to

Czechoslovakia is already in operation. The House will realise that the formal Treaty of guarantee has yet to be drawn up and completed in the normal way, and, as the Foreign Secretary has stated in another place, there are some matters which must await settlement between the Governments concerned. Until that has been done, technically the guarantee cannot be said to be in force. His Majesty's Government, however, feel under a moral obligation to Czechoslovakia to treat the guarantee as being now in force. In the event, therefore, of an act of unprovoked aggression against Czechoslovakia, His Majesty's Government would certainly feel bound to take all steps in their power to see that the integrity of Czechoslovakia is preserved,'—[OFFICIAL REPORT, 4th October, 1938; col. 303, Vol. 339.]

" That remained the position until yesterday, and I may say that recently His Majesty's Government have endeavoured to come to an agreement with the other Governments represented at Munich on the scope and terms of such a guarantee, but up to the present we have been unable to reach any such agreement. In our opinion the situation has radically altered since the Slovak Diet declared the independence of Slovakia. The effect of this declaration put an end by internal disruption to the State whose frontiers we had proposed to guarantee and, accordingly, the condition of affairs described by my right hon. Friend the Secretary of State for the Dominions, which was always regarded by us as being only of a transitory nature, has now ceased to exist, and His Majesty's Government cannot accordingly hold themselves any longer bound by this obligation.

" In the second place, I think the House would like to know the position as regards the financial assistance to the former Government of Czechoslovakia authorised by the Act of Parliament passed last month. As far as I have been able to ascertain, the present position is as follows. Section 1 of the Act provides that the Treasury shall repay to the Bank of England £10,000,000 which has been placed at the disposal of the National Bank of Czechoslovakia. That has been done. The amount that has been withdrawn by Czechoslovakia since the advance was first made available last October is £3,250,000, and the balance of £6,750,000 remains in the

Bank of England. As originally devised between ourselves and the French Government and the former Czechoslovakia Government it included the issue by the last-named Government of a loan on the London market by means of which the assistance given to that Government, so far as it took the form of loan, would be repaid. In the new circumstances, when it appears that the Government of Czechoslovakia has ceased to exist and the territory for which that Government was formerly responsible has been divided, it would seem impossible at present to say how the scheme can be carried through, and steps have been taken to request the Bank of England to make no further payments out of the balance until the situation has been cleared up and a definite conclusion reached."

MR. WEDGWOOD BENN : " What about the refugee fund ? "

THE PRIME MINISTER : " I may say that I have no reason to suppose that the £3,250,000 already drawn has been applied other than in accordance with the arrangements made by us and that a substantial proportion of the sum has been directly devoted to the assistance of refugees. In the third place, the House will be aware that the President of the Board of Trade and the Secretary to the Department of Overseas Trade were about to pay a visit to Berlin in connection with certain discussions which are now proceeding between the representatives of German and British industries. These discussions are still proceeding, and I believe are proceeding in a satisfactory manner. But, in the meantime, having regard to the effect on general conditions in Europe which the events I have described are bound to exert, His Majesty's Government feel that the present moment would be inappropriate for the proposed visit, which has been accordingly postponed, and the German Government have been so informed.

" In considering these events and their relation to the events which preceded them, we must remember that at Munich, and at the discussions which went on before it, we were not dealing with a situation which had just been created. We were dealing with events and with a set of circumstances which had resulted from forces set in motion twenty years earlier. I may remind the House that in July of last year, when it was apparent that a deadlock had taken place in the negotiations between the Czechoslovakian Government and the Sudeten

Germans, and that if the deadlock were not speedily broken, the German Government might intervene in the dispute, we were confronted with three alternative courses : we could have threatened to go to war with Germany if she attacked Czechoslovakia, or we could stand aside and let matters take their course, or, finally, we could attempt to find a peaceful solution through mediation. The first course was rejected, and I do not believe there was then, or that there is now, any considerable body of opinion in this country which would have been prepared to support any other decision. We had no treaty liabilities to Czechoslovakia ; we had always refused to accept any such obligations.

" The second alternative was also repugnant to us, and, realising that once hostilities had broken out they might spread very far, we felt it our duty to do anything in our power to find means of avoiding conflict, and, accordingly, we adopted the third course, that of mediation. I need not recall all the circumstances which led up to the final settlement arrived at on 29th September at Munich. I would only say that in the conditions of that time, and having regard to the alternatives open to us, I have no doubt that the course we took was right, and I believe it has received the approval of the vast majority of world opinion. The settlement has not proved to be final. The State which under that settlement we hoped might begin a new and more stable career, has become disintegrated. The attempt to preserve a State containing Czechs, Slovaks, as well as minorities of other nationalities, was liable to the same possibilities of change as was the Constitution which was drafted when the State was originally framed under the Treaty of Versailles. And it has not survived. That may or may not have been inevitable, and I have so often heard charges of breach of faith bandied about which did not seem to me to be founded upon sufficient premises, that I do not wish to associate myself to-day with any charges of that character.

" But I am bound to say that I cannot believe that anything of the kind which has now taken place was contemplated by any of the signatories to the Munich Agreement at the time of its signature. The Munich Agreement constituted a settlement, accepted by the four Powers and Czechoslovakia, of the Czechoslovak question. It provided for the fixation of the future frontiers of Czechoslovakia which has been effected, and laid down the limits of the German occupation, which the German Government accepted. They have now, without, so far as I know, any communication with the other three signatories to the Munich Agreement, sent their troops beyond the frontier there laid down. But even though it may now be claimed that what has taken place has occurred with the acquiescence of the Czech Government, I cannot regard the manner and the method by which these changes have been brought about as in accord with the spirit of the Munich Agreement.

" A further point which I would make is this : Hitherto the German Government in extending the area of their military control have defended their action by the contention that they were only incorporating in the Reich neighbouring masses of people of German race. Now for the first time they are effecting a military occupation of territory inhabited by people with whom they have no racial connection. These events cannot fail to be a cause of disturbance to the international situation. They are bound to administer a shock to confidence, all the more regrettable because confidence was beginning to revive and to offer a prospect of concrete measures which would be of general benefit.

" In a speech which I made at Birmingham on 30th January last I pointed out that we ought to define our aims and attitude, namely, our determination to search for peace. I added that I felt it was time now that others should make their contribution to a result which would overflow in benefits to many besides those immediately concerned. It is natural, therefore, that I should bitterly regret what has now occurred. But do not let us on that account be deflected from our course. Let us remember that the desire of all the peoples of the world still remains concentrated on the hopes of peace and a return to the atmosphere of understanding and good will which has so often been disturbed. The aim of this Government is now, as it has always been, to promote that desire and to substitute the method of discussion for the method of force in the settlement of differences. Though we may have to suffer checks and disappointments, from time to time, the object that we have in mind is of too great significance to the happiness of mankind for us lightly to give it up or set it on one side."

A HALT TO AGGRESSION

Two days later Mr. Chamberlain spoke at Birmingham on the eve of his 70th birthday to the annual meeting of the Birmingham Unionist Association. By that time he was in possession of fuller information as to the events of the past few days. His speech was broadcast to the Empire and America.

" IT has been rather indiscreetly disclosed to you that to-morrow I shall attain my seventieth birthday. I had hoped to keep that quiet, but, since the cat has been let out of the bag, I am not going to deny it; only I don't see what I can do about it, except to thank you all for your good wishes, and to say to you that, as I am still sound in wind and limb, I hope that I may have a few more years before me in which to give what service I can to the State if that should be wanted.

" I had intended to-night to talk to you upon a variety of subjects, upon trade and employment, upon social service, and upon finance. But the tremendous events which have been taking place this week in Europe have thrown everything else into the background, and I feel that what you, and those who are not in this hall but are listening to me, will want to hear is some indication of the views of His Majesty's Government as to the nature and the implications of those events.

" One thing is certain. Public opinion in the world has received a sharper shock than has ever yet been administered to it, even by the present regime in Germany. What may be the ultimate effects of this profound disturbance on men's minds cannot yet be foretold, but I am sure that it must be far-reaching in its results upon the future. Last Wednesday we had a debate upon it in the House of Commons. That was the day on which the German troops entered Czecho-slovakia, and all of us, but particularly the Government, were at a disadvantage, because the information that we had was only partial; much of it was unofficial. We had no time to digest it, much less to form a considered opinion upon it. And so it necessarily followed that I, speaking on behalf of the Government, with all the responsibility that attaches to that position, was obliged to confine myself to a very restrained and cautious exposition, on what at the time I felt I could make but little commentary. And, perhaps naturally, that somewhat cool and objective statement gave rise to a misapprehension, and some people thought that because I spoke quietly, because I gave little expression to feeling, therefore my colleagues and I did not feel strongly on the subject. I hope to correct that mistake to-night.

"But I want to say something first about an argument which has developed out of these events and which was used in that debate, and has appeared since in various organs of the Press. It has been suggested that this occupation of Czechoslovakia was the direct consequence of the visit which I paid to Germany last autumn, and that, since the result of these events has been to tear up the settlement that was arrived at at Munich, that proves that the whole circumstances of those visits were wrong. It is said that, as this was the personal policy of the Prime Minister, the blame for the fate of Czechoslovakia must rest upon his shoulders. That is an entirely unwarrantable conclusion. The facts as they are to-day cannot change the facts as they were last September. If I was right then, I am still right now. Then there are some people who say : ' We considered you were wrong in September, and now we have been proved to be right.'

" Let me examine that. When I decided to go to Germany I never expected that I was going to escape criticism. Indeed, I did not go there to get popularity. I went there first and foremost because, in what appeared to be an almost desperate situation, that seemed to me to offer the only chance of averting a European war. And I might remind you that, when it was first announced that I was going, not a voice was raised in criticism. Everyone applauded that effort. It was only later, when it appeared that the results of the final settlement fell short of the expectations of some who did not fully appreciate the facts—it was only then that the attack began, and even then it was not the visit, it was the terms of settlement that were disapproved.

" Well, I have never denied that the terms which I was able to secure at Munich were not those that I myself would have desired. But, as I explained then, I had to deal with no new problem. This was something that had existed ever since the Treaty of Versailles—a problem that ought to have been solved long ago if only the statesmen of the last twenty years had taken broader and more enlightened views of their duty. It had become like a disease which had been long neglected, and a surgical operation was necessary to save the life of the patient.

" After all, the first and the most immediate object of my visit was achieved. The peace of Europe was saved ; and, if it had not been for those visits, hundreds of thousands of families would to-day have been in mourning for the flower of Europe's best manhood. I would like once again to express my grateful thanks to all those correspondents who have written me from all over the world to express their gratitude and their appreciation of what I did then and of what I have been trying to do since.

" Really I have no need to defend my visits to Germany last autumn, for what was the alternative ? Nothing that we could have done, nothing that France could have done, or Russia could have done could possibly have saved Czechoslovakia from invasion and destruction. Even if we had subsequently gone to war to punish Germany for her actions, and if after the frightful losses which would have been inflicted upon all partakers in the war we had been victorious in the end, never could we have reconstructed Czechoslovakia as she was framed by the Treaty of Versailles.

" But I had another purpose, too, in going to Munich. That was to further the policy which I have been pursuing ever since I have been in my present position—a policy which is sometimes called European appeasement, although I do not think myself that that is a very happy term or one which accurately describes its purpose. If that policy were to succeed, it was essential that no Power should seek to obtain a general domination of Europe ; but that each one should be contented to obtain reasonable facilities for developing its own resources, securing its own share of international trade, and improving the conditions of its own people. I felt that, although that might well mean a clash of interests between different States, nevertheless, by the exercise of mutual good will and under-standing of what were the limits of the desires of others, it should be possible to resolve all differences by discussion and without armed conflict. I hoped in going to Munich to find out by personal contact what was in Herr Hitler's mind, and whether it was likely that he would be willing to co-operate in a programme of that kind. Well, the atmosphere in which

o

our discussions were conducted was not a very favourable one, because we were in the middle of an acute crisis ; but nevertheless, in the intervals between more official conversations I had some opportunities of talking with him and of hearing his views, and I thought that results were not altogether unsatisfactory.

" When I came back after my second visit I told the House of Commons of a conversation I had had with Herr Hitler, of which I said that, speaking with great earnestness, he repeated what he had already said at Berchtesgaden—namely, that this was the last of his territorial ambitions in Europe, and that he had no wish to include in the Reich people of other races than Germany. Herr Hitler himself confirmed this account of the conversation in the speech which he made at the Sportpalast in Berlin, when he said : ' This is the last territorial claim which I have to make in Europe.' And a little later in the same speech he said : ' I have assured Mr. Chamberlain, and I emphasise it now, that when this problem is solved, Germany has no more territorial problems in Europe.' And he added : ' I shall not be interested in the Czech State any more, and I can guarantee it. We don't want any Czechs any more.'

"And then in the Munich Agreement itself, which bears Herr Hitler's signature, there is this clause : ' The final determination of the frontiers will be carried out by the international commission '—the *final* determination. And, lastly, in that declaration which he and I signed together at Munich, we declared that any other question which might concern our two countries should be dealt with by the method of consultation.

" Well, in view of those repeated assurances, given voluntarily to me, I considered myself justified in founding a hope upon them that once this Czechoslovakian question was settled, as it seemed at Munich it would be, it would be possible to carry farther that policy of appeasement which I have described. But notwithstanding, at the same time I was not prepared to relax precautions until I was satisfied that the policy had been established and had been accepted by others, and therefore, after Munich, our defence programme was actually accelerated and it was expanded so as to remedy certain weaknesses which had become apparent during the crisis. I am convinced that after Munich the great majority of British people shared my hope, and ardently desired that that policy should be carried further. But to-day I share their disappointment, their indignation that those hopes have been so wantonly shattered.

" How can these events this week be reconciled with those assurances which I have read out to you ? Surely as a joint signatory of the Munich Agreement I was entitled, if Herr Hitler thought it ought to be undone, to that consultation which is provided for in the Munich declaration. Instead of that he has taken the law into his own hands. Before even the Czech President was received, and confronted with demands which he had no power to resist, the German troops were on the move, and within a few hours they were in the Czech capital.

" According to the proclamation which was read out in Prague yesterday, Bohemia and Moravia have been annexed to the German Reich. Non-German inhabitants, who of course include the Czechs, are placed under the German Protector in the German Protectorate. They are to be subject to the political, military, and economic needs of the Reich. They are called self-governing States, but the Reich is to take charge of their foreign policy, their Customs and their Excise, their bank reserves, and the equipment of the disarmed Czech forces. Perhaps most sinister of all, we hear again of the appearance of the Gestapo, the secret police, followed by the usual tale of wholesale arrests of prominent individuals, with consequences with which we are all familiar.

" Every man and woman in this country who remembers the fate of the Jews and the political prisoners in Austria must be filled to-day with distress and foreboding. Who can fail to feel his heart go out in sympathy to the proud and brave people who have so suddenly been subjected to this invasion, whose liberties are curtailed, whose national independence has gone ? What has become of this declaration of ' No further territorial ambition ' ? What has become of the assurance ' We don't want Czechs in the Reich ' ? What regard had been paid here to that principle of self-determination on which Herr Hitler argued so vehemently with me at Berchtesgaden when he was asking for the severance of Sudetenland from Czechoslovakia and its inclusion in the German Reich.

" Now we are told that this seizure of territory has been necessitated by disturbances in Czechoslovakia. We are told that the proclamation of this new German Protectorate against the will of its inhabitants has been rendered inevitable by disorders which threatened the peace and security of her mighty neighbour. If there were disorders, were they not fomented from without ? And can anybody outside Germany take seriously the idea that they could be a danger to that great country, that they could provide any justification for what has happened ?

" Does not the question inevitably arise in our minds, if it is so easy to discover good reasons for ignoring assurances so solemnly and so repeatedly given, what reliance can be placed upon any other assurances that come from the same source ?

" There is another set of questions which almost inevitably must occur in our minds and to the minds of others, perhaps even in Germany herself. Germany, under her present regime, has sprung a series of unpleasant surprises upon the world. The Rhineland, the Austrian *Anschluss*, the severance of Sudetenland—all these things shocked and affronted public opinion throughout the world. Yet, however much we might take exception to the methods which were adopted in each of those cases, there was something to be said, whether on account of racial affinity or of just claims too long resisted— there was something to be said for the necessity of a change in the existing situation.

" But the events which have taken place this week in complete disregard of the principles laid down by the German Government itself seem to fall into a different category, and they must cause us all to be asking ourselves : ' Is this the end of an old adventure, or is it the beginning of a new ? '

" ' Is this the last attack upon a small State, or is it to be followed by others ? Is this, in fact, a step in the direction of an attempt to dominate the world by force ? '

" Those are grave and serious questions. I am not going to answer them to-night. But I am sure they will require the grave and serious consideration, not only of Germany's neighbours but of others, perhaps even beyond the confines of

Europe. Already there are indications that the process has begun, and it is obvious that it is likely now to be speeded up.

"We ourselves will naturally turn first to our partners in the British Commonwealth of Nations and to France, to whom we are so closely bound, and I have no doubt that others, too, knowing that we are not disinterested in what goes on in South-Eastern Europe, will wish to have our counsel and advice.

"In our own country we must all review the position with that sense of responsibility which its gravity demands. Nothing must be excluded from that review which bears upon the national safety. Every aspect of our national life must be looked at again from that angle. The Government, as always, must bear the main responsibility, but I know that all individuals will wish to review their own position, too, and to consider again if they have done all they can to offer their service to the State.

"I do not believe there is anyone who will question my sincerity when I say there is hardly anything I would not sacrifice for peace. But there is one thing that I must except, and that is the liberty that we have enjoyed for hundreds of years, and which we will never surrender. That I, of all men, should feel called upon to make such a declaration—that is the measure of the extent to which these events have shattered the confidence which was just beginning to show its head and which, if it had been allowed to grow, might have made this year memorable for the return of all Europe to sanity and stability.

"It is only six weeks ago that I was speaking in this city, and that I alluded to rumours and suspicions which I said ought to be swept away. I pointed out that any demand to dominate the world by force was one which the democracies must resist, and I added that I could not believe that such a challenge was intended, because no Government with the interests of its own people at heart could expose them for such a claim to the horrors of world war.

"And indeed, with the lessons of history for all to read, it seems incredible that we should see such a challenge. I feel bound to repeat that, while I am not prepared to engage this country by new unspecified commitments operating under conditions which cannot now be foreseen, yet no greater mistake could be made than to suppose that, because it believes war to be a senseless and cruel thing, this nation has so lost its fibre that it will not take part to the utmost of its power resisting such a challenge if it ever were made. For that declaration I am convinced that I have not merely the support, the sympathy, the confidence of my fellow-countrymen and countrywomen, but I shall have also the approval of the whole British Empire and of all other nations who value peace indeed, but who value freedom even more."

A GUARANTEE AGAINST INVASION

A week later in the House of Commons Mr. Chamberlain stated that recent actions of the German Government had " raised the question whether that Government is not seeking by successive steps to dominate Europe, and perhaps even to go further than that," and that, " were this interpretation of the intentions of the German Government to prove correct, His Majesty's Government feel bound to say that this would rouse the successful resistance of this and other countries who prize their freedom, as similar attempts have done in the past." He mentioned that consultations were proceeding with other friendly Governments, but added that there was " no desire on the part of His Majesty's Government to stand in the way of any reasonable efforts on the part of Germany to expand her export trade . . . nor . . . to set up in Europe opposing blocks of countries with different ideals about the forms of their internal administration. We are solely concerned here with the proposition that we cannot submit to a procedure under which independent States are subjected to such pressure under threats of force as to be obliged to yield up their independence, and we are resolved by all means in our power to oppose attempts, if they should be made, to put such a procedure into operation."

On the 31st March the Prime Minister announced the first step in his new policy of safeguarding peace by guaranteeing the independence of those who might otherwise be the subject of attack.

"THE right hon. Gentleman the Leader of the Opposition (Mr. Attlee) asked me this morning whether I could make a statement as to the European situation. As I said this morning, His Majesty's Government have no official confirmation of the rumours of any projected attack on Poland and they must not, therefore, be taken as accepting them as true.

"I am glad to take this opportunity of stating again the general policy of His Majesty's Government. They have constantly advocated the adjustment, by way of free negotiation between the parties concerned, of any differences that may arise between them. They consider that this is the natural and proper course where differences exist. In their opinion there should be no question incapable of solution by peaceful means, and they would see no justification for the substitution of force or threats of force for the method of negotiation.

"As the House is aware, certain consultations are now proceeding with other Governments. In order to make perfectly clear the position of His Majesty's Government in the meantime before those consultations are concluded, I now have to inform the House that during that period, in the event of any action which clearly threatened Polish independence, and which the Polish Government accordingly considered it vital to resist with their national forces, His Majesty's Government would feel themselves bound at once to lend the Polish Government all support in their power. They have given the Polish Government an assurance to this effect.

"I may add that the French Government have authorised me to make it plain that they stand in the same position in this matter as do His Majesty's Government."

MR. ARTHUR GREENWOOD : "May I, in one sentence, transgress in order to say that I am quite sure that this House realises the potentialities that might arise from the statement which the right hon. Gentleman has made. It may prove to be in its consequences as momentous a statement as has been made in this House for a quarter of a century. It is very difficult with such recent statements before us to say very much, but may I ask the right hon. Gentleman one or two questions which I do not think he has made quite clear in his statement ? I would like to ask him whether the statement which he has now read is to be regarded as the first step in a developing policy to deter or restrain aggression, and, if so, will the Government take immediate, active and energetic steps to bring into this arrangement other Powers ? Will he especially think of the value of the Union of Soviet Socialist Republics together with other Powers, large and small ? Will he do so with the wider object of obtaining the maximum amount of co-operation in the defence of peace ? Will he consider now the advisability of an immediate conference of those Powers who might be prepared to range themselves on the side of peace as against aggression ?

THE PRIME MINISTER : " I will try to answer the questions which the right hon. Gentleman has put to me. I think the statement makes it clear that what I have said is intended to cover what I may call an interim period. The Government, as has already been announced, are in consultation with various other Powers, including, of course, the Soviet Government. My Noble Friend the Foreign Secretary saw the Soviet Ambassador this morning, and had very full discussions with him on the subject. I have no doubt that the principles upon which we are acting are fully understood and appreciated by that Government. The House is aware that we are expecting a visit next week from Colonel Beck, the Foreign Secretary of Poland. There will then be an opportunity of discussing with him the various further measures that may be taken in order, as the right hon. Gentleman has put it, to accumulate the maximum amount of co-operation in any efforts that may be made to put an end to aggression, if aggression were intended, and to substitute for it the more reasonable and orderly method of discussion."

MR. GREENWOOD : " There is a point to which the right hon. Gentleman did not refer—the possibilities of a conference. May I put this point, and I want to put it quite frankly, as I think the House will not be without a feeling of responsibility at this moment. Can the right hon. Gentleman say whether in his view he would welcome that maximum co-operation from all Powers, including the U.S.S.R. ? "

THE PRIME MINISTER : " Yes, we should welcome the maximum amount of co-operation. On the question of a conference, in our view it is simply a matter of practical expediency. We have no theoretical views about a conference. If it proved to be the best way we should not hesitate to use it. If we find that there is a more effective way of achieving our object, we might dispense with a conference."

MR. DENMAN ; " With regard to the Prime Minister's original statement, may I ask whether there has been time for full consultation with the Dominions ? "

THE PRIME MINISTER : " The Dominions have been kept fully informed."

MR. JOHN MORGAN : " Can the right hon. Gentleman give us an assurance that there are no ideological impediments between us and the U.S.S.R. ? "

THE PRIME MINISTER : " Yes, I have no hesitation in giving that assurance."

responsibility at this moment. Can he at all give him. Gentleman say whether in his view he would welcome that maximum co-operation from all Powers, including the U.S.S.R.?"

The Prime Minister : "... Yes, we should welcome the maximum amount of co-operation. On the question of a conference, in my view it is simply a matter of material expediency. We have no theoretical views about a conference. If it proved to be the best way we should not hesitate to use it. If we find that there is a more effective way of achieving our object, we might dispense with a conference."

Mr. Dennis : "... With regard to the Prime Minister's original statement, may I ask whether there has been any full consultation with the Dominions?"

The Prime Minister : "The Dominions have been kept fully informed."

Mr. John Morris : "Can the right hon. Gentleman give an assurance that there are no ideological impediments between us and the U.S.S.R.?

The Prime Minister : "Yes, I can. I can give that assurance in regard to assurance."

TO MAKE BRITAIN'S POSITION CLEAR

On 3rd April, on a motion for the Adjournment, the Prime Minister, following Mr. Arthur Greenwood, spoke at greater length on the policy—" a tremendous departure from anything which this country has undertaken hitherto "—which he had adopted in his continued attempt to save the peace of Europe.

"THE whole House will share the regret expressed by the right hon. Gentleman (Mr. Greenwood) at the cause which made it necessary for him to open the Debate this afternoon instead of the Leader of the Opposition. We all hope that the right hon. Gentleman who leads the Opposition will soon be restored to his usual health.

" The right hon. Gentleman who has just spoken promised us on Friday that the Debate which took place to-day would be carried on on a high level, and, if I may be allowed to say so, he has, as far as he is concerned, amply fulfilled that promise. And so, feeling as I think he does, that this is an occasion on which we should rather stress the points on which we agree than those on which we differ I shall, while noting his reference to the leonine character of those who sit around him, not attempt to go back to any matters of difference, but rather address myself to the situation that is before us. When my Noble Friend the Member for South Dorset (Viscount Cranborne) suggested on Friday that it might be a good thing if this Debate were to be postponed for a time, I confess that my first thought was rather to agree with him, not because I anticipated that any harm could be done by the Debate, but because I realised that nothing was likely to occur over the week-end which would enable me to give the House any new information.

" While, of course, the right hon. Gentleman opposite very rightly and properly put forward his ideas as to the manner in which the matter should be developed, he will recognise that it is not so easy for me, who am about to take part in conversations, to say in public what exactly are the lines on which we wish to go. If, as I hope may be the case, the result of this Debate is to show that fundamentally and generally this House is unanimous in its approval of the declaration which I made on Friday, and is united and determined to take whatever measures may be necessary to make that declaration effective, the Debate may well serve a very useful purpose. The declaration that I made on Friday has been described, in a phrase so apt that it has been widely taken up, as a cover note issued in advance of the complete insurance policy. I myself emphasised its transitional or temporary character, and the description of it as a cover note is not at all a bad one so far as it goes ; but where I think it is altogether incomplete is that, while, of course, the issue of a cover note does imply that it is to be followed by something more substantial, it is the nature of the complete insurance policy which is such a tremendous departure from anything which this country has undertaken hitherto. It does really constitute a new point—I would say a new epoch—in the course of our foreign policy.

"The commitments of this country, whether actual or potential, were stated some time ago by my right hon. Friend the Member for Warwick and Leamington (Mr. Eden) in a passage which is famous because it so clearly and carefully expressed the facts. The speech was made in the country. That was not so very long ago, and I think that if at that time it had been suggested that we should add to those commitments something affecting a country in the eastern part of Europe, it would, no doubt, have obtained some limited amount of support, but it certainly would not have commanded the approval of the great majority of the country. Indeed, to have departed from our traditional ideas in this respect so far as I did on behalf of His Majesty's Government on Friday constitutes a portent in British policy so momentous that I think it is safe to say it will have a chapter to itself when the history books come to be written.

"The right hon. Gentleman alluded just now to some misunderstanding of the meaning of that declaration. I confess that I was myself surprised that there should be any misunderstanding, for I thought it was clear and plain for all who run to read. Of course, a declaration of that importance is not concerned with some minor little frontier incident ; it is concerned with the big things that may lie behind even a frontier incident. If the independence of the State of Poland should be threatened—and if it were threatened I have no doubt that the Polish people would resist any attempt on it—then the declaration which I made means that France and ourselves would immediately come to her assistance. The right hon. Gentleman quoted a passage from a speech of mine which was made very recently, but perhaps I may be permitted to recall to the House that as long ago as last September I myself gave a warning of the possibility of such a departure as we are now contemplating. On that Tuesday, 27th September, at a moment when it hardly seemed possible to cherish any longer the hope that peace might be preserved, it was my duty to broadcast a message. I would like, if I may, to recall to the House one or two sentences that I spoke then :

" ' I am myself a man of peace to the depths of my soul. Armed conflict between nations is a nightmare to me ; but if I were convinced that any nation had made up its mind to dominate the world by fear of its force, I should feel that it must be resisted. Under such a domination life for people who believe in liberty would not be worth living.'

At that time I did not myself feel that the events that were taking place in connection with Czechoslovakia necessarily involved such an assumption as that. My opinion at that time was, as it is now, that war as it is waged in these days is such a frightful thing that I could not ask the country to accept new commitments which might involve us in war unless some really vital principle like that which I have just described were at stake. A little later, at the end of the year, hon. Members will recall that the President of the United States in a New Year's message dwelt on the same thought. At the end of that month I alluded to that New Year's message, and said that a challenge of that kind, a demand to dominate one by one other nations without limits to where that might go, was the only challenge which could endanger the peace of the world, but that if it were made, then I felt, like President Roosevelt, that it must be resisted.

" There were some at that time, indeed, there were some in September, who believed that the first steps had already been taken towards making that challenge. At that time it was possible to quote to those who held that view the assurances that had been given to me, and not to me only but to the world, that the foreign policy of the German Government was limited, that they had no wish to dominate other races, and that all they wanted was to assimilate Germans living in territory adjacent to their country. We were told that when that was done that was to be the end, and there were to be no more terrritorial ambitions to be satisfied. Those assurances have now been thrown to the winds. That is the new fact which has completely destroyed confidence and which has forced the British Government to make this great departure of which I gave the first intimation on Friday.

" It is true we are told now that there are other reasons for recent events in Czechoslovakia—historical associations, the fear of attack. Well, there may be excellent reasons, but they do not accord with the assurances which were given before. It is inevitable that they should raise doubts as to whether further reasons may not presently be found for further expansion. I am not asserting that to-day this challenge has been made. No official statement that I know of has ever formulated such ambitions, although there has been plenty of unofficial talk ; but the effect of these recent events has penetrated far beyond the limits of the countries concerned, and perhaps far further than was anticipated by those who brought them about. It is no exaggeration to say that public opinion throughout the world has been profoundly shocked and alarmed. This country has been united from end to end by the conviction that we must now make our position clear and unmistakable whatever may be the result.

" No one can regret more than I do the necessity to have to speak such words as those. I am no more a man of war to-day than I was in September. I have no intention, no desire, to treat the great German people otherwise than as I would have our own people treated. I was looking forward with strong hopes to the result of those trade discussions which had already begun in Germany, and which, I thought, might have benefits for both our countries and many other countries besides, but confidence which has been so grievously shaken is not easily restored. We have been obliged, therefore, to consider the situation afresh.

" It is not so long ago that I declared my view that this country ought not to be asked to enter into indefinite, unspecified commitments operating under conditions which could not be foreseen. I still hold that view; but here what we are doing is to enter into a specific engagement directed to a certain eventuality, namely, if such an attempt should be made to dominate the world by force. The right hon. Gentleman rightly said that the matter could not end where it stands to-day. If that policy were the policy of the German Government it is quite clear that Poland would not be the only country which would be endangered, and the policy which has led us to give this assurance to Poland, of course could not be satisfied or carried out if we were to confine ourselves to a single case which, after all, might not be the case in point. These recent happenings have, rightly or wrongly, made every State which lies adjacent to Germany unhappy, anxious, uncertain about Germany's future intentions. If that is all a misunderstanding, if the German Government has never had any such thoughts, well, so much the better. In that case any agreements which may be made to safeguard the independence of these countries will never have to be called upon, and Europe may then gradually simmer down into a state of quietude in which their existence even might be forgotten.

"Let me emphasise again, whatever the outcome of the discussions which are now taking place between His Majesty's Government and the Governments of other countries, they contain no threat to Germany so long as Germany will be a good neighbour. I am glad to hear what the right hon. Gentleman said about encirclement. It is fantastic to suggest that a policy which is a policy of self-defence can be described as encirclement if by that term is meant encirclement for the purpose of some aggressive action.

"I do not wish to-day to attempt to specify what Governments we may now, or in the near future, find it desirable to consult with on the situation, but I would make one allusion to the Soviet Union, because I quite appreciate that the Soviet Union is always in the thoughts of hon. Members opposite, and that they are still a little suspicious as to whether those so-called ideological differences may not be dividing us upon what otherwise it would obviously be in the interests of both to do. I do not pretend for one moment that ideological differences do not exist; they remain unchanged. But, as I said on Friday in answer to a question, our point is that whatever may be those ideological differences they do not really count in a question of this kind. What we are concerned with is to preserve our independence, and when I say ' our independence' I do not mean only this country's. I mean the independence of all States which may be threatened by aggression in pursuit of such a policy as I have described.

" Therefore, we welcome the co-operation of any country, whatever may be its internal system of government, not in aggression but in resistance to aggression. I believe that this nation is now united not only in approval of what we have said, but in approval of the aim and purpose that lie behind it. I believe that the whole Empire shares in that approval. The members of the British Empire beyond the seas have hitherto watched our efforts for peace with a fervent hope that they might be successful. All of them have had a growing consciousness that we cannot live for ever in that atmosphere of surprise and alarm from which Europe has suffered in recent months. The common business of life cannot be carried on in a state of uncertainty. As far as it is possible for His Majesty's Government to help to restore confidence by plain words, we have done our part. In doing so I am certain that we have expressed the will of this people. I trust that our action, begun but not concluded, will prove to be the turning point not towards war, which wins nothing, cures nothing, ends nothing, but towards a more wholesome era when reason will take the place of force and threats will make way for cool and well-marshalled arguments."